INSTANT
REFERENCE

# POLITICS

**ty** TEACH YOURSELF®

For UK orders: please contact Bookpoint Ltd., 130 Milton Park, Abingdon, Oxon 0X14 4SB. Telephone: (44) 01235 827720. Fax: (44) 01235 400454. Lines are open from 09.00–18.00, Monday to Saturday, with a 24-hour message answering service. E:mail address: orders@bookpoint.co.uk

For U.S.A. order enquiries: please contact McGraw-Hill Customer Services, P.O. Box 545, Blacklick, OH 43004-*0545*, U.S.A. Telephone: 1-800-722-4726. Fax: 1-614-755-5645.

For Canada order enquiries: please contact McGraw-Hill Ryerson Ltd., 300 Water St, Whitby, Ontario L1N 9B6, Canada. Telephone: 905 430 5000. Fax: 905 430 5020.

Long renowned as the authoritative source for self-guided learning – with more than 30 million copies sold worldwide – the *Teach Yourself* series includes over 300 titles in the fields of languages, crafts, hobbies, business and education.

*British Library Cataloguing in Publication Data*
A catalogue record for this title is available from The British Library.

*Library of Congress Catalog Card Number:* On file

First published in UK 2001 by Hodder Headline Plc., 338 Euston Road, London, NW1 3BH.

First published in US 2001 by Contemporary Books, A Division of The McGraw-Hill Companies, 4255 West Touhy Avenue, Lincolnwood (Chicago), Illinois 60712-1975 U.S.A.

The 'Teach Yourself' name and logo are registered trade marks of Hodder & Stoughton Ltd.

Picture Credits:
With special thanks to AKG:
6, 8, 9, 10, 15, 17, 18, 19, 23, 32, 40, 55, 58, 62, 64, 65, 79, 88, 90, 92, 94, 95, 100, 111, 118, 121, 122, 128, 135, 136, 140, 158, 169, 180, 181, 186, 188, 192, 200, 203

Text Editor: David Robertson
Typeset by TechType, Abingdon, Oxon
Printed in Great Britain for Hodder & Stoughton Educational, a division of Hodder Headline Plc, 338 Euston Road, London NW1 3BH by Cox & Wyman Ltd., Reading, Berkshire.

Impression number   10 9 8 7 6 5 4 3 2 1
Year                      2007      2006      2005      2004      2003      2002      2001

# Contents

Bold type in the text indicates a cross reference. A plural, or possessive, is given as the cross reference, i.e. is in bold type, even if the entry to which it refers is singular.

## absolutism or absolute monarchy

A system of government in which the ruler or rulers have unlimited power and are subject to no constitutional safeguards or checks. The principle of an absolute monarch, given a right to rule by God (the **divine right of kings**), was extensively used in Europe during the 17th and 18th centuries. Absolute monarchy contrasts with limited or constitutional monarchy, in which the sovereign's powers are defined or limited. Where

> In Plato's *Republic* the philosopher-king was to be granted absolute authority because only a trained philosopher was truly wise enough to rule; he was the shepherd of the human flock.

absolutism is a **tyranny** no theoretical justification may be offered. However, if the rule is claimed to be beneficial, justification may be offered on grounds of the ruler's access to privileged knowledge, or his or her claim to be sanctioned by a higher power.

## administration

One of the functions of **government** by which it implements legislation and policy and operates the governmental system in accordance with a country's constitution and those conventions underlying it. The government of a country is often referred to as an administration; for example the Major or Blair administration in Britain, or the Bush or Clinton administration in the USA. In countries with a parliamentary system of government, ministers are normally constitutionally responsible or answerable to the **legislature**. However, in countries such as the USA, which have a constitutional separation of powers, neither heads of executive departments nor the chief executive are constitutionally responsible to the legislature. Heads of executive departments are normally responsible solely to the chief executive (usually the president), and the chief executive is responsible to the people by virtue of his or her election. Nonetheless, the actions of the president of the USA and the various members of the presidential administration are subject to considerable scrutiny by Congress, mainly through its committees. In liberal democracies ministers or their political equivalents are normally almost fully liable for acts beyond their powers, including the actions of the civil servants for whom they are responsible. In a number of countries the administration of policy is also subject to the scrutiny of an **ombudsman**.

## administrative law

Law concerning the powers and control of government agencies or those agencies granted statutory powers of **administration**. These powers include those necessary to operate the agency or to implement its purposes, and making quasi-judicial decisions (such as determining tax liability, granting licences or permits, or hearing complaints against the agency or its officers). The vast increase in these powers during the 20th century in many countries has been widely criticized. In the UK, powers delegated to ministers of the crown are so wide that they sometimes enable ministers to make regulations that amend or override acts of Parliament. The courts can exercise some control over administrative action through **judicial review**, for example a declaration that certain regulations are void because they exceed their authority (ultra vires).

- The 1998 Human Rights Act provides an extra form of judicial control.
- In the USA the 1946 Administrative Procedure Act was an attempt to cope with the problem.

## advisory committee

In the UK, advisory committees are non-elected bodies whose members are answerable only to the minister who appointed them. They work in secret and are mainly made up of outside experts working part-time. Royal Commissions are included in this group.

The 807 advisory committees in existence in 1995 included:

- the Committee on the Safety of Medicines (CSM), which approves new drugs
- the Committee on Toxicity, which advises on food additives
- the Spongiform Encephalopathy Advisory Committee, which advises on BSE.

## affirmative action

Government policy of positive discrimination by the use of legal measures and moral persuasion that favours women and members of minority ethnic groups in such areas as employment and education. It is designed to counter the effects of long-standing **discrimination** against these groups. In Europe, Sweden, Belgium, the Netherlands, and Italy actively promote affirmative action through legal and financial incentives.

In India, the government's decision of 1990 to implement the recommendations of the Mandal Commission on job reservations for disadvantaged 'backward castes' provoked a bloody caste war in the cities of northern India.

In the USA, the Equal Opportunities Act of 1972 set up a commission to enforce the policy in organizations receiving public funds, and many private institutions and employers also adopted voluntary affirmative-action programmes at that time. In the 1980s the policy was sometimes not rigorously enforced and there were allegations of 'reverse discrimination' (individuals receiving preferential treatment solely because they belonged to a particular group); nevertheless, a review completed in 1995 reported that most programmes were justifiable. President Clinton reaffirmed his commitment to them, but Republicans have pledged to end such federal programmes.

## agrarian parties

Agrarian parties are political parties chiefly representing the interests of peasants or, more broadly, the rural sector of society. The extent to which they are important, or whether they even exist, depends mainly on two factors:

- the size of an identifiable peasantry, or the size of the rural relative to the urban population

- social integration: for agrarian parties to be important, the representation of countryside or peasantry must not be integrated with the other major sections of society.

Thus a country might possess a sizeable rural population, but have an economic system in which the interests of the voters were predominantly related to their incomes, not to their occupations or location; and in such a country the political system would be unlikely to include an important agrarian party. As agriculture has come to employ a progressively smaller percentage of Western populations, which concurrently become ever more urbanized, this sort of political party has tended either to decline in importance or to broaden its appeal by shifts in its policies. The politics of the Third Republic in France were, to a large extent, based on an urban/rural

**cleavage** leading to at least semi agrarian parties. These declined rapidly in the Fourth Republic and Fifth Republic.

## aid, foreign
Financial and other assistance given by richer, usually industrialized, countries to war-damaged or developing states.

## alienation
A sense of isolation, powerlessness, and therefore frustration. The feeling of loss of control over one's life or a sense of estrangement from society or even from oneself. As a concept it was developed by the German philosophers G W F **Hegel** and Karl **Marx**; the latter used it as a description and criticism of the condition that developed among workers in capitalist societies. It has come to be a widely used sociological concept, and a similar term, **anomie**, has also been used – in particular by French sociologist Emile **Durkheim,** who used it in his work *Suicide* (1897) to explain unrest in factories and to describe the sense of powerlessness felt by groups such as young people, black people, and women in Western industrial society.

## Althusser, Louis (1918–1990)
French philosopher and Marxist, born in Algeria, who argued that the idea that economic systems determine family and political systems is too simple. He attempted to show how the ruling class ideology of a particular era is a crucial form of class control.

Althusser divides each mode of production into four key elements – the economic, political, ideological, and theoretical – all of which interact. His structuralist analysis of capitalism sees individuals and groups as agents or bearers of the structures of social relations, rather than as independent influences on history. His works include *For Marx* (1965), *Lenin and Philosophy* (1969), and *Essays in Self-Criticism* (1976). He has influenced thinkers in fields as diverse as social anthropology, literature, and history.

## anarchism
The political belief that society should have no government, laws, police, or other authority, but should be a free association of all its members. The term is derived from the Greek *anarkhos*, 'without ruler'. It does not mean 'without order': anarchists maintain that order can be achieved by cooperation. Anarchist elements occur in social philosophies widely ranging from those of the Russian writer Leo Tolstoy to the Indian nationalist

Mahatma Gandhi. Perhaps the most influential anarchist of the 20th century was the US linguist Noam Chomsky.

Serious and responsible anarchist writing continues to explore the possibilities of gaining a piecemeal liberalization of various aspects of our social and political life. The resurgence of anarchist thinking at this level was one of the major features of post-war intellectual life in the West; its influence can be seen in the various 'liberation' movements, such as women's, gay, and prisoners'. From the 1960s there have been outbreaks of politically motivated violence popularly identified with anarchism, including the worldwide student unrest of May 1968.

> ❻ My political opinions lean more and more towards anarchy…The most improper job of any man, even saints, is bossing other men. ❾
>
> **J R R Tolkien**, English author, *Letters.*

## anomie
A term used in the social sciences, to describe a state of 'formlessness' created by the breakdown of commonly agreed standards of behaviour and morality. The concept was developed by French sociologist Emile **Durkheim.** He used 'anomie' to describe societies in transition during industrialization, and demonstrated that suicide rates were affected by anomie.

## anticlerical
An anti-clerical political outlook is one that is strongly opposed to the churches wielding any direct political influence or power. Anticlerical parties or politicians have had an important role in most Western societies at one time or another. Nowadays a clerical/anticlerical **cleavage** still exists in Italy and, to a lesser extent, France. In France, during the period 1870–1958, important sections of the electorate would automatically back certain political parties because they could be relied upon to oppose any clerical influence in politics. As the principal political voice of the Roman Catholic Church, the Mouvement Républicaine Populaire, ceased to be of influence early in the Fifth Republic the distinction became less vital. Other electors (nowadays especially the Christian Democrats in Italy) vote as they

do precisely because they feel that churches *should* play a significant role in the state.

In general it has been **Roman Catholicism** that has been the focus of anti-clerical politics, largely because it has historically been associated with conservative values and therefore seen as supporting upper classes. In the Dutch party system, however, anticlericalism applies to the general opposition to church influence in politics, especially since the development of interdenominational political groupings (which was itself a sign of the declining influence of the churches in politics and society in general). As the Catholic Church has changed and, particularly in the Third World, been seen as 'revolutionary' and an advocate of liberation theology, the traditional basis for anticlericalism has declined. The general secularization of modern society has further reduced concern about religious influence in the state. Thus some political parties (the German Christian Democrats, for example) have become pure Conservative parties, with religious affiliation playing no role in their support or rejection. However, religious **fundamentalism** has become both

**anticlericalism** *A 19th-century anticlerical picture satirizing the Roman Catholic Church and its perceived means of accruing wealth.*

stronger and politically more relevant since the 1970s, so there is no guarantee that a form of opposition to religious involvement in politics, such as is already developing in USA, will not become important again. This opposition will probably not deserve the title of anticlericalism as previously understood, because the fundamentalists support is based in **populism** rather than, supposedly, the interests of the upper classes.

## anti-Semitism

Prejudice or discrimination against, and persecution of, the Jews as an ethnic group. It is a form of racism that has been practised for almost 2,000 years by European christians. The most extreme form of anti-Semitism was Nazi Germany's genocide of the Jewish people. In the **Holocaust** (1933–45)

**CENTURIES OF PERSECUTION**

German religious reformer Martin Luther was one of the first major writers of anti-Semitic literature in Germany, claiming that Jewishness contaminated the soul of the German people. Legislation in the Middle Ages forbade Jews to own land or to become members of a craft guild; to earn a living they had to become moneylenders and traders (and were then resented when they prospered). Britain expelled many Jews in 1290, but they were formally readmitted in 1655 by Cromwell. From the 16th century Jews were forced by law in many cities to live in a separate area, or ghetto.

6 million Jews died in concentration camps and in local extermination programmes, such as the siege of the Warsaw ghetto. Anti-Semitism still exists widely and is promulgated by neo-fascist groups.

## apartheid

The racial-segregation policy of the government of South Africa 1948–94 (deriving from Afrikaans 'apartness'). Under the apartheid system, nonwhites – classified as Bantu (black), coloured (mixed), or Indian – did not share full rights of citizenship with the white minority. For example, black people could not vote in parliamentary elections and until 1990 many public facilities and institutions were restricted to the use of one race only.

**SUPPRESSION**

Anti-apartheid feeling resulted in many uprisings, including:

- the Sharpeville uprising of 1960, which took place during a campaign against the pass laws
- the Soweto riots of 1976, which were prompted by the government's ruling that Afrikaans was to be the language used in African schools
- unrest at the Crossroads squatter camps in 1986.

During this period, thousands of the regime's opponents were imprisoned without trial and many anti-apartheid leaders were exiled, while others joined guerrilla forces outside South Africa.

After years of internal dissent and the imposition of international trade sanctions by the United Nations (UN) and other organizations, President F W de Klerk repealed the key elements of apartheid legislation and by 1994 apartheid had ceased to exist. The term apartheid has also been loosely applied to similar movements and other forms of racial separation, for example social or educational, in other parts of the world.

## appeasement

Historically, the conciliatory policy adopted by the British government towards the Nazi and fascist dictators in Europe in the 1930s in an effort to maintain peace. The word has come to mean any policy that fails to stand firm against a potentially hostile country.

## Aquinas, St Thomas
### (1225–1274)

Italian philosopher and theologian, canonized in 1323. He was a Dominican monk, known as the 'Angelic Doctor'. In 1879 his works were recognized as the basis of Catholic theology. He assimilated the philosophy of **Aristotle** into Christian doctrine.

Aquinas's unfinished *Summa Theologica*, begun in 1265, deals with the nature of God, morality, and the work of Jesus. The philosophy of Aquinas is known as Thomism. His theories were held to justify the political order of the medieval world as necessary for Christianity to flourish.

**Aquinas** *The works of Sir Thomas Aquinas form the basis of Catholic theology.*

❝ It sometimes happens that someone is a good citizen who has not the quality according to which someone is also a good man. ❞

**St Thomas Aquinas**, Italian philosopher and theologian, quoted in Walter Ullmann, *A History of Political Thought: The Middle Ages.*

## arbitration

The submission of a dispute to a third, unbiased party for settlement. It may be personal litigation, a trade-union issue, or an international dispute.

---

**INTERNATIONAL ARBITERS**

Following the Hague Conventions of 1899 and 1907, the first permanent international court was established in The Hague in the Netherlands, and the League of Nations set up an additional Permanent Court of International Justice in 1921 to deal with frontier disputes and the like. The latter was replaced 1945 with the International Court of Justice under the United Nations.

---

## Aristotle (384–322 BC)

Greek philosopher, a student of **Plato**, who advocated reason and moderation. Unlike Plato he derived his political theory from the recognition that mutual aid is natural to humankind, and refused to set up any one constitution as universally ideal. His political works are *The Politics* and *Nicomachaean Ethics.*

Among his many contributions to political thought were the first systematic attempts to distinguish between different forms of government, ideas about the role of law in the state, and the conception of a science of politics, which he regarded as 'the Queen of Sciences'. Although he was no democrat, Aristotle's

**Aristotle** *Aristotle conceived of a science of politics which he regarded as 'the Queen of Sciences'.*

political theory gives a much more central role to citizens than does Plato's. In the Middle Ages, Aristotle's philosophy, and therefore many of his political ideas, were incorporated into Christian theology, especially by **Aquinas**.

> ❝ Man by nature is a political animal. ❞
>
> **Aristotle**, Greek philosopher, *Politics* bk I, 1253a 2–3.

## arms control

The attempt to limit the arms race between the **superpowers** by reaching agreements to restrict the production of certain weapons. Because complete **disarmament** has come to seem impossible, arms control is the most important way that international relations can hope to restrict war and its effects. From 1970 to the end of the 20th century, arms control largely involved the USA and USSR signing pacts to restrict the production of nuclear missiles.

## arms race

Competition between nations to build up armaments. There have been arms races several times in recent history, brought about by military equipment becoming highly dependent on technology. Perhaps the first important arms race was the competition between Britain and Germany at the turn of the century to build bigger and better battleships, the 'Dreadnoughts'. The major arms race since World War II has been the competition between the USA and the USSR to build up more powerful nuclear weaponry, especially ICBMs (Intercontinental Ballistic Missiles), in the hope of achieving a first strike capacity over the enemy. The arms race is a central part of **balance of power** theory. In more recent times the emphasis

**arms race** *A cartoon from 1908 depicting German naval expansion.*

has shifted to competition for more and more sophisticated and accurate conventional weapons; it was these weapons which gave the US-led forces in the **Gulf War** overwhelming superiority over the Iraqi forces.

## army

An organized military force for fighting on the ground. A national army is used to further a political policy by force either within the state or on the territory of another state. Most countries have a national army, maintained by taxation, and raised either by conscription (compulsory military service) or voluntarily (paid professionals). Although high technology air forces and navies were central to the **Cold War**, armies capable of patrolling the ground are increasingly returning to a central role because of the requirements of peacekeeping.

## assembly

An assembly is a collection of people who either directly comprise, or represent, a political or social entity. In a political sense, assemblies are decision-making or rule-passing groups. In many cases there is no real difference between an assembly and a **parliament**, house of representatives, chamber of **deputies**, or whatever the local terminology of the political system may be. There remains a shade of difference in the implication, however. Because a full assembly (as in school 'assembly') implies that *all* relevant people are present, calling a body an assembly implies less a meeting of representatives, perhaps with freedom of action, than a direct collection of all parties. In the **United Nations**, for example, the General Assembly contains all the member states, in contrast to the Security Council, which has only a few members. The authority of an assembly is accordingly greater than that of a council or set of representatives.

## asylum, political

The granting of refuge in another country to a person who, for political reasons, cannot return to his or her own country without putting himself or herself in danger. Under British immigration rules, asylum is granted only in cases where refugees can prove that if they return to their country of origin they will be persecuted for reasons of race, religion, nationality, membership of a particular group, or political opinion.

- In the first seven months of 1999 there were 37,000 applications for political asylum in the UK, involving chiefly

New legislation came into effect in the UK on 1 April 2000, which, among other changes, replaced welfare benefits with a food voucher system, worth £35 a week for an adult, and allowed asylum seekers to be forcibly dispersed into accommodation around the UK.

Kosovar refugees from Yugoslavia, and, in fewer numbers, Somalis, Sri Lankan Tamils, Afghans, and Turkish Kurds.

- By August 1999, there were 83,000 asylum seekers (not counting dependants) who were awaiting a decision on their status or who were appealing expulsion orders.

Home Office statistics suggested that only 17% of asylum applicants processed in 1998 were genuine refugees.

### Augustine of Hippo, St (Aurelius Augustinus; 354–430)
One of the early Christian leaders and writers known as the Fathers of the Church. He was converted to Christianity by Ambrose in Milan and became bishop of Hippo (modern Annaba, Algeria) in 396. Augustine's main politically relevant writing, in his vast output of at least 113 books and treatises, was *The City of God*, vindicating the Christian church and divine providence. His general sense of humankind was highly pessimistic and he regarded a firm state as a necessary instrument to force people to live by Christian rules.

### authoritarianism
Rule of a country by a dominant **élite** who repress opponents and the press in order to maintain their own wealth and power. They are frequently indifferent to activities not affecting their security, and rival power centres, such as **trades unions** and **political parties**, are often allowed to exist, although under tight control. An extreme form is **totalitarianism**.

### authority
In a political system, the right to make and enforce legitimate decisions. The nature, sources, and limitations of political authority have been much debated questions since the time of the ancient Greeks. Authority is a form of political power that depends ultimately on public acceptance rather than mere force.

### ayatollah
(Arabic 'sign of God') An honorific title awarded to Shiite Muslims in Iran by popular consent, as, for example, to Ayatollah Ruhollah Khomeini. It has become shorthand for those wielding political power and influence in Muslim countries.

## balance of power

The theory that the best way of ensuring international order is to have power so distributed among states that no single state is able to achieve a dominant position. During the nuclear stalemate of the **Cold War** it was often asserted that the balance of power had been replaced by a 'balance of terror'. Now that the USA is the only **superpower** the balance of power as a concept is more likely to be applied at a regional level.

## ballot

(Italian *ballotta*, diminutive of *balla*, 'a ball') The process of voting in an election. In democracies ballots are usually secret. Ballot rigging is a term used to describe elections that are fraudulent because of interference with the voting process or the counting of votes. Secret voting at elections of members of Parliament was advocated by English reformers in the early 19th century; it was included in the draft of the Reform Bill of 1832, a bill on the

Under the Athenian and other democracies in ancient Greece small balls were used for secret voting; this method was known as *psephisma* (from *psephos*, a pebble, the original instrument of balloting). It was used on all questions affecting the status of individuals. These were of two kinds: lawsuits and proposals of ostracism. Thus psephology is the name for that part of political science which deals with the study of elections.

subject having been introduced by Daniel O'Connell in 1830. It was also among the demands of the Chartists, and frequent attempts were made to introduce it between 1832 and 1872. The secret ballot was first used in

❝ The ballot is stronger than the bullet. ❞

**Abraham Lincoln,** former US president, speech, 19 May 1856.

England in 1870, in the London School Board elections. Two years later, William Forster's Ballot Act introduced it into parliamentary and municipal elections.

## Baltic States

The collective name for the states of Estonia, Latvia, and Lithuania. They were formed as independent states after World War I out of former territories of the Russian Empire. The government of the USSR recognized their independence in peace treaties signed in 1920, but in 1939 forced them to allow occupation of important military bases by Soviet troops. In the following year, the Baltic States were absorbed into the Soviet Union as constituent republics. They regained their independence in September 1991 after the collapse of the Soviet Union.

## behaviouralism

Those approaches in **political science** that became important in post-war America and spread to some university departments in Europe. Technically, a behavioural approach is one that concentrates on explaining overt political or social behaviour in terms of other overt or express phenomena. For example, when considering **voting**, the only part of the process which can be subjected to a behavioural study is the actual casting of the vote, which can be observed externally and objectively; the ideology of the voter cannot be studied as here more subjective matters are involved. Other objective factors, such as class, religion, region, and age can be taken into consideration when describing the voting process, but individual policy preferences or attitudes to issues are much more difficult to study.

## Bell, Daniel (1919– )

Leading US sociologist who tried to show how the West, as a result of welfare state and mixed economy, had come to the 'end of the ideological age', in *The End of Ideology* (1960). Over 30 years later the same thesis was proclaimed after the collapse of the Soviet Union.

## Bentham, Jeremy (1748–1832)

English philosopher, legal and social reformer, and founder of **utilitarianism,** a political philosophy still highly important and developed by his colleague **James Mill**, and James's son **John Stuart Mill**. The essence of Bentham's political philosophy, pronounced in his *Principles of Morals* *and Legislation* (written in 1780, published in 1789) was that the object of all legislation should be 'the greatest happiness for the greatest number'. Bentham declared that the 'utility' of any law is to be measured by the extent to which it promotes the pleasure, good, and happiness of the people concerned. In 1776 he published *Fragments on Government.* He championed annual elections, the secret **ballot**, and universal male suffrage.

**Bentham** *Jeremy Bentham, English philosopher and founder of **utilitarianism**.*

> ❛ The greatest happiness of the greatest number is the foundation of morals and legislation. ❜
>
> **Jeremy Bentham**, English philosopher and legal and social reformer, *The Commonplace Book.*

### Bentley, Arthur Fisher (1870–1957)
US political scientist. In *The Process of Government* (1908), he laid down the theory that '**pressure groups**' influence all governments. This theory, developed by subsequent generations of political science, lies at the heart of the modern political science theories of **pluralism** and **corporatism**.

### Bill of Rights (UK)
In Britain, an act of Parliament of 1689, which established Parliament as the primary governing body of the country. It made provisions limiting royal prerogative with respect to legislation, executive power, money levies, courts, and the army, and stipulated Parliament's consent to many government functions. The Bill of Rights is the nearest approach to a written constitution that the United Kingdom possesses. Since 1998 the Human Rights Act, incorporating the European Convention on Human Rights into UK law, has given UK citizens the sort of protections that the US Bill of Rights gives.

---

### THE UK BILL OF RIGHTS

The 1688 Bill of Rights embodied the Declaration of Rights which contained the conditions on which William and Mary were offered the throne in the Glorious Revolution. The act made illegal:

- the suspension of laws by royal authority without Parliament's consent
- the power to dispense with laws
- the establishment of special courts of law
- levying money by royal prerogative without Parliament's consent
- the maintenance of a standing army in peacetime without Parliament's consent.

It also asserted a right to petition the sovereign, freedom of parliamentary elections, freedom of speech in parliamentary debates, and the necessity of frequent parliaments.

---

## Bill of Rights (USA)

In the USA, the first ten amendments to the US Constitution, incorporated in 1791. These rights were not originally part of the draft of the Constitution. The Bill of Rights was mooted during the period of ratification. Twelve amendments were proposed by Congress in 1789; the ten now called the Bill of Rights were ratified in 1791. Originally they only applied to the

---

### The US Bill of Rights

| | |
|---|---|
| **1** | Guarantees freedom of worship, of speech, of the press, of assembly, and to petition the government |
| **2** | Grants the right to keep and bear arms |
| **3** | Prohibits billeting of soldiers in private homes in peacetime |
| **4** | Forbids unreasonable search and seizure |
| **5** | Guarantees none be 'deprived of life, liberty, or property without due process of law' or compelled in any criminal case to be a witness against himself or herself |
| **6** | Grants the right to speedy trial, to call witnesses, and to have defence counsel |
| **7** | Grants the right to trial by jury of one's peers |
| **8** | Prevents the infliction of excessive bail or fines, or 'cruel and unusual punishment' |
| **9**, **10** | Provides a safeguard to the states and people for all rights not specifically delegated to the central government. |

Federal Government. A major part of US constitutional development was the process, known as incorporation, from the end of the Civil War until the 1960s, by which the **Supreme Court** came to apply the Bill of Rights to state governments as well as the federal powers.

### Bismarck, Otto Eduard Leopold von (1815–1898)

German politician, prime minister of Prussia 1862–90 and chancellor of the German Empire 1871–90. He pursued an aggressively expansionist policy, waging wars against Denmark (1863–64), Austria (1866), and France (1870–71), which brought about the unification of Germany. More than any one else, he laid the foundations for the power of Germany in European politics ever since. In the process he proclaimed the German Empire in 1871, after defeating France in the Franco-Prussian War 1870–71, and annexing Alsace-Lorraine. These later moves helped make World War I almost inevitable.

**Bismarck** *Otto von Bismarck, German politician who laid the foundation for Germany's power in European politics.*

### Bodin, Jean (1530–1596)

French political philosopher whose six-volume *De la République* (1576) is considered the first work on political economy. Bodin, a lawyer by profession, developed a highly authoritarian political theory emphasizing obedience to a sovereign ruler. As such his work was seen as a precursor to the ideas of Thomas **Hobbes**.

### Bolshevik

(From Russian *bolshinstvo* 'a majority') Originally a member of the majority of the Russian Social Democratic Party who split from the **Mensheviks** in 1903. The Bolsheviks, under **Lenin**, advocated the destruction of capitalist political and economic institutions and the setting up of a socialist state with power in the hands of the workers. The Bolsheviks set the Russian Revolution of 1917 in motion. They changed their name to the Russian Communist Party in 1918. The word has come to mean any very left wing group or political programme.

### bourgeoisie

(French 'the freemen of a borough') In Marxist political theory the social **class** above the workers and peasants, and below the nobility. It has come more loosely to mean the middle class. 'Bourgeoisie' and bourgeois have also acquired a contemptuous sense, implying commonplace, philistine respectability. Some socialists use it to refer to the whole propertied class, as distinct from the **proletariat**.

**bourgeoisie** *A late 19th-century cartoon, showing the contemporary conception of the bourgeoisie as exploitative moneymakers.*

### Bukharin, Nikolai Ivanovich (1888–1938)

Soviet politician and theorist. A moderate, he was the chief **Bolshevik** thinker after **Lenin**. He drafted the Soviet constitution of 1936, but in 1938 was imprisoned and tried for treason in one of Stalin's show trials. He pleaded guilty to treason, but defended his moderate policies and denied criminal charges. He was executed nevertheless, as were all other former members of Lenin's Politburo except **Trotsky**, who was murdered, and **Stalin** himself. In 1988 he was posthumously exonerated.

> 6 We might have a two-party system, but one of the two parties would be in office and the other in prison. 9
>
> **Nikolai Ivanovich Bukharin,** Soviet politician and theorist, attributed remark.

### bureaucratic state

German sociologist Max **Weber** and many later social theorists argued that political systems would become increasingly similar as they all underwent a process of increasing 'bureaucratization'. According to this theory the especial suitability of bureaucratic forms of administration for running complex and large-scale organizations would make the development of a bureaucratic state essential, regardless of official ideologies. One theory derived from Weber, the **convergence thesis**, claimed that even such apparently opposed systems as the USA and the USSR were growing increasingly alike as bureaucracy took over. Political changes in the 1980s undermined this theory. Not only did the communist economies collapse from inefficiency, to be replaced by attempts at free-market capitalism, but liberal, conservative and even social democrat governments throughout the West set out to 'deregulate' their own economies, reducing the role of the **state** considerably.

## Burke, Edmund (1729–1797)

British politician and political theorist, born in Dublin, Ireland. During a parliamentary career spanning more than 30 years, he was famous for opposing the government's attempts to coerce the American colonists and for supporting the emancipation of Ireland. However, he was a vehement opponent of the French Revolution, which he denounced in his most famous political work, *Reflections on the Revolution in France* (1790). (The English radical Thomas Paine, in *The Rights of Man* (1791–92), famously countered this.) Burke is often seen as the first theorist of British

**Burke** *Edmund Burke is often seen as the first theorist of British Conservatism.*

Conservatism because of his basic political credo – that **liberty** is only possible within the strict framework of law and order. He also stressed the limitations on human reason in politics and the need for tradition.

> ❝ Liberty, too, must be limited in order to be possessed. ❞
>
> **Edmund Burke**, Anglo-Irish political theorist and Whig politician, letter to the Sheriffs of Bristol.

## cabinet

The group of ministers who hold a country's highest executive offices and decide government policy. In Britain the cabinet system originated under the Stuarts, where the term was used for 'a small room, implying secrecy'. Under William III it became customary for the king to select his ministers from the party with a parliamentary majority.

The US cabinet, unlike the British, does not initiate legislation, and its members, appointed by the president, must not be members of Congress. In the UK the cabinet is collectively responsible to Parliament for the policy it pursues, and, in theory, the members of the cabinet are obliged to stand or fall together, and to act as one on all questions relating to the executive government. A significant part of the cabinet's work, however, is carried out through its committee system that was important in both World Wars and has been extensively used since 1945. As the prime minister appoints the committee members, and as in many cases the real decision may be taken by a committee rather than at cabinet level, this has become a major source of prime ministerial power.

*Cabinet Collective Responsibility*

Constitutionally the cabinet is bound to offer, through the prime minister, unanimous advice to the sovereign, who is constitutionally bound to accept that advice. Ministers are collectively responsible to Parliament for the conduct of the government and for its policies. In addition, however, each minister is also individually responsible for the running of his or her department and for its policies.

Individual and collective ministerial responsibility is constitutionally important in enabling Parliament to secure information and to question and criticize the government and its policies, but the doctrine of ministerial responsibility tends to be overshadowed by party solidarity. An attack on an individual minister normally means an attack on the government, and an attack on the government usually brings its parliamentary supporters rallying to its defence and the government's majority will normally safeguard it from defeat.

## capitalism

An economic system in which the principal means of production, distribution, and exchange are in private (individual or corporate) hands and competitively operated for profit. A mixed economy combines the private enterprise of capitalism and a degree of state monopoly, as in nationalized industries and welfare services. Most capitalist economies are actually mixed economies, but some (such as the US and Japanese) have a greater share of the economy devoted to free enterprise. The worldwide trend since the 1980s has been for a restoration of large areas of state monopoly to private enterprise, and thus an increase in capitalism, especially as the old Soviet-style economies of the USSR and Eastern Europe have become almost entirely free enterprise.

> ❝ Making capitalism out of socialism is like making eggs out of an omelette. ❞
>
> **Vadim Bakatin**, candidate in his first Russian presidential election, speech, May 1991.

## capital punishment

Legally endorsed punishment by death. Capital punishment is retained in 92 countries and territories (1990), including the USA (38 states), China, and Islamic countries. It was abolished in the UK in 1965 and is not practised anywhere in Western Europe. Those opposed to capital punishment argue not only that it is immoral, but that its finality, in an age when the failure of the criminal justice system to bring in safe verdicts is so often apparent, makes it entirely unsafe in a democracy. Those in favour of capital punishment argue that it is a more effective deterrent to crime than imprisonment, though criminologists have never been able to demonstrate this convincingly.

According to human rights organization Amnesty International, in 1998 China executed at least 1,769 people, which was more than the rest of the world combined. Executions in China were performed upon convicted criminals, including political prisoners and drunk drivers.

❝ I am dismayed that such learned people, with all the facts before them, have taken so long to come to the conclusion that, I guess, most people around the world formed 30 years ago. ❞

**Dennis Bentley**, on the quashing of the conviction of his older brother Derek Bentley, an epileptic of 19 with a mental age of 11, who had been hanged in 1953 for being the accomplice to the murder of PC Sidney Miles. Christopher Craig, who fired the shot while Bentley himself was under arrest, was detained for 10 years as he was 16 at the time and too young to be executed. The Court of Appeal quashed Bentley's conviction on 30 July 1998; *Daily Telegraph*, 31 July 1998.

## caste

A system of stratifying a society into ranked groups defined by marriage, descent, occupation, or **ethnicity**. Most common in South Asia, caste systems are also found in other societies such as in Mali and Rwanda, and in the past, in Japan, in South Africa under apartheid, and among the Natchez. The term dervives from the Portuguese *casta* 'race' and the most famous caste system, the one most studied by sociologists, is the Hindu system.

The system in Hindu society dates from ancient times and is divided into four main classes known as 'varnas':

- Brahmans (priests)
- Kshatriyas (nobles and warriors)
- Vaisyas (traders and farmers)
- Sudras (servants)
- plus a fifth group, Harijan ('untouchables').

Because castes are fixed by birth, there is no real social mobility of the type known in class based societies where individuals can rise above the birth origins. The modernizing of the Indian economy has partially weakened the caste system, though most Hindus still oppose intercaste marriages. In other ways the system has been rejuvenated since Independence through extensive caste quotas in public life, and by democratic politics, which encourages the mobilization of caste loyalties for electoral support.

## Castro (Ruz), Fidel
(1927– )
Cuban communist politician, prime minister 1959–76, and president for life from 1976. After two unsuccessful attempts he led the revolution that overthrew the right-wing regime of the dictator Fulgencio Batista, 1959. He developed his own brand of Marxism, but was forced into alliance with the USSR because of US opposition. This led to the Cuban Missile Crisis of 1961 that cemented US hostility. The USA has made many attempts to overthrow Castro, who has

**Castro** *Fidel Castro remains a hugely popular leader in Cuba, despite economic problems.*

remained enormously popular in Cuba despite major economic problems, especially since 1990, when the country was deprived of the support of the USSR. Castro has, however, faced increasing pressure for reform as the long term US trade embargo has continued to bite.

> ❛ A revolution is not a bed of roses. A revolution is a struggle to the death between the future and the past. ❜
>
> **Fidel Castro**, Cuban communist president, speech given on the second anniversary of the revolution, Havana, January 1961.

## catch-all party
A Catch-all party is a political party which has no very clear base in terms of the social characteristics of the people who vote for it, unlike, for example, most socialist parties with their predominantly working-class base. Critics see them as predominantly motivated by the desire to put together as large a voting support as possible in order to maximize their chances of winning elections. Catch-all parties are unlikely to stand far from the centre of the political spectrum in which they operate, but may well espouse a set of policies which do not fit in the left and right framework (see **left wing**

and **right wing**). In practice, these parties have usually been right-of-centre, standing for support of the economic and social status quo. They have, therefore, denied any **class** orientation.

Typical of parties often defined as catch-all were the **Gaullist** parties in post-war France, especially during the early years of the Fifth Republic, and the Italian Christian Democrats

## censorship

The suppression by authority of material considered immoral, heretical, subversive, libellous, damaging to state security, or otherwise offensive. It is generally more stringent under **totalitarian** or strongly religious regimes and in wartime. Historically censorship has been the norm. Only since the mid-20th century has there been a widespread belief that the state has no right to control what an individual reads, writes, or watches. Not only legislation such as the **Official Secrets Act** and broadcast control laws, but laws relating to obscenity, libel, and blasphemy act as forms of censorship. In the USA, despite First Amendment protection of free speech, attempts at censorship are made by government agencies or groups; the question is often tested in the courts, especially with respect to sexually explicit material. Recently, efforts have been made to suppress certain pieces of music and works of art, on such grounds as racial harassment and social depravity.

> 6 You can cage the singer but not the song. 9
>
> **Harry Belafonte**, US singer and civil-rights activist, *International Herald Tribune,* 3 October 1988.

---

**HISTORICAL CENSORSHIP**

In China 213 BC the first emperor Qin ordered that all books of history be destroyed so that he could not be criticized. A mid-18th-century emperor had 2,665 books destroyed that contained content he disapproved of. In England under the Tudors and Stuarts, the crown claimed a monopoly on printing presses, and publication could be carried out only under licence until 1695.

*censorship of the Internet*

Concerns over the ready availability of sensitive national security material, pornography, and other issues have led a number of countries to pass laws attempting to censor the Internet. These include the US Communications Decency Act (1996).

In 2000, a survey by the US organization Freedom House found that 63% of countries restrict print and electronic journalists. The French monitoring service Reporters sans Frontières states that the following countries totally or largely restrict Internet access: Azerbaijan, Belarus, Burma, China, Cuba, Iran, Iraq, Kazakhstan, Kyrgystan, Libya, North Korea, Saudi Arabia, Sierra Leone, Sudan, Syria, Tajikistan, Tunisia, Turkmenistan, Uzbekistan, and Vietnam.

**central bank**

The bank responsible for issuing currency in a country. Often it is also responsible for foreign exchange dealings on behalf of the government and for supervising the banking system in the country (it holds the commercial reserves of the nation's clearing banks).

Although typically independent of central government, a central bank will work closely with it, especially in implementing monetary policy through the control of interest rates. The earliest bank to take on the role of central bank was the Bank of England, which, having been taken into state control by the Labour government of 1945, was given its independence back by the Labour government of 1997. In the USA the Federal Reserve System was established in 1913.

## Central Intelligence Agency (CIA)

The CIA is the USA's main intelligence organization, established in 1947. It has actively intervened overseas, generally to undermine left-wing regimes or to protect US financial interests, for example in the Democratic Republic of Congo (formerly Zaire) and Nicaragua. Concerns over its power led to an attempt at legislative control in 1980, since when all covert activity by the CIA had by law to be reported to Congress, preferably beforehand, and to be authorized by the president. The CIA was originally intended solely for use overseas in the **Cold War** (domestic intelligence functions are performed by the Federal Bureau of Investigation). It was involved in, for example, the restoration of the Shah of Iran in 1953, South Vietnam (during the Vietnam War), Chile (the coup against President Allende), and Cuba (the Bay of Pigs). On the domestic front, it was illegally involved in the

Watergate political scandal and in the 1970s lost public confidence when US influence collapsed in Iran, Afghanistan, Nicaragua, Yemen, and elsewhere.

---

**CIA** FAILURE

Details emerged in April 1997 of one of the CIA's greatest failures since its operations began. Up to 300 Iraqis died as the result of a failed attempt by the CIA to overthrow Saddam Hussein, the Iraqi leader. The CIA financed an Iraqi opposition group (the Iraqi National Accord) which killed 100 people in a bombing campaign against civilian targets in Baghdad and other cities, and fomented a military coup against the Iraqi leader. In June 1996 Saddam Hussein struck first, crushing the CIA-backed coup with ease; as many as 80 officers were executed or died under torture.

---

## centralization

A tendency to concentrate administrative functions in the hands of the principal departments of the state, as opposed to allowing local autonomy. Centralization seeks to establish uniformity in institutions and standards of services offered by state organizations. It has frequently been ideologically associated with **socialism** or **communism**, but is also widely associated with increasing government intervention in the affairs of society, especially during the 20th century. Centralization, like bureaucracy, almost inevitably creates problems for democratic government and personal liberty, but it remains part of the constant struggle between democracy and liberty on the one hand and efficient and effective government on the other.

## charisma

A special, indefinable power perceived in certain leaders by their followers. 'Charisma' was originally a theological term meaning the divine grace bestowed on a Christian in order to fulfil his or her mission. The term was appropriated by the German sociologist Max **Weber** to describe the inspirational power of some individuals. Leaders as diverse as **Hitler** and Ghandi have been regarded as charismatic.

## Charter 77

A Czechoslovak human rights movement founded in 1977 to lobby for Czech conformity to the UN Declaration of Human Rights. It is named after the 1977 human rights manifesto signed by over 700 intellectuals and former party officials in response to the 1975 Helsinki Conference on Security and Cooperation in Europe (CSCE). The manifesto prompted a renewed crackdown on dissidents by the communist government and Charter 77 was forced to operate largely as an underground movement. Charter 77 remained active throughout the 1980s and played a key part in the largely peaceful overthrow of the communist regime in 1989–90.

## Christian Democracy

An ideology of a number of parties active in Western Europe since World War II, especially in Italy, the Federal Republic of Germany, and France, and (since 1989) in central and Eastern Europe. Christian Democrats are essentially moderate Conservatives who believe in a mixed economy and in the provision of social welfare. Their original political ties to the Catholic Church have largely evaporated or weakened to the point that they are entirely politically independent. Their original strength came from the fact that the churches were amongst the few institutions to retain public confidence in Europe after World War II had made existing Conservative parties unacceptable.

## Christianity

World **religion** derived from the teaching of Jesus, as found in the New Testament, during the first third of the 1st century. It has a present-day membership of about 1 billion, and is divided into groups or denominations that differ in some areas of belief and practice. Its main divisions are the Roman Catholic, Eastern Orthodox, and Protestant Churches. The Christian churches have been integral to the politics of Western societies, and to a lesser extent eastern European and Russian countries since the early Middle Ages. **Secularization** in the 20th century has largely weakened their political influence, but a residual political impact of Christianity can be seen in most countries, and in some, particularly North America, politicians treat any issue that might excite religious interests very carefully. More recently Christianity has come to be allied with radical politics, especially through Roman Catholic **liberation theology** in Latin America.

## Christian Socialism

A 19th-century movement stressing the social principles of the Bible and opposed to the untrammelled workings of *laissez-faire* capitalism. Its founders, all members of the Church of England, were Frederick Denison Maurice, Charles Kingsley, and the novelist Thomas Hughes. In Europe, the establishment of Christian Socialist parties (the first was in Austria) was a direct response to the perceived threat of more extreme socialism and therefore contained many conservative features. The large-scale alienation of the industrial working class in Europe from organized religion limited the potential political influence of this movement.

## citizenship

The legal status as a member of a state. In most countries citizenship may be acquired either by birth or by naturalization. The status confers rights such as voting and the protection of the law and may also impose responsibilities such as military service.

The UK has five different categories of citizenship, with varying rights; in particular rights of abode in the UK differ widely for each category.

- British citizen, basically, anyone born in the UK to a parent who is a British citizen, or to a parent who is lawfully settled in the UK
- British dependent territories citizenship
- British overseas citizenship
- British subject
- Commonwealth citizen.

## civil defence or civil protection

The organized activities by the civilian population of a state to mitigate the effects of enemy attack. Civil defence was very important in all European countries during World War II in dealing with the effect of air raids. Although civil defence protection was continued for some time after 1945, it became apparent that the impact of a nuclear attack would swamp any organized efforts at protection. In the UK the Civil Defence Corps and Auxiliary Fire Service were disbanded in 1968. Skeleton arrangements continue under the authority of the Home Office, and regulations came into force in 1983 compelling local authorities to take part in civil defence exercises. Councils have to train staff, provide blast-proof bunkers and communication links, and take part in the exercises.

## civil disobedience

The deliberate breaking of laws considered unjust, a form of nonviolent direct action. The term was coined by the US writer Henry Thoreau in an essay of that name in 1849. Mahatma Gandhi advocated it to prompt peaceful withdrawal of British power from India. Civil disobedience has since been employed by, for instance, the US civil rights movement in the 1960s and the peace movement in the 1980s. It is important to distinguish civil disobedience, where one deliberately breaks the law complained of, from simply disobeying laws, for example regulations on street protests, in order to draw attention to other problems.

## civil liberties

Civil liberties are freedoms or rights that are thought to be especially valuable in themselves and vital to the functioning of a liberal and democratic society. Emphases vary, but most lists of basic civil liberties will include freedom of speech, freedom of religion and of thought, freedom of movement, freedom of association, the right to a fair trial, and freedom of the person. These rights and liberties are essential protections against the arbitrary acts of government and are fundamental to free political association. In some countries these freedoms are enshrined in a written document or constitutional code, sometimes known as a **Bill of Rights**, enforced by a special court. In the USA a powerful body of legal doctrine has been developed around the first ten amendments to the Constitution, especially the first amendment, the fourth amendment, the due process clause of the fifth amendment and also, more recently, the equal protection clause of the fourteenth amendment. In many democracies a **pressure group** exists specifically to protect such liberties; the UK has Liberty (the National Council for Civil Liberties), and the USA the American Civil Liberties Union.

## civilization

Refers to highly developed human society with a structured division of labour, from the Latin *civis* 'citizen'. The earliest known civilizations include:

- Sumer in 3500 BC
- Egypt in 3000 BC
- Indus Valley in 2500 BC
- China in 2200 BC
- Mesoamerica – the Olmec in 1200 BC
- Peru – the Chavin in 800 BC

In the social sciences civilization is defined as an advanced socio-political stage of cultural evolution, whereby a centralized government (of a city, ceremonial centre, or larger region called a state) is supported by the taxation of surplus production, and rules the agricultural and, often, mercantile base. Those who do not produce food become specialists who govern, lead religious ritual, impose and collect taxes, and execute public works such as irrigation systems, roads, bridges, buildings, and tombs. These institutions require leisure time for such an upper social class to develop writing, mathematics, the sciences, engineering, architecture, philosophy, and the arts.

## civil law

One of the two main European legal systems, English **(common) law** being the other. Civil law concerns criminal law, but also matters other than criminal law, such as contract and tort. During the Middle Ages, Roman law was adopted, with local modifications, all over Europe, mainly through the Christian church's influence. Its later diffusion was due largely to the influence of the French *Code Napoléon*, based on Roman law, which was adopted in the 19th century by several states of Eastern Europe and Asia, and in Egypt. Inside the Commonwealth, Roman law forms the basis of the legal systems of Scotland and Québec and influences the state law of Louisiana in the USA. It is also the basis of South African law.

## civil rights

The rights of the individual citizen, largely but not entirely rights against the state, such as rights to freedom of speech, rights to a fair trial, and rights against racial or other discrimination. In many countries they are specified (as in the **Bill of Rights** of the US constitution or the **Human Rights** Act in the UK) and guaranteed by law to ensure equal treatment for all citizens. In the USA, the struggle to obtain civil rights for former slaves and their descendants, both through legislation and in practice, has been a major theme since the **Civil War**. In Europe the European Convention of Human Rights, drafted shortly after World War II, has been incorporated into the domestic law of most countries.

## civil rights movement

The general term for efforts by African-American people to affirm their constitutional rights and improve their status in society after World War II. Having made a significant contribution to the national effort in wartime, they began a sustained campaign, often involving **civil disobedience**, for full civil rights that challenged racial discrimination and segregation; the Civil Rights Commission was created by the Civil Rights Act of 1957. Further favourable legislation followed, such as the Civil Rights Act of 1964 and the 1965 Voting Rights Act. Other civil rights movements have included those of women and homosexuals. **See also:** *women's movement; gay politics.*

## civil service
The body of administrative staff appointed to carry out the policy of a government. In the USA, federal employees are restricted in the role they may play in political activity, and they retain their posts (except at senior levels) when there is a change in administration. Members of the UK civil service may not take an active part in politics, and do not change with the government. Continental countries tend to a combination of the US and British systems.

---

**SIZE AND SCOPE OF THE UK CIVIL SERVICE:**

- A basic distinction is usually drawn between nonindustrial and industrial staff in the civil service.
- There are about 476,000 civil servants, a decrease of 37% from a peak of 751,000 in 1976.
- About half of all civil servants are engaged in the provision of public services, a further quarter are employed in the Ministry of Defence, and the rest are divided between central administrative and policy duties, support services, and largely self-supporting services, such as National Savings and the Royal Mint.
- The Diplomatic Service is a separate service, employing some 5,800 people for the Foreign and Commonwealth Office and diplomatic missions abroad.

---

## civil society
That part of a society or culture outside the government and state-run institutions. For Karl **Marx** and G W F **Hegel**, civil society was that part of society where self-interest and materialism were rampant, although Scottish economist Adam Smith believed that enlightened self-interest would promote the general good. Classical writers and earlier political theorists such as John **Locke** used the term to describe the whole of a civilized society. The term re-emerged in political theory at the end of the 20th century, especially to help analyse problems of post-communist society.

## civil war

War between rival groups within the same country. Major civil wars such as that in the UK (1642–51) or the USA (1860–64) have far-reaching consequences for the political and social structures of their societies, and are often comparable to the effect of major revolutions like the French or Russian revolution.

## class

The main grouping of social stratification in industrial societies, based primarily on economic and occupational factors, but also referring to people's style of living or sense of group iden-tity. It is perhaps the most important single analytic sociological

**class** *A late 19th-century image of the class gulf and the exploitative relationship between the upper and lower classes.*

concept. Within the social sciences, class has been used both as a descrip-tive category and as the basis of theories about industrial society. Theories of class may see such social divisions either as a source of social stability (**Durkheim**) or social conflict (**Marx**). The most widely used descriptive classification in the UK divides the population into five main classes, with the main division between manual and non-manual occupations. Max **Weber's** work on social class lies behind most modern sociological research using such a schema. Such analysis is also widely used in indus-trial research and by advertising and market research agencies.

## cleavage

Cleavage is a vital concept in political science, especially in relation to vot-ing behaviour and the formation and working of party systems. It means a division between groups within a society, based on some more or less fixed attributes: cleavages exist along lines of **class**, **religion**, language, and race. The patterns of social cleavages fix competitive politics and generally influ-ence the stability and functioning of the political system. To a large extent this sort of patterning is still crucial. In origin most political parties repre-sent a given side on one or more cleavage lines, and are likely to be opposed by parties representing the other side. Some kinds of cleavage patterns make for more violent political life, and less stable government, than if other cleavages dominate. For example, racial or religious cleavages, if at all strong, are much harder to manage by bargaining and compromise than class cleavages, because they tend to produce absolute demands.

## coalition

An association of political groups, usually for some limited or short-term purpose. The primary use is to describe a grouping of political parties that collectively form a government when one party has failed to secure a majority in a **legislature**. Coalition government is the norm in democratic politics, and is by no means as unstable as critics often claim. In fact, only a simple plurality (see **pluralism**) electoral system such as that in the UK and USA is likely to produce non-coalition governments.

## coalition theory

Coalition theory, much of which developed from **game theory**, is part of the rational choice tradition in political science, which tries to explain political activity. There are two main areas of political activity to which coalition theories apply. The best worked out is the creation of a coalition of minority parties in a parliament. The other covers military and diplomatic alliances. For government formation coalition theories have been quite successful, especially when applied to party systems where the number and sizes of parties, as well as the ideological spectrum of the nation's politics, leaves no obvious coalition grouping.

- One of the two principal rules to emerge from early work in this sphere was that the most likely coalition to form will be what is called a 'minimum-winning' coalition.
- The other principal rule is of 'ideological connectedness'. Parties will try to cooperate with others nearest to their own political values.

## cohabitation

Cohabitation is a term used to describe the periods like that between 1986 and 1988, when a socialist French president, François Mitterrand, and a centre-right coalition headed by prime minister Jacques Chirac, together formed the government of France. This is not a problem unique to France. It can arise in any political system where a president with real political power is elected separately, from the parliament. In the USA, for example, it is relatively rare for a Republican president to enjoy a majority in

Congress, where both Houses usually have a Democratic majority, but the Republicans often win the presidency. French politicians had always feared this situation arising. In the end, a very uneasy truce was worked out in which the centre-right government would not try to repeal much of its socialist predecessor's work, and would accept that Mitterrand had a supremacy in certain areas traditionally viewed as in the president's prerogative. Cohabitation proved possible, and when the same situation occurred at the end of the 1990s, the French began to see many advantages.

## Cold War

Ideological, political, and economic tensions between 1945 and 1989 between the USSR and Eastern Europe on the one side and the USA and Western Europe on the other. The Cold War was fuelled by propaganda, undercover activity by intelligence agencies, and economic sanctions, and was intensified by signs of conflict anywhere in the world. Arms-reduction agreements between the USA and USSR in the late 1980s, and a reduction of Soviet influence in Eastern Europe, led to a reassessment of positions, and the 'war' was officially ended in December 1989. Part of the cause was an inability by the USSR and the USA to understand each other's reasons for keeping large military forces in central and western Europe after World War II. In essence both sides were defending against imaginary threats. The terrible threat of nuclear instability made it impossible for either side to take the risk of trusting the other.

> The term 'Cold War' was first used by Bernard Baruch, advisor to US president Harry S Truman, in a speech made in April 1947. He spoke about Truman's intent for the USA to 'support free peoples who are resisting attempted subjugation by armed minorities or by outside pressures'.

## collective responsibility

The doctrine found in governments modelled on the British system of **cabinet** government. It is based on convention, or usage, rather than law, and requires, once the cabinet has reached a decision, that all members of the government are bound by it and must support it or resign their posts. From time to time prime ministers have to allow exceptions, when an issue, such as British membership of the **European Union** in the 1970s, cuts across normal political lines and an insistence on collective responsibility would make it impossible to form a successful cabinet at all.

## collectivism

An ideological position, in which the collective (such as the state) has priority over its individual members. It is the opposite of individualism. Collectivism, impossible to attain in a pure form, would transfer all social and economic activities to the state, which would assume total responsibility for them. In practice, it is possible to view collectivism as a matter of degree and argue that the political system of one state is more, or less, collectivist than that of another, for example in the provision of state-controlled housing. Collectivism was the hallmark of moderate left wing parties like the British **Labour party** in the period from 1945 until the 1980s. As a policy, collectivism denotes the advocacy of substantial state intervention in the economy for the benefit of the whole community, as opposed to a *laissez-faire* attitude. Historically the term came into vogue as a reaction to some of the more extreme variants of individualism. It can cover a wide range of social policy positions from interventionism to complete state ownership.

## collectivization

The policy pursued by the Soviet leader Joseph **Stalin** in the USSR, after 1928, to reorganize agriculture by taking land into state ownership or by creating collective farms. Much of this was achieved during the first two five-year plans but only by forcible means and with much loss of life amongst the peasantry. It involved combining numerous peasant holdings into huge agricultural enterprises run along industrial lines. Resistance to collectivization was so strong, especially among the prosperous peasants or 'kulaks', that productivity remained low on the new farms. Many peasants killed their livestock and destroyed their farm equipment before joining the collectives, while the mass deportations of those who refused to give up their private land deprived the country of experienced farmers.

## command economy or planned economy

An economy where resources are allocated to factories, by the state, through central planning. This system is unresponsive to the needs and whims of consumers and to sudden changes in conditions (for example, crop failure or fluctuations in the world price of raw materials). For example, in the former USSR, state planners decided what was to be produced. They passed orders down to factories, allocating raw materials, workers, and other factors of production to them. Factories were then told how much they should produce with these resources and where they should be sent. If there were a shortage of goods in the shops, then goods would be rationed through queuing.

In theory, the time and money expended on advertising and marketing in a market-led economy can instead be devoted to producing something useful in a command economy. However, historical experience in the 20th century suggests that planned economies have not produced as high growth as free-market or mixed economies.

## Common Agricultural Policy (CAP)

System of financial support for farmers in **European Union** (EU) countries. The most important way in which EU farmers are supported is through guaranteeing them minimum prices for part of what they produce. CAP has been criticized for its role in creating overproduction, and consequent environmental damage, and for the high price of food subsidies. The objectives of CAP were outlined in the Treaty of Rome:

- to increase agricultural productivity
- to provide a fair standard of living for farmers and their employees
- to stabilize markets
- to assure the availability of supply at a price that is reasonable to the consumer.

---

**THREE-YEAR REFORMATION**

**1992**  In response to the alarming rate at which surpluses were increasing, a package of reforms was initiated to cut prices and compensate farmers for the loss of income through direct subsidies. Cereals farmers who took land out of production received 'set-aside' payments.

**1995**  The three-year reform of CAP was completed, with the result that mountains of unsold cereals, butter, and beef had shrunk to almost nothing. European farm prices, previously two to three times world-market levels, fell sharply. The reforms cut prices but also pushed up farm spending from 31 billion ecus in 1992 to more than 40 billion in 1996. In 1994 nearly half (49.3%) of EU spending still went to farmers.

In the 1970s and 1980s CAP became extremely expensive due to over-production of those agricultural products that were subsidized. In many years, far more was produced than could be sold and it had to be stored, creating 'mountains' and 'lakes' of produce. This put CAP under intense financial and political strain, and led to mounting pressure for reform.

## common law

That part of the English law and of some Commonwealth countries not embodied in legislation. It consists of rules of law based on common custom and usage and on judicial decisions. Originally English common law was the basis of law in the USA and many other English-speaking countries. Common law developed after the Norman Conquest in 1066 as the law common to the whole of England, rather than local law. As the court system became established (under Henry II), and judges' decisions became recorded in law reports, the doctrine of precedent developed. This means that, in deciding a particular case, the court must have regard to the principles of law laid down in earlier reported cases on the same, or similar points, although the law may be extended or varied if the facts of the particular case are sufficiently different. Hence, common law (sometimes called 'case law' or 'judge-made law') keeps the law in harmony with the needs of the community where no legislation is applicable or where the legislation requires interpretation.

## Commons, House of

The lower chamber of the UK Parliament (and of the Canadian Parliament). It consists of around 650 elected members of Parliament, each of whom represents a constituency. Its functions are to debate, legislate, and to scrutinize the activities of government. Constituencies are kept under continuous review by the Parliamentary Boundary Commissions of 1944. The House of Commons is presided over by the Speaker. Proceedings in the House of Commons began to be televised from November 1989. After the 2001 election, the Commons included 117 women members, including 7 women in senior

Since 1945, general elections have been held approximately every three years, but in practice some Parliaments have lasted four or five years (for example 1945–1950, 1959–64, 1966–70, and 1992–98), whereas others have been of much shorter duration (for example 1950–51, 1964–66, February–October 1974).

government positions. The members of the House of Commons are directly elected by universal adult suffrage. Under the Parliament Act of 1911 the maximum period between general elections is five years, but the prime minister may advise a dissolution at any time during a Parliament's lifetime. Typically the prime minister will try to time the election to maximize his or her party's electoral chances. In order to remain in office the prime minister and his or her government must retain the confidence of a majority of the members of the House of Commons. It may not have, and does not need to retain, the confidence of a majority of the peers in the **House of Lords**. The majority of ministers are drawn from the House of Commons and it is there that the government must defend its actions and policies. Major legislation is introduced first in the House of Commons and any resolution or bill proposing an increase in taxation or public expenditure must be moved in the Commons by a minister of the Crown. If the House of Lords declines to pass financial legislation within a month of its being passed by the lower house, then it may nonetheless receive the royal assent under the Parliament Act of 1911. The House of Commons is therefore constitutionally and politically much the more important of the two Houses of Parliament.

> ❝ The Commons, faithful to their system, remained in a wise and masterly inactivity. ❞
>
> **James Mackintosh**, Scottish lawyer, philosopher, and historian, *Vindiciæ Gallicæ*.

### commonwealth
A body politic founded on law for the common 'weal' or good. Political philosophers of the 17th century, such as Thomas **Hobbes** and John **Locke**, used the term to mean an organized political community. In Britain it was specifically applied to the regime (the Commonwealth) of Oliver Cromwell in 1649–60. In the 20th century it came to mean principally the British Commonwealth, a loose association of countries that had once been part of the British Empire.

### communalism
A society in which **ethnicity**, **religion**, or other social identity completely determines the entire life of a subculture in question: people will not only marry, reside, speak, and carry out their entire private life inside their sub-

culture, but this pattern may carry through to social, economic, and political institutions. For example, separate wings of political parties and **trades unions** entirely committed to one subculture may exist. States may provide for separate education and even media structures to mirror the subcultures, as in the Netherlands.

## commune

Generally a group of people or families living together, sharing resources and responsibilities. There have been various kinds of commune through the ages, including a body of burghers or burgesses in medieval times, a religious community in the USA, and a communal division in communist China. The word nowadays has two main referents:

- any local government division in Italy and in some other European countries
- a group of ideologically motivated people trying to live a life by different principles from those characteristic of their society.

## communism

A form of revolutionary **socialism** based on the theories of the political philosophers Karl **Marx** and Friedrich **Engels**, emphasizing common ownership of the means of production and a planned economy. The principle is that each should work according to his or her capacity and receive according to his or her needs. Politically, it seeks the overthrow of **capitalism** through a proletarian (see **proletariat**) revolution. The first communist state was the USSR after the revolution of 1917. Revolutionary socialist parties and groups united to form communist parties in other countries during the interwar years. After World War II, communism was enforced in those countries that came under Soviet occupation. China emerged after 1961 as a rival to the USSR in world communist leadership, and other countries attempted to adapt communism to their own needs. The late 1980s saw a movement for more individual freedoms in many communist countries, culminating in the abolition or overthrow of communist rule in Eastern European countries and Mongolia, and further state repression in China. By 1991 communism had ceased to be the official doctrine in Russia with the disintegration of the USSR; it now survives in only a few countries, notably China, Cuba, North Korea, Laos, and Vietnam, and even in these countries, market forces are being encouraged in the economic sphere. The classic text of communism is Marx's *Communist Manifesto* (1848), which argues that human society, having passed through successive stages of slavery,

**feudalism**, and capitalism, must advance to communism. The term is derived from French *commun* 'common, general'.

## community

In the social sciences, the sense of identity, purpose, and companionship that comes from belonging to a particular place, organization, or social group. The concept dominated sociological thinking in the first half of the 20th century. Much early sociology, like that of **Weber** and **Durkheim**, is concerned to understand the collapse of community in favour of other forms of social organization and solidarity consequent on the industrial revolution.

## comparative government or comparative politics

Comparative government is one of the main branches of politics. Its aim is to compare the ways in which different societies cope with various problems to develop an understanding of how different institutional mechanisms work within their contexts, and, more ambitiously, to develop general theories concerning government. One might ask whether the French or US presidencies enjoy the most power, or ask for a comparison of the roles of the parliaments in Britain and Germany. Considerable progress has been made in some areas. The effect of different electoral systems on the party system is well understood from wide-ranging comparisons; and predictive theories have been developed which work quite well in relationship to coalition membership in multi-party systems. The main problem for comparative government as a science is that it lacks a general theoretical framework to identify what the principal tasks of a political system are. Researchers have therefore relied heavily on **functionalism**.

## Comte, (Isidore) Auguste Marie François Xavier
(1798–1857)

French philosopher regarded as the founder of sociology, a term he coined 1830. He sought to establish

**Comte** *Auguste Comte, French philosopher.*

sociology as an intellectual discipline, using a scientific approach ('positivism') as the basis of a new science of social order and social development. In his six-volume *Cours de philosophie positive* (1830–42), Comte argued that human thought and social development evolve through three stages: the theological, the metaphysical, and the positive or scientific. He sought to proclaim society's evolution to a new golden age of science, industry, and rational morality.

> ❝ Men are not allowed to think freely about chemistry and biology, why should they be allowed to think freely about political philosophy? ❞
>
> **Auguste Comte**, French philosopher, *Positive Philosophy*.

## confederation
A form of union of individual states or societies. Confederation insists on the individual independence of each state or society in a common union, while **federation** insists on the supremacy of the common government. Thus the British Commonwealth, as at present constituted, is a confederation, as was the German confederation established at the Congress of Vienna in 1815. The 'federal' versus 'confederal' distinction can be crucially important – the American Civil War was fought not only on the slavery question but also on the question of whether the union should be confederate or federate. Often confederations are formed when there is not common purpose to persuade member states to give up the degree of sovereignty required for a federation. Thus many of the debates about the future of the **European Union** are really debates about whether it should have a federal or confederal nature.

## confessional politics
Political party system, whose voters belong to a specific religious denomination. The label 'confessional party' is restricted to those political movements where the appeal is intentionally to voters with a specific commitment to an overall religious creed, and not simply policy attitudes that correlate with aspects of religious beliefs. The principal role of such parties is to support policies specifically in the interest of, or influenced by, their faith. There are two main types of confessional party.

- One, often known as a clerical party, exists in a political system where there is a high degree of religious uniformity among those who subscribe to a religious belief at all, but where there is also an **anticlerical** political movement which is opposed to the influence of any religious body on national politics.
- An alternative version of a confessional party is where a society is split by religious identities, so that political parties evolve to support a particular religious community against both a potentially secular state, and against parties promoting a rival religious community.

## confidence vote

A test of support for the government in the **legislature**. In most parliamentary democracies the survival of a government depends on assembly support. The opposition may move a vote of 'no confidence'; if the vote is carried, it requires the government, by convention, to resign. Constitutions often seek to limit the ease with which an opposition can pass a no confidence vote, to avoid governmental instability. For example, in Germany, a 'constructive vote of no confidence' is held in which a majority of assembly members are required to vote positively in favour of an alternative executive leader (or chancellor) rather than simply against the current one. The last UK prime minister to be defeated in the House of **Commons** and forced to resign was Labour prime minister James Callaghan in 1979. He lost the subsequent general election to Margaret Thatcher.

## Congress

The national **legislature** of the USA, consisting of the House of Representatives (435 members, apportioned to the states of the Union on the basis of population, and elected for two-year terms) and the Senate (100 senators, two for each state, elected for six years, one-third elected every two years). Congress meets in Washington, DC, in the Capitol Building. An act of Congress is a bill passed by both houses. In 19th-century history, the term 'congress' refers to a formal meeting or assembly, usually for peace, where delegates assembled to discuss or settle a matter of international concern, such as the Congress of Vienna 1815, which divided up Napoleon's empire after the Napoleonic Wars.

> The Congress of the United States met for the first time on 4 March 1789. It was preceded by the Congress of the Confederation representing several states under the Articles of Confederation 1781–89.

## conservation

Action taken to protect and preserve the natural world, usually from pollution, overexploitation, and other harmful features of human activity. The late 1980s saw a great increase in public concern for the environment, with membership of conservation groups, such as Friends of the Earth, Greenpeace, and the US Sierra Club, rising sharply. **See also:** *environmentalism*; *green movement*.

Globally the most important conservation issues include:

- the hole in the ozone layer caused by depletion of atmospheric ozone by the action of chlorofluorocarbons (CFCs)
- global warming, the build-up of carbon dioxide in the atmosphere
- destruction of habitats and a reduction in species biodiversity.

Conservation groups in Britain originated as early as the 1860s. They include:

- the Commons Preservation Society (1865), which fought successfully against the enclosure of Hampstead Heath (1865) and Epping Forest (1866) in London
- the National Footpaths Preservation Society (1844)
- the National Trust (1895)
- English Heritage (1983)
- English Nature (1991, formerly the Nature Conservancy Council).

> 6 The Earth only has so much bounty to offer and inventing ever larger and more notional prices for that bounty does not change its real value. 9
>
> **Ben Elton**, English writer and comedian, *Stark*, 'Dinner in Los Angeles'.

## constitution

Body of fundamental laws of a state, laying down the system of government and defining the relations of the **legislature**, **executive**, and **judiciary** to each other and to the citizens. Constitutions also often list inalienable rights citizens must have against the state. Since the French Revolution (1789–99) almost all countries (the UK is an exception) have adopted written constitutions; that of the USA (1787) is the oldest. Of all the world's states, 69 have adopted their current constitutions in the period since 1989.

Constitutions are the rules of the political game, and must be understood in their cultural context: often there are large unwritten aspects even to a written constitution.

The constitution of the UK does not exist as a single document, but there are several constitutionally vital texts:

In the contemporary world 24 states have federal constitutions: Argentina, Australia, Austria, Belgium, Bosnia-Herzegovina, Brazil, Canada, The Comoros, Ethiopia, Germany, India, Malaysia, Mexico, Micronesia, Nigeria, Pakistan, the Russian Federation, St Kitts and Nevis, Sudan, Switzerland, the United Arab Emirates, the USA, Venezuela, and Yugoslavia.

- Magna Carta 1215
- the Petition of Right 1628
- Habeas Corpus Act 1679, limiting the royal powers of taxation and of imprisonment
- the Bill of Rights 1689
- the Act of Settlement 1701, establishing the supremacy of Parliament and the independence of the judiciary
- the Parliament Acts 1911 and 1949, limiting the powers of the Lords.
- The Triennial Act 1694, the Septennial Act 1716, and the Parliament Act 1911 limiting the duration of Parliament
- the Reform Acts of 1832, 1867, 1884, 1918, and 1928 extending the electorate.

## constitutional law

That part of the law relating to the **constitution**. It sets out the rules defining the powers, limits, and rights of government. In countries without a written constitution, such as the UK, constitutional law is a mixture of legislation, judicial precedent, and accepted conventional behaviour. Many countries have either a specialized court system, or a special 'top court' to interpret written constitutions, which therefore wield considerable political power. Examples are the French Constitutional Council and the German Constitutional Court as well as the US Supreme Court. Judges on these bodies may be more powerful even than senior elected politicians.

## containment

The policy (adopted from 1947) designed to prevent the spread of **communism**; first stated by George Kennan (1904–    ), then a State

Department official, and later US ambassador to Moscow. Communism was to be 'contained' within the boundaries that it had then achieved. Any apparent expansion of communist influence justified US involvement, which lead rapidly to problems with the Korean and later the Vietnam wars.

## convergence thesis

The theory, developed in the 1950s but foreshadowed by **Weber**, that **socialist** and **capitalist** societies would inevitably grow more and more alike. Much of this theory relied on ideas about bureaucracy (see **bureaucratic state**) and the kind of organization needed to ensure rational policies and effective decision-making.

The basic thesis is that the Russian Revolution led to monolithic administrative and policy control by the communist party, while in the West efficient and powerful **civil services** have developed and close control is exercised over the everyday activities of business, workers, and others.

The responses of bureaucrats and planners charged with achieving particular goals are seen as transcending overt ideological differences between the two societies. The thesis has been very influential even though, in its original application, (contrasting US and USSR models), the theory has simply proved to be wrong. However much planning and state power may have grown in capitalism, it ultimately became necessary for the Soviet-style economies to be abandoned and replaced with market economies.

## convertibility

The arrangement under which the currency of one nation can be freely sold, at prices determined by the market, for another currency. Convertibility has come to be a particular problem for the post-communist economies of Eastern Europe and the former USSR. The rouble and other Eastern European currencies were not subject to market forces, because the government fixed their external prices at quite absurdly artificial prices. Nonconvertibility was more than merely setting an absurd price, however, it also involved refusing to exchange roubles for other currencies. Convertibility was the currency equivalent of **free trade**.

## corporatism

The belief that the state in capitalist democracies should intervene to a large extent in the economy to ensure social harmony. In Austria, for example, corporatism results in political decisions often being taken after discussions between chambers of commerce, **trades unions**, and the government. Britain in the 1970s was often accused of becoming corporatist.

## corporative state

A state in which the members are organized and represented not on a local basis as citizens, but as producers working in a particular trade, industry, or profession. Originating with the **syndicalist** workers' movement, the idea was superficially adopted by the fascists during the 1920s and 1930s. Catholic social theory, as expounded in some papal encyclicals, also favours the corporative state as a means of eliminating **class** conflict. The concept arose in the political theories of the syndicalist movement of the early 20th century, which proposed that all industries should be taken over and run by the trades unions, a federation of whom should replace the state. Certain features of syndicalist theory were adopted and given a right-wing flavour by the fascist regime in Italy. Employers' and workers' organizations were represented in the National Council of Corporations, but this was completely dominated by the Fascist Party and had no real powers. Corporative institutions were set up by the Franco and Salazar regimes in Spain and Portugal, under the influence of fascist and Catholic theories.

## Council of Europe

A body constituted in 1949 to achieve greater unity between European countries, to facilitate their economic and social progress, and to uphold the principles of parliamentary democracy and respect for **human rights**. It comprises a:

- Committee of foreign ministers
- Consultative Assembly
- Parliamentary Assembly (with members from national parliaments)
- European Commission on Human Rights, (now the unified European Court of Human Rights).

The founder members were the UK, France, Italy, Belgium, the Netherlands, Sweden, Denmark, Norway, the Republic of Ireland, Luxembourg, Greece, and Turkey; Iceland, Germany, Austria, Cyprus, Switzerland, Malta, Portugal, Spain, Liechtenstein, Finland, and San Marino joined subsequently. With the collapse of **communism** in Eastern Europe, the council acquired a new role in assisting the establishment of Western-style democratic and accountable political systems in the region, and several former communist countries entered into membership. Hungary joined in 1990, Czechoslovakia and Poland in 1991 (the Czech and Slovak republics were given separate status in 1993), Bulgaria in 1992, Estonia, Lithuania, Romania, Slovakia, and Slovenia in 1993, Andorra in 1994, and

Albania in 1995. Latvia, Moldova, Ukraine, Macedonia, and Russia were admitted in 1996, bringing the membership to 39.

## coup d'état

French for 'stroke of state' (often shortened to 'coup'), it is the forcible takeover of the government of a country by elements from within that country, generally carried out by violent or illegal means. It differs from a **revolution** in typically being carried out by a small group (for example, of army officers or opposition politicians) to install its leader as head of government, rather than being a mass uprising by the people.

Recent coups include:

- 1973 the overthrow of the socialist government of Chile by a right-wing junta
- 1983 the military seizure of power in Nigeria
- 19–22 August 1991 the short-lived removal of Mikhail Gorbachev from power in the USSR by hardline communists,
- February 1998 the overthrow of President Ahmad Tejan Kabbah in Sierra Leone in.

## criminal law

That body of law that defines the public wrongs (crimes) that are punishable by the state and establishes methods of prosecution and punishment. It is distinct from **civil law**, which deals with legal relationships between individuals (including organizations), such as contract law. The laws of each country specify what actions or omissions are criminal. These include serious moral wrongs, such as murder; wrongs that endanger the security of the state, such as treason; wrongs that disrupt an orderly society, such as evading taxes; and wrongs against the community, such as dropping litter.

---

### GOING TO COURT

In England and Wales crimes are either:
- indictable offences (serious offences triable by judge and jury in a crown court)
- summary offences dealt with in magistrates' courts
- hybrid offences tried in either kind of court according to the seriousness of the case and the wishes of the defendant.

An action may be considered a crime in one country but not in others, such as **homosexuality** or drinking alcohol.

## Cuban missile crisis

The confrontation in international relations in October 1962 when Soviet rockets were installed in Cuba and US president Kennedy compelled Soviet leader Nikita Khrushchev, by military threats and negotiation, to remove them. This event prompted an unsuccessful drive by the USSR to match the USA in nuclear weaponry.

Following reports that the USSR was constructing launching sites for nuclear missiles in Cuba, the USA imposed a naval 'quarantine' around the island on 22 October 1962, and the two **superpowers** came closer to possible nuclear war than at any other time. Soviet inferiority in nuclear weapons forced a humiliating capitulation to Kennedy's demands on 2 November, when Kennedy announced that Soviet missile bases in Cuba were being dismantled.

## Cultural Revolution

Refers to a series of Chinese mass movements from 1966 to 1969 begun by Communist Party leader **Mao Zedong**, directed against the upper middle class – bureaucrats, artists, and academics – who were killed, imprisoned, humiliated, or 'resettled'. Intended to 'purify' Chinese **communism**, it was also an attempt by Mao to renew his political and ideological pre-eminence inside China. Half a million people are estimated to have been killed. The 'revolution' was characterized by the violent activities of the semi-military Red Guards, most of them students. Although the revolution was brought to an end in 1969, the resulting bureaucratic and economic chaos had many long-term effects.

## decentralization

In politics, the **devolution** of power and decision-making authority to sub-state units, usually regional or local government. It may also mean the breaking up of a large state institution into smaller and more local departments so that administrative decisions, as well as political authority, are concentrated more locally.

## decolonization

The gradual achievement of independence by former colonies of the European imperial powers, which began after World War I. The process of decolonization accelerated after World War II with 43 states achieving independence from 1956 to 1960, 51 from 1961 to 1980, and 23 from 1981. The movement affected every continent: India and Pakistan gained independence from Britain in 1947; and Algeria gained independence from France in 1962.

## decree

A legal rule or regulation, having all the power of parliamentary legislation, but issued directly by a government department. They are a particular feature of continental European constitutional law, particularly in France. For example the constitution of the French Fifth Republic was intended to limit parliamentary power, and thus the ability to make binding laws in many areas was transferred to the administrative branch of government. This is a rather wider transfer of power away from an elected body than is to be found in **common law** systems. The real difference is one of subjective tone, as 'decree' carries with it a suggestion of autocratic power.

## de Gaulle, Charles André Joseph Marie (1890–1970)

French general and later first president of the Fifth Republic (1958– 69). He organized the Free French troops fighting the Nazis (1940–44), was head of the provisional French government 1944–46, and leader of his own **Gaullist** party. In 1958 the national assembly asked him to form a government to solve the crisis in Algeria where the army had mutinied in support of the French settlers. He became president at the end of 1958, having changed the constitution to provide for a presidential system, and served until 1969. As wartime leader of the 'Free French' he entered Paris in 1944 in triumph and was briefly head of the provisional government before resigning over the new constitution of the Fourth Republic in 1946. In 1947 he founded the Rassemblement du Peuple Français, a nonparty constitutional reform movement. He then withdrew from politics in 1953 until recalled and given power in 1958. His policies all concentrated on retaining French independence from both the USA and USSR, and seeking a leadership role in Europe.

> ❝ A great country worthy of the name does not have any friends. ❞
>
> **Charles de Gaulle**, French general and first president of the Fifth Republic, *Time*, 28 May 1965.

## delegation

The passing of the responsibility for carrying out a task down the chain of command. For example, a managing director may delegate control of finances to the company secretary. A foreman may delegate responsibility for supervising a group of machines to a worker. Politically, delegation often means that an electoral body or other political group delegates to one member the right to cast a vote in an assembly to which he or she is elected according to specific instructions, rather than electing one member to exercise his or her own judgement on their behalf.

## democracy

Government by the people, usually through elected representatives (from Greek *demos* 'the community', *kratos* 'sovereign power'). In the modern world, democracy has developed from the American and French revolutions, although forms of representative parliamentary government existed in Iceland from the 10th century and in England from the 13th century. The other main form of democracy, in theory at least, is **direct** (or **participatory**) **democracy** where the whole body of citizens makes decisions collectively. What is commonly called **liberal democracy** is perhaps the main modern form, which combines the right to representative government with the right to individual freedom, and limitations on the invasion of this freedom by government. In practice the features of a liberal democratic system include:

- representative institutions based on majority rule
- free and fair elections
- a choice of political parties
- accountability of the government to the electorate
- freedom of expression, assembly, and the individual, guaranteed by an independent judiciary
- limitations on the power of government.

> ❡ Democracy is the fig leaf of elitism. ❡
>
> **Florence King**, US writer. *Reflections in a Jaundiced Eye.*

## Democratic Party

One of the two main political parties of the USA. It tends to be the party of the working person, as opposed to the **Republicans**, the party of big business, but the divisions between the two are not clear cut. Its stronghold since the Civil War has traditionally been industrial urban centres and the Southern states, but conservative Southern Democrats were largely supportive of Republican positions in the 1980s and helped elect President Reagan. Bill Clinton became the first Democrat president for 13 years in 1993.

**20th century Democrat presidents:**

- Grover Cleveland
- Franklin D Roosevelt
- John F Kennedy
- Jimmy Carter
- Woodrow Wilson
- Harry S Truman
- Lyndon B Johnson
- Bill Clinton.

From the 1930s the Democratic Party pursued a number of programmatic reforms. They included Roosevelt's **New Deal** and Kennedy's 'New Frontier' (which was implemented by Lyndon Johnson). The New Deal aimed at pulling the country out of the 1930s depression and putting it back to work. The 'Great Society' programme – encompassing the Economic Opportunity Act, the Civil Rights Act 1964, the Medicare and Voting Rights Act 1965, and the Housing, Higher Education, and Equal Opportunities acts – sought to make the USA a better place for the ordinary, often disadvantaged, citizen. The Party has always had a tendency to factions and internal divisions. Currently it contains:

- the Conservative Democratic Forum (CDF)
- the northern liberals, moderate on military matters but interventionist on economic and social issues
- the radical liberals of the Midwest agricultural states
- the Trumanite 'Defense Democrats', liberal on economic and social matters but military hawks
- the non-Congressional fringe, led by Jesse Jackson and seeking a 'rainbow' coalition of African-Americans, Hispanics, feminists, students, peace campaigners, and southern liberals.

## demonstration

Political protest, sometimes illegal, and always involving mass participation. The official response to demonstrations in Britain was first codified by the Public Order Act of 1936, (largely replaced by the Public Order Act of 1986). This was provoked by the Cable

An estimated 280,000 attended the Countryside March in London of March 1998 in protest against the new Labour government's policies affecting rural areas.

Street riot of that year, when an anti-Jewish march through east London by Oswald Mosley and 2,500 of his Blackshirts gave rise to violent clashes. Later famous demonstrations include:

- the nonstop anti-apartheid presence in front of South Africa House in London April 1986-February 1990
- the women's peace camp at Greenham Common
- the picketing of the News International complex in Wapping, east London, by print workers in 1986
- the anti-poll-tax demonstrations in Trafalgar Square, London, in March 1990.

During the 1990s resort to 'direct action', through demonstrations, has spread to include environmentalists, for example protesting against housing developments, rubbish dumps, new road building, notably the Newbury bypass, and extension of Manchester airport; and animal welfare groups, protesting against fox-hunting and vivisection.

## dependency thesis

Dependency theory was a popular radical critique of Western capitalist nations in their relations with the **Third World** during the 1960s and 1970s, and still has its advocates. It derives from a theory of economic imperialism, and is also used as a critique of foreign aid programmes. The basic idea is that major capitalist powers such as the USA and leading members of the European Union have not really given up colonialism, but in fact exercise enormous political control over Third World countries. They control them by the use of economic pressure and by exploiting their superior market position to extract unfair advantage in international trade. The theory holds that, as most of the finance for industrial and agricultural development in the Third World has to come from the money markets in the developed capitalist states, that development is tied to the economic interests of the West. An extreme version claims that outright foreign aid gifts are suspect, because the funding is used to develop Third World economies in such a way that they remain totally dependent on markets in the **First World**.

## détente

The reduction of political tension and the easing of strained relations between nations; for example, the ending of the **Cold War** in 1989–90. The term (from the French for 'relaxation') was first used in the 1970s to describe the easing of East–West relations in the form of trade agreements and cultural exchanges.

## deterrence

The key concept underlying the nuclear arms race: the belief that a potential aggressor will be discouraged from launching a 'first strike' nuclear attack by the knowledge that the adversary is capable of inflicting 'unacceptable damage' in a retaliatory strike. This doctrine is widely known as that of mutual assured destruction **(MAD)**. Three essential characteristics of deterrence are the 'capability to act', 'credibility', and the 'will to act'. In general, military policies rely on deterrence when the costs of waiting for an attack and then defending against it are prohibitive.

## devolution

The delegation of authority and duties from a central political institution to regional ones. In the UK a bill for the creation of Scottish and Welsh assemblies was introduced in 1976 and rejected by referenda in Scotland and Wales in 1979. The Labour government that took office in May 1997 introduced legislation to establish Scottish and Welsh assemblies. The Scottish Parliament is located in Edinburgh and the National Assembly for Wales in Cardiff. The word was first widely used in this sense in connection with Ireland, with the Irish Nationalist Party leader John Redmond claiming in 1898 that the Liberals wished to diminish home rule into 'some scheme of devolution or federalism'. Devolution is different from **federalism** because it is, ultimately, the creation of the central government, which remains potentially supreme.

In practice, however, devolution and federalism may operate in a similar fashion. In a devolved system it may not be practical to alter the division of powers because the resistance of the regional authorities may be such that the whole system would be undermined if the central authority attempted any change. Most **liberal democracies** experienced pressure for some degree of devolution in the last decades of the 20th century.

## dialectical materialism

The political, philosophical, and economic theory of the 19th-century German thinkers Karl **Marx** and Friedrich **Engels** that lies at the heart of **Marxism**. It stresses the material (or the physical and economic) causation of all society, including ideas, and the way history develops by contradictions building up between opposed socio-economic forces (the dialectic).

## dictatorship

Absolute rule by one ruler, overriding the **constitution**. In ancient Rome a dictator was a magistrate invested with emergency powers for six months. Although dictatorships were common in Latin America during the 19th century, the only European example during this period was the rule of Napoleon III. The 20th century produced many dictatorships, including:

- Atatürk (Turkey)
- Pilsudski (Poland)
- Mussolini (Italy)
- Hitler (Germany)
- Primo de Rivera (Spain)
- Franco (Spain)
- Salazar (Portugal)
- Stalin (Soviet Union)
- Saddam Hussein (Iraq).

As a term of political analysis the word 'dictator' now has little value owing to its wholly derogatory overtones and lack of precision; it tends to disguise the way in which even in apparent dictatorships, effective power is seldom actually held by one independent ruler.

## dictatorship of the proletariat

A Marxist term for a revolutionary dictatorship established during the transition from capitalism to **communism** after a socialist revolution. In the USSR the communist rule from 1917 until the adoption of the Stalin Constitution in 1936, was officially termed the dictatorship of the **proletariat**. The idea is that the working classes are too strongly affected by the ideological manipulation of the past to see their own interests clearly immediately after an election, and have to be lead, if necessary forced, along the proper revolutionary road.

**dictatorship of the proletariat** *A poster depicting Russian communist revolutionary Lenin leading the working class.*

## diplomacy

The process by which states attempt to settle their differences through peaceful means such as negotiation or arbitration. More generally it is the continual process of negotiation and communication, carried out by foreign policy professionals, which underlies the whole of international relations.

## direct democracy

According to the theory of direct democracy, all concerned citizens must directly participate in the making of decisions and the passing of laws, and this function can neither be delegated to others, nor carried out by other elected representatives. The idea comes from classical Greek democracy and by admirers of that system such as French philosopher Jean-Jacques **Rousseau**. To Rousseau, for example, direct democracy is necessary for true freedom, because one is only free when obeying a law which oneself has 'willed'. Others argue that direct involvement in politics, has an educative influence. No political system; today comes anywhere near operating direct democracy at the national level, nor has one ever done so. At times, local government may have approached this system; the Town Meetings of early New England states are the best example.

## disarmament

The reduction of a country's weapons of war. Most disarmament talks since World War II have been concerned with nuclear-arms verification and reduction, but biological, chemical, and conventional weapons have also come under discussion at the United Nations and in other forums. Attempts to limit the **arms race** (initially between the USA and the USSR and, since 1992, between the USA and Russia) have included the Strategic Arms Limitation Talks (SALT) of the 1970s and the Strategic Arms Reduction Talks (START) of the 1980s and 1990s. The enormous cost in lives and materials of World War I provided a considerable stimulus to efforts to reduce the arms race that had played a crucial role before 1914. Major, but ultimately fruitless, attempts were made by the League of Nations to secure a limitation on armaments, and limited disarmament treaties were made between some states (for example by Britain, the USA, and Japan on naval forces in 1930). What progress there was consisted of nuclear arms limitation treaties, only with the reduction in importance of nuclear weapons at the end of the **Cold War** did conventional disarmament return to the fore.

Following a recommendation of the UN General Assembly, the Conference on Disarmament (CD) was set up in 1978. Its objective is to promote the attainment of general and complete disarmament under effective international control. It held its first meeting in 1979, building on the 1963 Test Ban Treaty, the 1970 Non-proliferation Treaty, the 1972 Seabed Arms Control Treaty, and the 1972 Biological and Toxin Weapons Convention. In 1992 it introduced its own Chemical Weapons Convention, and is now the world's principal multilateral disarmament negotiating forum. It is based in Geneva.

### Disarmament: Key Dates

| | |
|---|---|
| **1930s** | League of Nations attempt to achieve disarmament fails. |
| **1968** | US president Lyndon B Johnson's proposals for Strategic Arms Limitation Talks (SALT) are delayed by the Soviet invasion of Czechoslovakia. |
| **1972–77** | SALT I is in effect. |
| **1979–85** | SALT II, signed by the Soviet and US leaders Brezhnev and Carter, is never ratified by the US Senate, but both countries abide by it. |
| **1986** | US president Ronald Reagan revokes this pledge, against the advice of his European NATO partners. |

| | |
|---|---|
| **1987** | Reagan and the Soviet leader Mikhail Gorbachev agree to reduce their nuclear arsenals by 4% by scrapping intermediate-range nuclear weapons. |
| **1990** | Treaty signed between the USA and the USSR limiting both NATO and the Warsaw Pact to greatly reduce conventional weapons systems in Europe. |
| **January 1991** | US president George Bush announces decision to halve US military presence in Europe. |
| **30–31 July 1991** | Bush and Gorbachev sign Strategic Arms Reduction Treaty (START), which limits both sides to no more than 6,000 nuclear warheads. |
| **September–October 1991** | Bush announces the unilateral reduction of about 2,400 US nuclear weapons, asking the USSR to respond in kind. Gorbachev offers a package of unilateral cuts and proposals that surpasses the broad arms-control initiative presented by Bush. |
| **January 1992** | Bush and Russia's president Boris Yeltsin promise additional (60–80%) cuts in land- and sea-based long-range nuclear missiles. In addition, Bush promises an accelerated withdrawal of US troops from Europe and the halting of future production of the advanced B-2 bomber. Yeltsin announces that Russian long-range missiles will no longer be targeted on US cities. |
| **June 1992** | Yeltsin consents to the abandonment of strategic parity (equal balance of arms) and announces, with Bush, bilateral cuts in long-term nuclear weapons that far surpass the terms of the 1991 START treaty. By 2003, it is promised, US warheads will be cut from 9,986 to 3,500, and Russian warheads from 10,237 to 3,000. |
| **January 1993** | START II treaty signed by Bush and Yeltsin in Moscow, committing both countries to reduce long-range nuclear weapons by two-thirds by the year 2003 and to do away with land-based, multiple warheads. |
| **May 1995** | Negotiations to review Non-Proliferation Treaty (NPT) continue in New York. The treaty was originally signed in 1970 to limit the spread of nuclear weapons for 25 years; the 1995 negotiations aim to renew the treaty on an indefinite basis, rather than for a limited period. |

> ❛ To adopt nuclear disarmament would be akin to behaving like a virgin in a brothel. ❜
>
> **David Penhaligon**, British Liberal politician, *The Guardian*, 1980.

## discrimination

A distinction made on social, economic, political, legal, religious or other grounds between individuals or groups such that one has the power to treat the other unfavourably. Discrimination has often been based on stereotype, including **anti-Semitism**, **apartheid**, and discrimination based on **caste**, **race**, and sex. There exists also the idea of positive discrimination, or **'affirmative action'**, sometimes practised in an attempt to counteract the effects of previous long-term discrimination. Not only minorities but, in some cases, majorities have been targets for discrimination.

Legislation has been to some degree effective in forbidding racial discrimination, against which there is a United Nations convention (1969). The problem for anti-discrimination policies is that much legislation necessarily involves treating people differently according to some attribute; pensions involve age distinctions, for example. How does one justify one sort of characteristic based differentiation and not others?

National legislation in the UK includes the race-relations acts of 1965 and 1976 and the Sex Discrimination Act of 1975.

## dissent

A strongly held opposition on moral grounds by a minority against an important law, or influential idea strongly supported by the majority. Dissent is often applied to issues like a state's foreign or military policy, or to issues traditionally seen as evoking moral outrage such as abortion, capital punishment, or interference with religious freedom. Alternatively dissent may be towards the entire basis of a state and how it operates, in which case dissenters do not accept the basic **legitimacy** of the state. The noun 'dissenter' has a long history in political theory, probably originally meaning someone who opposes a religious orthodoxy, and came to be applied to, among others, opponents of the regime in **totalitarian** societies such as the former USSR.

## divine right of kings

The Christian political doctrine that hereditary monarchy is the system approved by God, and thus hereditary right cannot be forfeited. Monarchs are accountable

**divine right of kings** *Pepin, who was anointed in 751 by the Pope after he usurped the throne of the Franks, starting the doctrine of the divine right of kings.*

to God alone for their actions, and rebellion against the lawful sovereign is therefore blasphemous. The doctrine had its origins in the anointing of Pepin in 751 (in what would today be France) by the Pope after Pepin had usurped the throne of the Franks. It was at its peak in 16th- and 17th-century Europe as a weapon, this time against the claims of the papacy. In 17th-century England the doctrine was maintained by the supporters of the Stuarts in opposition to the democratic theories of the Puritans and Whigs. The most influential exposition of divine right in English is to be found in Sir Robert Filmer's *Patriarcha* (1680). The success of John **Locke's** *Two Treatises on Government* (1690) signalled the decline of the theory of divine right in England, although versions are found, especially in France, until 1789 when **Rousseau** opposed it.

## division of labour

The system of work where a task is split into several parts and done by different workers. For example, on a car assembly line, one worker will fit doors, another will make the engine block, and another will work in the paint shop. The division of labour is an example of specialization. More generally it refers to the increasing specialization of economic roles in contrast to traditional craftwork. Division of labour also exists in traditional societies where men and women perform gender-related tasks (a sexual division of labour). Many sociologists, including **Marx** and **Durkheim**, have taken the division of labour to be crucial in the development of society, but perceived it often to be a cause of serious malfunctioning in those societies.

## domino theory

An idea popularized by US president Dwight D Eisenhower in 1954 that if one country came under communist rule, adjacent countries were likely to fall to communism as well. Used in the USA and Australia to justify intervention in southeast Asia, belief in the theory was a main cause of the Vietnam War. The domino theory has also been invoked in reference to US involvement in Central America. Political science experts in international relations have never regarded it as valid thesis.

## doves

Doves and their opposites, hawks, came into prominence in the USA during the **Vietnam War**. Hawks were those who favoured tough military activities and a generally forceful solution to problems. Doves were those who took a gentle, conciliatory, or pacifistic stance on any issue. Hawks, for example, would be in favour of President Nixon's bombing of

Cambodia in 1971, and might oppose arms control negotiations unless sure that the USA would gain an advantage. Since then, the terms hawks and doves have been used more generally to contrast any tough approach to almost any problem to a softer or more conciliatory one. For example, the stringent regulation of picket lines in industrial disputes could be hawkish; urging the police to avoid arrests would be a dove's response. The emphasis is essentially on contrasting the use of force and coercion to diplomacy and negotiation. The terminology may be fading from political discourse: it was notable that the hawk–dove metaphor was absent in the USA during the often fierce debates as to whether or not to go to war over Iraq's invasion of Kuwait.

### Downs, Anthony (1930– )
US political scientist, responsible for starting an entirely new line of research in politics with just one book, *An Economic Theory of Democracy.* At a time when most empirical research was influenced by sociology and psychology, he argued for the use of economic style analysis to explain political behaviour. Downs's approach, which came to be known as the rational-choice theory, is based on taking 'political man' as a creature who seeks to achieve maximum satisfaction through choices based on rational calculation, just as 'economic man' does. Downs showed that much of the behaviour of voters and political parties in Western democracies could be explained very satisfactorily by a few simple assumptions of this rational-choice sort. Work by others in the USA and Britain has considerably developed the theory, and has produced formulations that even have a certain predictive value. Unlike most political theory, Downsian models have repeatedly been tested in research on European and US politics with considerable success.

### due process of law
Legal principle, dating from the Magna Carta, (the charter of rights granted by King John of England 1215). Now enshrined in the fifth and fourteenth amendments to the US Constitution, it states that no person shall be deprived of life, liberty, or property without due process of law (a fair legal procedure). In the USA, the provisions have been given a wide interpretation, to include, for example, the right to representation by an attorney. It can sometimes be made into a more substantive doctrine – at one stage laws regulating wage rates were held in the USA to be a breach of due process, because they involved taking away the employer's 'property' with-

out trial. All developed legal systems have an equivalent doctrine – in the UK it is often referred to as the rules of **natural justice**.

## Durkheim, Emile (1858–1917)

French sociologist, one of the founders of modern sociology, who also influenced social anthropology. He worked to establish sociology as a respectable and scientific discipline, capable of diagnosing social ills and recommending possible cures. His four key works are:

- *De la division du travail social/The Division of Labour in Society* (1893), comparing social order in small-scale societies with that in industrial ones

- *Les Régles de la méthode/The Rules of Sociological Method* (1895), outlining his own brand of **functionalism**

- *Suicide* (1897), showing social causes of this apparently individual act

- *Les Formes élémentaires de la vie religieuse/The Elementary Forms of Religion* (1912), a study of the beliefs of Australian Aborigines, showing the place of religion in social solidarity.

## dystopia

An imaginary society whose evil qualities serve as a moral or political warning. The term was coined in 1868 by the English philosopher John Stuart **Mill**, and is the opposite of a **utopia**. George Orwell's *1984* (1949) and Aldous Huxley's *Brave New World* (1932) are examples of novels about dystopias. Dystopias are common in science fiction. The film *Metropolis* (1927) by the Austrian director Fritz Lang shows, like most dystopias, a highly mechanized society in which individual rights are suppressed by a ruling elite. This society could be either capitalist, as in Jack London's novel *The Iron Heel* (1907), or socialist, as in Ayn Rand's *Anthem* (1938). Other dystopian novels are *Fahrenheit 451* (1953) by Ray Bradbury and *A Clockwork Orange* (1962) by Anthony Burgess. It is interesting that dystopias are often much better defined and described than utopias.

## egalitarianism

The belief that all citizens in a state should have equal rights and privileges. Interpretations of this can vary, from the notion of equality of opportunity to equality in material welfare and political decision-making. Some states reject egalitarianism; most accept the concept of equal opportunities but recognize that people's abilities vary widely. Even those states that claim to be socialist find it necessary to have hierarchical structures in the political, social, and economic spheres. Egalitarianism was one of the three core principles of the French Revolution along with **liberty** and **fraternity**.

## election

The process of appointing a person to public office or a political party to government by voting. Elections were occasionally held in ancient Greek democracies and Roman tribunes were regularly elected. Free and fair elections are part of the very definition of **democracy**. The qualifications for voting in elections were liberalized during the 20th century. New Zealand was the first country to give women the vote, in 1893 and, among economically advanced states, Switzerland was the last, in 1971. The minimum age for voting has been almost universally lowered to 18.

**election** *This 18th-century painting by Hogarth depicts a candidate in a local election canvassing for votes.*

**STATES WITH NO ELECTIONS**

Among all the sovereign contemporary states, only six – Brunei, Oman, Qatar, Saudi Arabia, the United Arab Emirates, and the Vatican City State – do not have, and never have had, any political institutions that can, even in the loosest sense, be described as popularly representative. In other countries citizens have the right to vote for a government but they do not necessarily have a free or wide choice.

## electoral college

In the US government, the indirect system of voting for the president and vice-president. The people of each state officially vote not for the presidential candidate, but for a list of electors nominated by each party. The whole electoral-college vote of the state then goes to the winning party (and candidate). A majority is required for election.

The USA has as many electors as it has senators and representatives in Congress, so that the electoral college numbers 538 (535 state electors and 3 from the District of Columbia), and a majority of 270 electoral votes is needed to win. The process is now a formality, but originally members of the electoral college might exercise their own judgement. Several political systems have used electoral colleges in this way, and they can be used inside a political party to choose its leader

## élite

A small group with power in a society, having privileges and status above others. An élite may be cultural, educational, religious, political (also called 'the **establishment**' or 'the governing circles'), or social. Sociological interest has centred on how such **minorities** get, use, and hold on to power, and on what distinguishes élites from the rest of society. Most political scientists would agree that some degree of élite rule exists even in modern democracies. The real problems tend to occur when the élites are interlocking, rather than competing with each other. The political science theory of **pluralism** is a modern version of élite theory.

## emergency powers

Special powers granted to a government that allow normal legislative procedures or judicial remedies to be suspended. In democracies, such emergency powers are usually strictly controlled by the **legislature** and are permitted only for the duration of the emergency. They are intended to cope with war or some other national security crisis, though this could be internal conflict – revolutionary outbreaks or general strikes. The British Conservative government of 1970–74 declared five states of emergency to deal with industrial unrest, which is an equivalent act.

In France, emergency powers may be exercised under Article 16 of the 1958 constitution by the president, although he must consult the prime minister, the presidents of the Senate and the National Assembly, and the Constitutional Council before declaring a state of emergency. These powers were in fact used only once, during the period April to September 1961, at the time of the Algerian war of independence. In the USA emergency powers can, and have, been taken. Although the US constitution makes no reference to such emergency powers, President Abraham Lincoln suspended the right of habeas corpus during the Civil War, and Franklin Roosevelt interned Japanese-Americans during World War II.

## empire

The collective name for a group of countries under the control of a single country or dynasty. Major empires in Europe have included the Roman Empire and the British Empire, and in Asia the Ottoman Empire and Mogul Empire. The British Empire was created in the 17th and 18th centuries, and included India, Canada, Australia, and South Africa. In the scramble for Africa in the late 18th century, seven European countries – Belgium, Britain, France, Germany, Italy, Portugal, and Spain – occupied or controlled all of Africa except for Ethiopia and Liberia. The African lands finally regained their independence in the years after World War II.

**empire** *A satirical cartoon depicts a greedy Britain trampling over the countries of its empire, such as South Africa, in its pursuit of gold.*

---

**EMPIRES IN HISTORY**

The earliest empires were established between 4,000 and 2,000 years ago in the Middle East, by the rulers of Sumeria, Babylon, and Assyria. Egypt also ruled an extensive empire. The next great empire was that of Persia, which was overthrown by Alexander the Great of Macedonia (Greece); his empire crumbled when he died at the age of 32. The Romans created a huge empire in Europe, which extended as far as Britain. The greatest land empire that has ever existed was that of the Mongols in the 13th century, whose rule extended across Asia from China in the east to Eastern Europe.

---

## Engels, Friedrich
### (1820–1895)

German social and political philosopher, most famous for his collaboration with Karl **Marx** on *The Communist Manifesto* (1848) and other key works. His later interpretations of **Marxism**, and his own philosophical and historical studies such as *Origins of the Family, Private Property, and the State* (1884) (which linked patriarchy with the development of private property), developed such concepts as historical materialism. His use of positivism and Darwinian ideas gave Marxism a scientific and deterministic flavour, which was to influence Soviet thinking. After Marx's death Engels was largely responsible for the wider dissemination of his ideas; he edited the second and third volumes of Marx's *Das Kapital* in 1885 and 1894. Although Engels

**Engels** *Friedrich Engels is best known for his collaboration with Karl Marx on* The Communist Manifesto, *the title page of which is shown here.*

himself regarded his ideas as identical with those of Marx, discrepancies between their works are the basis of many Marxist debates.

## Enlightenment

The European intellectual movement that reached its high point in the 18th century. Enlightenment thinkers were believers in social progress and in the liberating possibilities of rational and scientific knowledge. They were often critical of existing society and were hostile to religion, which they saw as keeping the human mind chained down by superstition. The American and French revolutions were justified by Enlightenment principles of human natural rights. Leading representatives of the Enlightenment were Voltaire, Gotthold Lessing, and Denis Diderot, but others like **Rousseau** and **Kant** are often associated with the movement's more political aspects.

## environmentalism

Theory that emphasizes the primary influence of the environment on the development of groups or individuals. It stresses the importance of the physical, biological, psychological, or cultural environment as a factor influencing the structure or behaviour of animals, including humans. In politics this has given rise in many countries to Green parties, which aim to 'preserve the planet and its people'. Environmentalism has been adopted into the programmes of major parties as a result of electoral threats from such specialist parties. **See also:** *conservation, green movement.*

## equality

The condition of being equal or the same in given respects, as advocated, for example, in some aspects of liberalism, and more obviously in **socialism**, and the **women's movement**. The efforts of these and other ideologies and movements have brought increased social and political awareness of the condition and secured a basis in law for equality on racial, sexual, and other grounds. Absolute equality is rarely advocated. Instead, debates about equality concern to what extent individuals or groups ought to have equality of opportunity, of respect, of rights, of treatment, equality before the law, and so on. **See also**: *equal opportunities.*

> 6 All animals are created equal but some animals are more equal than others. 9
>
> **George Orwell**, British novelist, *Animal Farm.*

### equal opportunities

The right to be employed, or considered for employment, without discrimination on the grounds of race, gender, physical or mental disability, and sometimes age.

In 1946 a Royal Commission in the UK favoured equal pay for women in Britain. The Equal Pay Act of 1970 guaranteed (in theory) equal pay for equal work. The Sex Discrimination Act of 1975 made it illegal to discriminate between men and women in a number of areas (though there were some exceptions). In 1975 the Equal Opportunities Commission was founded, with the power to oversee the operation of both the Equal Pay Act and the Sex Discrimination Act. The Commission was able to examine allegations of **discrimination** and to take legal action if necessary. Membership of the **European Union** has meant continued pressure to ensure equal opportunities, and the Human Rights Act of 1998 furthers this movement. In origin, equal opportunities referred to the idea that, while absolute equality of condition could never be guaranteed, a basis aspect of democracy was that everyone of a given talent level should have an equal chance of success, regardless of social origins.

### equal-opportunity policy

Plan of action that spells out what constitutes unfair **discrimination**, in order to guide employment practices and to ensure that the organization is working within the legislation on equal pay, sex, and race discrimination. Many private organizations, such as universities, have elaborate codes to ensure an absence of discrimination in, for example, hiring and promotion.

### escalation

In modern military strategy, especially nuclear war theory, the increasing violence or force in the response of a protagonist towards its enemy. Thus a war might start with purely conventional weapons but when one side finds itself doing badly, it might 'escalate' by using tactical nuclear weapons. At this point the other side may move to the same stage, or even to the use of major strategic weapons, thus 'escalating' the war further.

### establishment, the

Mainly journalistic expression to cover a perceived **élite** of the professional and governing classes (judges, civil servants, politicians, and so on) that collectively symbolize authority and the status quo. It can also include influential members of the media and even of the arts and entertainment.

## establishment of religion

The granting of special legal rights and protection by the state to a religious denomination, which then becomes, to some extent, controlled by the state. The best example is the established church in England, which is the Anglican church, formally called the Church of England. This title says nothing at all about its theology or organization but concentrates entirely on its political identity and demonstrates the nature of established churches quite clearly. The government of the day is directly involved in running the Church of England, with appointments to bishoprics being made by the prime minister. The monarch is officially the head of the church and legislation from the church's own controlling council, (for example, that introducing women priests in 1992) requires enactment by parliament.

The establishment of a religion has been seen as highly illiberal, and was one of the first things to be forbidden by the US constitution, in the First **Amendment** (1791). This was probably influenced by English philosopher John **Locke's** *Letter on Toleration* (1689); the English philosopher's liberal principles and opposition to strong state power were generally influential in the drafting of the **constitution**.

## ethnicity

A people's own sense of cultural identity (from Greek *ethnos* 'a people'). As a social science term it overlaps with such concepts as **race**, nation, **class**, and **religion**. Social scientists use the term ethnic group to refer to groups or societies that feel a common sense of identity, often based on a traditional shared culture, language, religion, and customs. It may or may not include common territory, skin colour, or common descent. The USA, for example, is often described as a multi-ethnic society because many members would describe themselves as members of an ethnic group (Jewish, black, or Irish, for example) as well as their national one (American). It is in practise extremely difficult to define, and some theories suggest that ethnicities are often partially invented, rather than having a genuine long-term historical identity.

## Eurocommunism

The policy followed by communist parties in Western Europe to seek power within the framework of competitive electoral politics, rather than by revolutionary means. Eurocommunism enabled these parties to free themselves from total reliance on the USSR. It was most successful in Italy, where the Communist party often won over 30% of the vote by identifying a clear national orientation and advocating gradual socio-economic change.

## European Court of Human Rights

The court that hears cases arising under the European Convention of Human Rights of the Council of Europe. Originally it took cases referred from the European Commission of Human Rights, if the Commission failed to negotiate a friendly settlement in a case where individuals' rights were violated by a member state, and had to make a formal decision for one party or the other. The process has now been unified so that the Court hears all stages of a case. The court sits in Strasbourg and comprises one judge for every state that is a party to the 1950 convention, but sits in panels selected from the full court. Court rulings have had extensive impact on the internal politics of member states, including forcing the Republic of Ireland to drop its constitutional ban on **homosexuality**, and forcing Germany to cease to exclude political left- and right-wingers from the **civil service**.

Originally Britain refused to ever incorporate the Human Rights Convention into its laws, which meant that a statute that directly contradicted the convention would prevail over a Strasbourg decision in a British court. Britain has had the second-worst record of violations of the convention in recent years; by 1991, 191 cases had been brought against the UK, and violations of the convention were found in two-thirds of these. Since the passing of the Human Rights Act in 1998, however, the UK has incorporated the convention on Human Rights, which can now be applied by UK Courts.

## European Court of Justice

The court of the **European Union** (EU), which is responsible for interpreting Community law and ruling on breaches of that law by member states and others. It sits in Luxembourg with judges from the member states. A ruling given to a national court on the meaning of EU legislation must be followed. Most of the court's work reaches it in the form of questions asked by national courts troubled by issues of Community law. The EU Commission can also complain to the court about a member country's failure to perform its obligations under that law. Additionally, member countries, EU institutions, and citizens can ask the court to annul acts of EU bodies. Finally, people can claim compensation from the court for losses suffered as a result of illegal acts of the EU.

When it entered the European Community (now the European Union) in 1973, the UK agreed to be bound by decisions of the Court of Justice and incorporated the Community treaties into its legal system. Where the court has found UK laws to contravene EU standards, the government has made the necessary changes. Courts in the UK also interpret existing laws to conform, where possible, to EU standards. The judges of the European Court have been amongst those most convinced of the need for uniformity in European law, and have often led the development of Europeanization.

## European Economic Community (EEC)
The EEC, popularly called the Common Market, was the forerunner of the **European Union.** It was established 1957 with only six members, with the aim of creating a single European market for the products of member states by the abolition of tariffs and other restrictions on trade. The Treaty of Rome, which set it up, is the founding legislation of the now much bigger and more policy-extensive successor.

## European Free Trade Association (EFTA)
An organization established in 1960 consisting today of Iceland, Norway, Switzerland, and (from 1991) Liechtenstein, previously a nonvoting associate member. There are no import duties between members. Of the original EFTA members, Britain and Denmark left (1972) to join the European Community (EC), as did Portugal (1985); Austria, Finland, and Sweden joined the EC's successor, the European Union (EU) in 1995. In 1973 the EC signed agreements with EFTA members, setting up a **free-trade** area of over 300 million consumers. Trade between the two groups amounted to over half of total EFTA trade. A further pact signed in October 1991 between the EC and EFTA provided for a European Economic Area (EEA), allowing EFTA greater access to the EC market by ending many of the restrictions. The EEA came into effect in January 1994. In December 1995 EFTA signed a free-trade pact with the Baltic States (Estonia, Latvia, and Lithuania). The pact, effective since June 1996, eliminates tariffs on industrial materials, fish and other maritime products, and processed agricultural goods.

## European Union (EU)
Political and economic alliance, formerly (to 1993) the European Community (EC). This in turn had consisted of the European Coal and Steel Community (1952), the **European Economic Community** (EEC), popularly called the Common Market, 1957), and the European Atomic Energy Community (Euratom, 1957).

The EU is rapidly developing into much more than a merely economic or trade association. A European Charter of Social Rights was approved in December 1991 by all members except the UK. At the same meeting at

Maastricht, agreement was reached on a treaty framework for European union, including political and monetary union, and for a new system of police and military cooperation. The Maastricht Treaty on European union came into effect on 1 November 1993, and the new designation of European Union was adopted, embracing not only the various bodies of its predecessor, the EC, but also two intergovernmental 'pillars', covering common foreign and security policy (CFSP) and cooperation on justice and home affairs. Most of the EU's members merged their currency systems into a single currency, called the euro, governed by a Europe wide Central Bank that came into effect in 1999.

The EU consists of the following institutions:

- the European Commission who initiate Union policy
- the Council of Ministers of the European Union, which makes decisions on the Commission's proposals
- the European Parliament, directly elected from 1979
- the Economic and Social Committee, a consultative body
- the Committee of Permanent Representatives (COREPER), consisting of civil servants temporarily seconded by member states to work for the Commission
- the **European Court of Justice**, to safeguard interpretation of the Rome Treaties (1957) that established the original alliance.

## Members of the EU:

- Belgium (1956)
- West Germany (1956)
- Luxembourg (1956)
- UK (1973)
- Republic of Ireland (1973)
- Spain (1981)
- East Germany (on reunification; 1990).
- Finland (1995)

- France (1956)
- Italy (1956)
- Netherlands (1956)
- Denmark (1973)
- Greece (1981)
- Portugal (1986)
- Austria (1995)
- Sweden (1995)

❝ It is now up to us to see that we embark on the next stage leading to political unity, which I think is ... the consequence of European unity. ❞

**Jacques Santer**, President of the European Commission, on the launch of the euro, *Daily Telegraph*, 1 January 1999.

## executive

One of the three traditional branches of government, the others being the **legislature** and the **judiciary**. In a sovereign state the executive consists of the person or body with the power to determine the policy of the state. In most modern states the composition and powers of the executive are defined in a written **constitution**. The major exception to this is the UK, which does not have a written constitution, but the composition and powers of the executive remain constitutionally limited by tradition, convention, **common law**, and statute. These policies however can only take effect to the extent that the executive can persuade the legislature to embody them in law, though in some countries the executive has a limited right to issue decrees directly. A major difference between modern political systems is the extent to which the executive and legislature are completely separate, (the USA is the best example), or partly joined (as in the UK where members of the executive, the prime minister and **cabinet**, must themselves be members of the legislature).

## existentialism

Philosophical position based on the situation of the individual in an absurd or meaningless universe where humans have free will. Existentialists argue that people are responsible for, and the sole judge of, their actions as they affect others. The origin of existentialism is usually traced back to the Danish philosopher Kierkegaard; among its proponents were Martin Heidegger in Germany and Jean-Paul Sartre in France.

All self-aware individuals can grasp or intuit their own existence and freedom, and individuals must not allow their choices to be constrained by anything, not even reason or morality. This freedom to choose leads to the notion of nonbeing, or nothingness, which can provoke angst or dread. Existentialism has many variants. Kierkegaard emphasized the importance of pure choice in ethics and Christian belief; Sartre tried to combine existentialism with **Marxism**. To the extent that it has had political influence existentialism has tended towards radical anarchy.

# F

### Fabian Society
UK socialist organization for research, discussion, and publication, founded in London in 1884. Its name is derived from the Roman commander Fabius Maximus, and refers to the evolutionary methods by which it hopes to attain **socialism** by a succession of gradual reforms. Early members included the playwright George Bernard Shaw and English social reformers Beatrice and Sidney Webb. The society helped to found the Labour Representation Committee in 1900, which became the **Labour Party** in 1906. Although socialism is no longer the programme of any major British party, the Fabians continue to be an important source of reformist ideas.

> ❝ Britain is not a country that is easily rocked by revolution.... In Britain our institutions evolve. We are a Fabian Society writ large. ❞
>
> **William Hamilton**, Scottish Labour politician, *My Queen and I* (1975).

### Falange
(Spanish 'phalanx'). Former Spanish Fascist Party (also known as Falange Española), founded in 1933 by José Antonio Primo de Rivera (1903–1936), son of military ruler Miguel Primo de Rivera. It was closely modelled in programme and organization on the Italian fascists and on the Nazis. In 1937, when **Franco** assumed leadership, it was declared the only legal party, and altered its name to Traditionalist Spanish Phalanx. The name 'falange' has continued to be used for right wing Christian inspired political movements elsewhere, notably in the Lebanon during the 1980s.

### false consciousness
A situation in which people's beliefs and values are seen as 'false', that is, artificially created by their culture or society. For example, a conflict between **trades unions** inside a work-force might be seen as a false consciousness on the grounds that workers 'ought' to realize that unity in the face of capitalists is in the 'true interests' of all workers. Where affluent workers might vote

Conservative, a 'true consciousness' would have them supporting their less affluent fellow workers. It comes from the theory of **ideology**, and especially from arguments on this subject within **Marxism**. It is an evaluative concept, and one that requires a very powerful theory to support it. Otherwise we can all describe anything someone else wants as a 'false' interest. Nevertheless, there are clear examples of people suffering false consciousness, believing that some policy will help them when it will not, or holding values and attitudes that one can easily trace to ideological conditioning or media manipulation.

### Fanon, Frantz Omar (1925–1961)

French political writer whose experiences in Algeria during the war for liberation in the 1950s led to the writing of *Les Damnés de la terre/The Wretched of the Earth* (1964), which calls for violent revolution by the peasants of the **Third World**. His writings continue to influence radical activists on questions of racial conflict.

> ❡ However painful it may be for me to accept this conclusion, I am obliged to state it: for the black man there is only one destiny. And it is white. ❡
>
> **Frantz Fanon**, Martiniquan psychiatrist, philosopher, and political activist, *Black Skins, White Masks*, Introduction.

### fascism

Political ideology that denies all rights to individuals in their relations with the state; specifically, the **totalitarian** nationalist movement founded in Italy in 1919 by **Mussolini** and followed by **Hitler's** Germany in 1933. Fascism was essentially a product of the economic and political crisis of the years after World War I. Units called *fasci di combattimento* (combat groups) were originally established to oppose communism. The fascist party, the *Partitio Nazionale Fascista*, controlled Italy from 1922 to 1943. Fascism protected the existing social order by forcible suppression of the working-class movement and by providing scapegoats for popular anger such as minority groups like Jews, foreigners, or blacks; it also prepared the citizenry for the economic and psychological mobilization of war. The term 'fascism' is also applied to similar organizations in other countries, such as the Spanish **Falange** and the British Union of Fascists under Oswald Mosley. Neo-fascist groups still exist in many countries, in the USA (the **Ku Klux Klan** and several small armed vigilante groups), France (National Front), Germany (German People's Union), Russia (Pamyat), and elsewhere. Germany experienced an upsurge in neo-fascist activity in 1992 and again in 1998, with rioting in several major cities.

In Italy the discrediting of the Christian right-of-centre parties resulted in a triumph for right-wing groups, including the neo-fascist National Alliance, in the 1994 elections. However, by 1998 the National Alliance had adopted a less extremist programme and claimed to be a mainstream conservative party. The loose employment of 'fascist' as a term of abuse for political opponents of whatever complexion to the right has tended to erode the analytical utility of the term.

> ❝ Facism is a religion; the 20th century will be known as the century of Fascism. ❞
>
> **Benito Mussolini**, Italian fascist dictator, February 1933.

## federalism

System of government in which two or more separate states unite into a federation under a common central government. A federation should be distinguished from a **confederation**, a looser union of states for mutual assistance. The USA is the prime example of federal government. In the USA each of the 50 states retains rights and privileges that overlap with those of the branches of the federal government. When jurisdiction is challenged, cases are decided by the US Supreme Court of the **judiciary** branch, thus creating **constitutional law**. Federations can be created out of unitary states, but are mainly found when ex-colonies or long-term independent political units of a common culture join together. Some countries are federal, however, largely because their enormous geographical size makes it hard for central government to rule the whole territory effectively in many policy areas. Federations vary enormously in how powerful the federal central government is vis à vis the sub units.

### Major Federal Countries:

| | | | |
|---|---|---|---|
| • Switzerland | • Argentinia | • Germany | • Nigeria |
| • Canada | • Austria | • India | • Pakistan |
| • Australia | • Belgium | • Mexico | • Russia |
| • Malaysia | • Brazil | • Micronesia | • Venezuela |

## feminism

The active belief in **equal opportunities** and rights for women. It sometimes extends to being a complete theory of social and political life, explaining most modern problems on the basis of historic male supremacy. Essentially feminists vary between merely supporting equal rights for women in the current social set up, and wanting a radical restructuring of societies and cultures they see as wholly dominated by male understanding and interests.

> ❝ I became a feminist as an alternative to becoming a masochist. ❞
>
> **Sally Kempton**, US writer, *Esquire*, July 1970.

## feudalism

The main form of social organization in medieval Europe (Latin *feudem* 'fief', coined 1839). It was a system based primarily on land, involving a hierarchy of authority, rights, and power that extended from the monarch downwards. An intricate network of duties and obligations linked royalty, nobility, lesser gentry, free tenants, villeins, and serfs. Feudalism was reinforced by a complex legal system and supported by the Christian church. With the growth of commerce and industry from the 13th century, feudalism gradually gave way to the class system as the dominant form of social ranking. The crux was the need for the monarch to raise troops. In return for military service the monarch allowed powerful vassals to hold land, and often also to administer justice and levy taxes. They in turn 'sub-let' such rights. At the bottom of the system were the serfs, who worked on their lord's manor lands in return for being allowed to cultivate some for themselves, and so underpinned the system.

## First Amendment

Part of the **Bill of Rights**, the first ten ammendments to the US **constitution**. It guarantees freedom of religion, of speech, of assembly, and of the press. Adopted in 1791, the First Amendment is often quoted on the Internet, even by non-US citizens, in arguments over international attempts at **censorship**. It has been rigorously upheld by the Supreme Court in the development of the US constitution, especially its ban on state involvement in religion, which remains controversial in US politics.

## First World

Another name for the developed world.

### fiscal policy

That part of government policy concerning **taxation** and other revenues, public spending, and government borrowing – for example the public sector borrowing requirement. Governments have to decide how much to spend; how resources should be allocated between different spending programmes; how much to raise in taxes and borrowing; as well as what taxes to levy. Fiscal policy can also be used to direct the economy, and to achieve indirect goals. For example, value-added tax (VAT) and excise duty on tobacco discourages cigarette smoking; the level of petrol tax can be used to control pollution. At a macroeconomic level, more public spending and less taxation will stimulate total spending in the economy, probably leading to a fall in unemployment but with the risk of a rise in inflation.

British governments after 1945 customarily made frequent adjustments to fiscal policy in order to regulate the level of economic activity. However, since 1979 all governments have placed greater emphasis on monetary policy, the control of the money supply, mainly by interest rate policies.

### flexible response

Strategic doctrine, which holds that in a war, a whole range of possible defensive and offensive strategies should be available, so that **escalation** need not proceed too rapidly. It is principally opposed to the doctrine of massive retaliation that was the mainstay of US defence thinking at the beginning of the nuclear age. The doctrine requires that a country should be able to meet an attack with increasing but highly specific degrees of force, working gradually up, if necessary, by clear stages to a major nuclear attack. The doctrine calls for subtle targeting and accurate weapons-delivery systems to avoid the need for massive retaliation. Though the period of **superpower** nuclear stalemate has ended, the doctrine itself may become even more important, because of the need of major powers to maintain the widest possible array of military capacities in order to respond appropriately to any level of crisis, such as the need to intervene in contexts such as the **Gulf War**.

### *force majeure*

The use of force rather than the seeking of a political or diplomatic solution to a problem (French 'superior force'). By this principle, a government could end a strike by sending in troops, instead of attempting to conciliate the strikers. Governments rarely admit to such a policy, and in international politics it is avoided wherever possible.

## foreign relations

A country's dealings with other countries. In medieval England, foreign affairs, together with home affairs, were dealt with by the king's principal secretary. Later, foreign relations were split off, and they remain a separate civil service in most countries. Specialized diplomatic bodies first appeared in Europe during the 18th century. After 1818 diplomatic agents were divided into:

- ambassadors
- papal legates and nuncios
- envoys extraordinary
- ministers plenipotentiary and other ministers accredited to the head of state
- ministers resident
- chargés d'affaires, who may deputize for an ambassador or minister, or be themselves the representative accredited to a minor country.

## Foucault, Michel Paul (1926–1984)

French philosopher and social thinker who argued that human knowledge and subjectivity are dependent upon specific institutions and practices, and that they change through history. In particular, he was concerned to subvert conventional assumptions about 'social deviants' – the mentally ill, the sick, and the criminal – who, he believed, are oppressed by the approved knowledge of the period in which they live. Foucault rejected many currents of modern thought, including **existentialism**, and his ideas challenge the ideas of **Marxism**. He was deeply influenced by the German philosopher Friedrich Nietzsche, and developed an analysis of the operation of power in society using Nietzschean concepts. Unusually for French thinkers, often isolated in their impact, Foucault has a major following in Western social science in all countries. His publications include *Histoire de la folie/ Madness and Civilization* (1961) and *Les Mots et les choses/The Order of Things* (1966).

> ❛ Freedom of conscience entails more dangers than authority and despotism. ❜
>
> **Michel Foucault**, French philosopher, *Madness and Civilization*.

## franchise

The eligibility, right, or privilege to vote at public elections, especially for the members of a legislative body, or parliament. For most of history the franchise has been restricted to male property owners. From the late 19th century onwards the franchise was extended, piecemeal, in all the countries which became democratic. In the UK, adult citizens are eligible to vote from the age of 18, with the exclusion of peers, the insane, and criminals. The voting age for adults in the USA was lowered from 21 to 18 by the 26th Amendment in 1971, and the Voting Rights Act of 1965 eliminated local laws that restricted full participation by minorities. It was 1918 before all men in the UK had the right to vote, and 1928 before women were enfranchised; in New Zealand women were granted the right as early as 1893.

### Franco, Francisco Paulino Hermenegildo Teódulo Bahamonde (1892–1975)

Spanish dictator from 1939. As a general, he led the insurgent Nationalists to victory in the Spanish Civil War 1936–39, supported by Fascist Italy and Nazi Germany, and established a dictatorship. In 1942 Franco reinstated a Cortes (Spanish parliament), which in 1947 passed an act by which he became head of state for life.

Once secure in office he curbed the growing power of the **Falange** Española (the fascist party), and in later years slightly liberalized his regime. In 1969 he nominated Juan Carlos as his successor and future king of Spain. He relinquished the premiership in 1973, but remained head of state until his death.

**Franco** *Francisco Franco established a dictatorship over Spain in the Spanish Civil War, supported by Fascist Italy and Nazi Germany.*

### fraternity

The literal translation of the French *fraternité,* one of the three slogans of the French Revolution; a better translation might be 'brotherhood'. The idea of brotherhood, with its implications of communal life and mutual support and respect, has been mainly part of communist ideology. Unlike liberty and equality, the other two cries of the French revolution, fraternity has been less discussed in political theory. While equality and liberty are essentially negative rights, denying the government or others the right to do certain things, brotherhood actually demands positive actions from ordinary people. The structure of Western states, and the overall nature of their ideologies, is geared away from such values and towards an individualism and rational self-satisfaction that fits ill with such demands. As a revolutionary cry it was splendid, but as a practical value in the French regimes that followed the revolution it was harder to achieve.

## freedom

The personal liberty to act according to the individual will and without any physical or other form of restraint. The absence of restraint is known in philosophical terms as negative freedom; a concrete example is the freedom of a prisoner released from jail. Positive freedom refers to the state of self-mastery or self-realization; for example, breaking an addictive habit, overcoming temptation to live by one's conscience. It may also refer to an absence of restrictions on people; an ability to act as they wish because of the absence of unfair social and economic restrictions which fall short of legal prohibitions.

John **Locke**, J S **Mill**, and Thomas **Hobbes** are among philosophers who hold the negative view of freedom; Jean-Jacques **Rousseau** and Georg **Hegel** (who influenced **Marx**) were the leading exponents of a positive view of freedom. The negative view of freedom tends to be held by liberal thinkers, whilst left wing theorists are attracted to positive liberty conceptions.

> 6 But what is Freedom? Rightly understood,
> / A universal licence to be good. 9
>
> **Hartley Coleridge**, English poet and essayist, *Liberty*.

## free trade

Economic system where governments do not interfere in the movement of goods between countries and there are thus no taxes on imports. In the modern economy, free trade tends to hold within economic groups such as the **European Union** (EU), but not generally, despite such treaties as the General Agreement on Tariffs and Trade (GATT) (1948) and subsequent agreements to reduce tariffs. The opposite of free trade is **protectionism**. The case for free trade, first put forward in the 17th century, received its classic statement in Adam Smith's *Wealth of Nations* (1776). According to traditional economic theory, free trade allows nations to specialize in those commodities that can be produced most efficiently. The modern free trade system dates from the post-war GATT agreement. Further international tariff reductions were agreed in the Kennedy Round Conference 1964–67, and the Tokyo Round 1974–79 gave substantial incentives to developing countries. In the 1980s recession, prompted by increased world oil prices and unemployment, swung the pendulum back towards protectionism, which discourages foreign imports by heavy duties, thus protecting home products. Within the EU, all protectionist tariffs were abolished 1993.

## functionalism

Theory that depicts society as a system made up of a number of interrelated parts, all interacting on the basis of a common value system or consensus about basic values and common goals. Every social custom and institution is seen as having a function in ensuring that society works efficiently; deviance and crime are seen as forms of social sickness. Functionalists often describe society as an organism with a life of its own, above and beyond the sum of its members. The French sociologists Auguste **Comte** and Emile **Durkheim** and the US sociologist Talcott Parsons assumed functionalist approaches for their studies. The approach is often criticized as inherently conservative because of its stress on stability and the difficulty it has explaining social change.

## fundamentalism

In terms of religion, an emphasis on basic principles or articles of faith. Christian fundamentalism emerged in the USA just after World War I (as a reaction to theological modernism and the historical criticism of the Bible) and insisted on belief in the literal truth of everything in the Bible. Islamic fundamentalism insists on strict observance of Muslim Shari'a law. Christian fundamentalists (in the sense used by most US 20th-century fundamentalist churches) also believe in the divinity of Christ, the virgin birth, the atonement, and the resurrection of Christ as essential parts of their faith. Liberal Christian theologians have questioned all these points. Islamic fundamentalism has a more direct political implication because of Islamic teaching that the state is subject to religious law and ought to be organized and controlled by religious leaders. Hence Islamic fundamentalism has come to be a threat to peaceful relations between states in many parts of the world. It is essentially incompatible with **democracy**.

## game theory

Group of mathematical theories, developed in 1944 by German-born US mathematician Oscar Morgenstern (1902–1977) and Hungarian-born US mathematician John Von Neumann, that seeks to abstract from invented game-playing scenarios and their outcome the essence of situations of conflict and/or cooperation in the real political, business, and social world. A feature of such games is that the rationality of a decision by one player will depend on what the others do; hence game theory has particular application to the study of oligopoly (a market largely controlled by a few producers). Considerable progress has been made in areas of political science, for example **coalition theory**, and in international relations, especially strategic theory, by applying game theory.

## Gaullism

Political philosophy deriving from the views of Charles **de Gaulle**, but not necessarily confined to Gaullist parties, or even to France. Its basic tenets are the creation and preservation of a strongly centralized state and an unwillingness to enter into international obligations at the expense of national interests. President Chirac's Rally for the Republic is an influential neo-Gaullist party in contemporary France, and was the first main political party in France to appoint a woman as head, when Michèle Alliot-Marie was elected its leader in November 1999. Most Gaullist political groups in France are, in other respects, orthodox Conservative parties, but they were originally influential left wing Gaullists.

## gay politics

Political activity by homosexuals in pursuit of **equal opportunities** and rights and an end to **discrimination**. A gay political movement first emerged in the late 1960s in New York with the founding of the Gay Liberation Front. It aimed to counter negative and critical attitudes to homosexuality and encouraged pride and solidarity among homosexuals. The appearance of the AIDS virus in the early 1980s produced a new wave of hostility towards homosexuals, but also put them in the forefront of formulating an effective response to the epidemic and raising the public's awareness of its dangers.

> ❝I have no doubt that, despite the publicity, your puerile conduct will soon be forgotten, although your cause may not be.❞

**Michael Kelly**, stipendiary magistrate, fining Peter Tatchell £18.60 (under the 1860 Ecclesiastical Courts Jurisdiction Act) for disrupting the Archbishop of Canterbury's Easter Sunday sermon as a protest on behalf of gay clergy; *Daily Telegraph*, 2 December 1998.

## General Agreement on Tariffs and Trade (GATT)
An organization within the United Nations, founded in 1948 with the aim of encouraging **free trade** between nations by reducing tariffs, subsidies, quotas, and regulations that discriminate against imported products. GATT was effectively replaced by the World Trade Organization in January 1995.

## general will
Concept in political thought introduced by Jean-Jacques **Rousseau in** his *Social Contract.* It is the collective decision of all the people in a state when they tried to consider only what is good for the whole society rather than what they want as individuals. He contrasts the general will with 'the will of all', which is the sum of the separate self interested desires of the citizens. He thought that liberty could only be assured when each person only had to obey those laws he or she created and accepted. It was his theory that, if a society could be organized so that it was ruled by the general will, by this collective view of what was best for all, then everyone would be free, because no one could oppose such a decision. This would ensure **freedom**, without **anarchy**.

## Geneva Convention
Convention originally referred to in the international agreement of 1864, regulating the treatment of those wounded in war. It was later extended to cover the types of weapons allowed, the treatment of prisoners and the sick, and the protection of civilians in wartime. The rules were revised at conventions held in 1906, 1929, and 1949, and by the 1977 Additional Protocols.

## genocide
The deliberate and systematic destruction of a national, racial, religious, or ethnic group defined by the exterminators as undesirable. The term is

commonly applied to the policies of the Nazis during World War II (what they called the 'final solution' – the extermination of all 'undesirables' in occupied Europe, particularly the Jews). In 1948 the United Nations General Assembly adopted a convention on the prevention and punishment of genocide, as well as the Universal Declaration of Human Rights. Genocide is not only an international crime, but also one which national courts will punish in support of international law even if the country in which genocidal activities took place will not act itself.

**See also**: *Holocaust.*

## gerrymander

To rearrange constituency boundaries to give an unfair advantage to the ruling party. The term derives from US politician Elbridge Gerry (1744–1814), who in 1812, while governor of Massachusetts, reorganized an electoral district shaped like a salamander in favour of his party. The restructuring of local authorities in Scotland 1995 was perceived as an instance of gerrymandering by the Conservative Party, who nonetheless did not control a single council after the subsequent election. In the USA, there have been Republican complaints of the 'racial gerrymandering' of congressional districts in Texas, Louisiana, and North Carolina so as to produce majority black districts.

## *glasnost*

Soviet leader Mikhail **Gorbachev's** policy of liberalizing various aspects of Soviet life, such as introducing greater freedom of expression and information and opening up relations with Western countries. It was paired in his thinking with *perestroika*, a decentralization of administrative power. *Glasnost* (Russian for 'openness') was introduced and adopted by the Soviet government in 1986. It involved the lifting of bans on books, plays, and films, the release of political dissidents, the tolerance of religious worship, a reappraisal of Soviet history (de-Stalinization), the encouragement of investigative journalism to uncover political corruption, and the sanctioning of greater candour in the reporting of social problems and disasters (such as Chernobyl). Under legislation introduced in 1990, most **censorship** of mass media was abolished; however, publication of state secrets, calls for the overthrow of the state by force, incitement of national or religious hatred, and state interference in people's private lives were prohibited. Journalists' rights to access were enshrined, and the right of reply instituted. Citizens gained the right to receive information from abroad.

## Gorbachev, Mikhail Sergeyevich (1931– )

Soviet president, in power 1985–91. He was a member of the **Politburo** from 1980. As general secretary of the Communist Party (CPSU) 1985–91 and president of the Supreme Soviet 1988–91, he introduced liberal reforms at home (**perestroika** and **glasnost**), proposed the introduction of multiparty democracy, and attempted to halt the **arms race** abroad. He became head of state in 1989. He was awarded the Nobel Peace Prize in 1990. Although he rose to power in the usual non-democratic and Soviet way, Gorbachev radically changed the style of Soviet leadership. He encountered opposition to the pace of change from both conservatives and radicals, but failed both to realize the depth of hostility this aroused against him in the CPSU, and to distance himself from the party. Following an abortive coup attempt by hardliners in August 1991, international acceptance of independence for the **Baltic States**, and accelerated moves towards independence in other republics, Gorbachev's power base as Soviet president was greatly weakened and in December 1991 he resigned. He contested the Russian presidential elections in June 1996, but attracted a humiliating 0.5% of the vote

❻ The market came with the dawn of civilization and is not the invention of capitalism. If the market leads to the improvement of people's daily lives, then there is no contradiction with socialism. ❾

**Mikhail Gorbachev**, Soviet president, rebutting the complaints of his conservative rivals that he was attempting to restore capitalism in the Soviet Union, June 1990.

## government

Any system whereby political authority is exercised. Modern systems of government distinguish between **liberal democracies**, **totalitarian** (one-party) states, and autocracies (authoritarian, relying on force rather than ideology). The Greek philosopher **Aristotle** was the first to attempt a systematic classification of governments. His main distinctions were between government by one person, by few, and by many (monarchy, oligarchy, and democracy), although the characteristics of each may vary between states and each may degenerate into tyranny (rule by an oppressive élite in the case of **oligarchy** or by the mob in the case of democracy). A further influential general categorization was that of the French philosopher **Montesquieu** who distinguished between constitutional governments – whether monarchies or republics – which operated under various legal and other constraints, and despotism, which was not constrained in this way. Many of the words used (dictatorship, tyranny, totalitarian, democratic) have acquired negative or positive connotations that make it difficult to use them objectively.

The main modern categories of government are:

- Liberal democracy: Western types of democracy. Its principal characteristics are the existence of more than one political party, relatively open processes of government and political debate, and a separation of powers.
- Totalitarian: including both fascist and communist states – a system where all power is centralized in the state, which in turn is controlled by a single party that derives its legitimacy from an exclusive ideology.
- Autocracy: a form of government that has emerged in a number of **Third World** countries, where state power is in the hands either of an individual or of the army; normally ideology is not a central factor, individual freedoms tend to be suppressed where they may constitute a challenge to the authority of the ruling group, and there is a reliance upon force.

> ❢ Every country has the government it deserves. ❢
> **Joseph de Maistre**, French monarchist, *Lettres et opuscules inédits.*

---

**GOVERNMENT TYPES IN THE WORLD**

In 1995, 73 of the world's 192 sovereign states were liberal democracies and 72 were emergent democracies, 13 had authoritarian nationalist regimes, 12 absolutist, 8 nationalistic-socialist, 7 military, 5 communist, and 2 Islamic-nationalist.

---

## Gramsci, Antonio (1891–1937)

Italian Marxist, who attempted to unify social theory and political practice. He helped to found the Italian Communist Party in 1921 and was elected to parliament in 1924, but was imprisoned by the fascist leader **Mussolini** from 1926; his *Quaderni di carcere/Prison Notebooks* were published posthumously in 1947. Gramsci believed that politics and ideology were independent of the economic base, that no ruling class could dominate by economic factors alone, and that the working class could achieve liberation by political and intellectual struggle. His concept of hegemony argued that real class control in capitalist societies is ideological and cultural rather than physical, and that only the working class 'educated' by radical intellectuals could see through and overthrow such bourgeois propaganda. His humane and gradualist approach to **Marxism**, specifically his emphasis on the need to overthrow bourgeois ideology, influenced European Marxists in their attempt to distance themselves from orthodox determinist Soviet communism. He was in some ways the founding father of **Eurocommunism**.

## green movement
Collective term for the individuals and organizations involved in efforts to protect the environment. The movement encompasses political parties such as the Green Party and organizations like Friends of the Earth and Greenpeace. Despite a rapid growth of public support, and membership of environmental organizations running into many millions worldwide, political green groups have failed to win significant levels of the vote in democratic societies. In 1996, Real World, a new political group, was formed in the UK from a coalition of 32 campaigning charities and pressure groups, including Oxfam, Friends of the Earth, Christian Aid, and the World Wide Fund for Nature. Claiming more than 2.1 million supporters, its aim is to lobby to influence party manifestos, raise issues of the environment and international development, and advocate constitutional reform. **See also**: _conservation, environmentalism_.

## green revolution
The change in methods of arable farming instigated in the 1940s and 1950s in **Third World** countries. The intention was to provide more and better food for their populations, albeit with a heavy reliance on chemicals and machinery. It was abandoned by some countries in the 1980s. Much of the

High-yield varieties of cereal plants require 70–90 kg/154–198 lb of nitrogen per hectare, more than is available to small farmers in poor countries. The rich farmers therefore enjoy bigger harvests, and the gap between rich and poor in the Third World has grown.

food produced was exported as cash crops, so the local diet did not always improve. The green revolution tended to benefit primarily those landowners who could afford the investment necessary for such intensive agriculture. In terms of production, the green revolution was initially successful in southeast Asia; India doubled its wheat yield in 15 years, and the rice yield in the Philippines rose by 75%. However, yields have levelled off in many areas; some countries that cannot afford the dams, fertilizers, and machinery required, have adopted intermediate technologies.

### Grotius, Hugo (1583–1645)

A Dutch jurist and politician also known as Huig de Groot. His book *De Jure Belli et Pacis/On the Law of War and Peace* (1625) is the foundation of international law. Grotius held that the rules governing human and international relations are founded on human nature, which is rational and social. These rules constitute a natural law binding on citizens, rulers, and God. Grotius was born in Delft and educated at the University of London. He became a lawyer and later received political appointments. In 1618 he was arrested as a republican and sentenced to imprisonment for life. His wife contrived his escape in 1620 and he settled in France, where he composed *De Jure Belli*. He was Swedish ambassador in Paris 1634–45.

**Grotius** *Hugo Grotius's book* On the Law of War and Peace *is the foundation of international law.*

### Group of Seven (G7)

The seven leading industrial nations of the world: the USA, Japan, Germany, France, the UK, Italy, and Canada, which account for more than three-fifths of global GDP. Since 1975 their heads of government have met once a year to discuss economic and, increasingly, political matters; annual summits are also attended by the president of the European Commission and, from 1991, Russia. Finance ministers and **central bank** governors from G7 member states meet four times a year.

The group formed during the 1970s with the aim of coordinating international management of exchange rates. However, its intervention in the mid-1980s was later blamed for the 1987 stock-market crash, and annual summits increasingly became forums for discussion of topical issues rather than policy-formulating sessions.

## guerrilla

An irregular soldier fighting in a small, unofficial unit, typically against an established or occupying power, and engaging in sabotage, ambush, and the like, rather than pitched battles against an opposing army. Guerrilla tactics have been used both by resistance armies in wartime (for example by the Resistance in France after 1940), by national liberation groups, and militant political extremists (for example, the Tamil Tigers). The term (Spanish 'little war') was first applied to the Spanish and Portuguese resistance to French occupation during the Peninsular War 1808–14. Guerrilla techniques were widely used in World War II – for example, in Greece and the Balkans. Political activists who resort to violence, particularly urban guerrillas, tend to be called 'freedom fighters' by those who support their cause, 'terrorists' by those who oppose it. Despite their earlier condemnation, many guerrilla leaders have eventually entered the political process; Robert Mugabe in Zimbabwe is an example.

### Leading modern guerrilla groups

- Action Directe, French
- Amal Shiite Muslim militia in Lebanon
- Armed Islamic Group (GIA) Islamic extremist group in Algeria
- Armed Revolutionary Nuclei (NAR) neofascist group, Italy
- Black September Palestinian group
- Bougainville Revolutionary Army secessionist force active in Papua New Guinea's island province of Bougainville since 1989
- Contras right-wing guerrillas in Nicaragua
- Euskadi ta Askatasuna (ETA), Basque separatist movement in northern Spain
- Fretilin (Revolutionary Front of East Timor) separatist group fighting, since the late 1970s, for East Timor's independence from Indonesia
- Hezbollah Shiite Muslim militia organization in Lebanon
- Palestine Liberation Organization (PLO) organization originally committed to the creation of a separate Palestinian state, but from 1993 pledged to peaceful coexistence with Israel
- Red Army Faction (RAF) active in western Germany from 1968. Popularly known as the Baader–Meinhof gang, it officially disbanded in 1998.

## Guevara, Che (Ernesto)
(1928–1967)

Latin American revolutionary. He was Argentinian, but left his homeland in 1953 because of his opposition to the right-wing president Juan Perón. In effecting the Cuban revolution of 1959 against the Cuban dictator Fulgencio Batista, he was second only to Castro and Castro's brother Raúl. Between 1961 and 1965, he served as Cuba's ministry of industry. In 1965 he went to the Congo to fight against white mercenaries, and then to Bolivia, where he was killed in an unsuccessful attempt to lead a peasant rising near Vallegrande. He was an orthodox Marxist and renowned for his guerrilla techniques. Always a romantic figure, he was idolized by many sectors of the left worldwide, especially amongst radical student movements.

**Guevara** *Latin American revolutionary Che Guevara.*

## Gulf War

The US-led war of 16 January–28 February 1991 between Iraq and a coalition of 28 UN member nations. A dispute over a shared oilfield and the price of oil was one of the main reasons for Iraq's invasion of Kuwait. Resolutions made in August 1990 by the United Nations Security Council for immediate withdrawal of Iraqi troops went unheeded. The UN Security Council authorized the use of force if Iraq did not withdraw before 15 January 1991. Within 24 hours of the deadline, US and allied forces launched massive air bombardments against Baghdad. The ground war started on 24 February and by the end of February the war was over, Iraq defeated, and Kuwait once more independent. The Gulf War was the first large-scale demonstration of modern technological warfare, with a foregone conclusion. The most technical and competent troops in the world were deployed against a Third World army. The real importance of the Gulf war was in showing that, now the **Cold War** was over, the UN was capable of wielding force to ensure international peace and to redress illegal national violence.

## Havel, Václav (1936– )

Czech dramatist and politician, president of Czechoslovakia 1989–92 and of the Czech Republic from 1993. His plays include *The Garden Party* (1963) and *Largo Desolato* (1985), about a dissident intellectual. Havel became widely known as a human rights activist. He was imprisoned 1979–83 and again in 1989 for support of **Charter 77**, a human-rights manifesto. As president of Czechoslovakia he sought to preserve a united republic, but resigned in recognition of the break up of the federation in 1992. In 1993 he became president of the newly independent Czech Republic. In December 1996 he underwent surgery for lung cancer but was re-elected president, by the Czech parliament, in January 1998.

## Hayek, Friedrich August von (1899–1992)

Austrian economist who taught at the London School of Economics 1931–50. His *The Road to Serfdom* (1944) was a critical study of socialist trends in Britain. He won the 1974 Nobel Prize for Economics with Gunnar Myrdal. *The Road to Serfdom* set out to combat the wartime vogue for **collectivism**, and argued that economic freedom was the necessary precondition for political freedom and democracy. His ideas were enthusiastically devoured by the leaders of the resurgent free-market conservatism of the late-1970s and 1980s, although these disciples did not always share Hayek's commitment to liberal values.

## head of state

Someone who carries out formal and ceremonial powers and responsibilities, such as receiving visiting monarchs and other heads of state. The head of state usually has some minor political powers, typically the head of state selects a leading elected politician as the **head** of government or prime minister. In the world's few remaining monarchies, the monarch is the head of state. In others it is usually a president, whose political powers may vary considerably. In some countries, such as Israel or Germany, the degree of real political power is very limited except when, as occurs frequently, in Italy for example, coalition formation requires the exercise of discretion selecting a potential prime minister likely to be able to form a government. In some systems the roles of chief executive, with real political power, and head of state are merged, and this is the case in the USA. There is no tidy pattern to the structure of states and governments, and the roles of their heads can be very complex. This headship need not even be held by one person alone. The Yugoslavian presidency after the death of Tito, for example, operated as a collective body of eight members with its leadership rotating among them.

### Hegel, Georg Wilhelm Friedrich (1770–1831)

German philosopher who conceived of mind and nature as two abstractions of one indivisible whole, Spirit. His system, which is a type of idealism, traces the emergence of Spirit in the logical study of concepts and the process of world history. His principal modern importance is through the influence he had on Marxist thought (see **Marxism**). In particular he influenced the logic of Marx's thought. He argued that the development of a concept involves three stages, which he calls *dialectic*. The dialectic moves from the thesis, to the

**Hegel** *Georg Hegel, known for his influence on Marxist thought, despite Marx's description of himself as 'standing Hegel on his head'.*

antithesis, and then to the synthesis. Hegel's works include *The Phenomenology of Spirit* (1807), *Encyclopaedia of the Philosophical Sciences* (1817), and, the main politically relevant text, the *Philosophy of Right* (1821). His own political theory is essentially right wing, lauding the state, and attaching a very high value to private property. Of all the great

> ❝ Hegel filled the universe with copulating contradictions. ❞
>
> **Bertrand Russell,** English philosopher and mathematician, *History of Western Philosophy*, ch. 22.

philosophers, Hegel is the most difficult to understand. Even so, his influence has been immense: not only amongst **Marx** and Feuerbach, but also, for example Benedetto Croce and Jean-Paul Sartre.

## hegemony
Political dominance of one power over others in a group in which all are supposedly equal (Greek *hegemonia* 'authority'). The term was first used for the dominance of Athens over the other Greek city states, later applied to Prussia within Germany, and, in more recent times, to the USA and the USSR with regard to the rest of their **Cold War** allies.

## Helsinki Conference
International meeting in 1975 at which 35 countries, including the USSR and the USA, attempted to reach agreement on cooperation in security, economics, science, technology, and human rights. This established the Conference on Security and Cooperation in Europe.

## Hiroshima
Japanese city on the south coast of Honshu island that was destroyed by the first wartime use of an atomic bomb on 6 August 1945. Casualties totalled at least 137,000 out of a population of 343,000: 78,150 were found dead, others died later. By 1995 the death toll, which included individuals who had died from radiation-related diseases in recent years, had climbed to 192,000. An annual commemorative ceremony is held on 6 August.

## Hitler, Adolf (1889–1945)
Infamous German Nazi dictator, born in Austria. He was Führer (leader) of the Nazi Party from 1921 and wrote *Mein Kampf/My Struggle* (1925–27). As chancellor of Germany from 1933 and head of state from 1934, he created a dictatorship by playing party and state institutions against each other and continually creating new offices and appointments. Hitler spent his early years in poverty in Vienna and Munich. After serving as a volunteer in the German army during World War I, he was employed as a spy by the military authorities in Munich and in 1919 joined, in this capacity, the German Workers' Party. By 1921 he had assumed its leadership, renamed it the National Socialist German Workers' Party (Nazi Party for short), and provided it with a programme that mixed nationalism with **anti-Semitism**. Having led an unsuccessful uprising in Munich in 1923, he served nine months in prison, during which he wrote his political testament, *Mein*

*Kampf*. The party did not achieve national importance until the elections of 1930; by 1932, it formed the largest group in the Reichstag (parliament) and Hitler became chancellor in a Nazi–Nationalist coalition on 30 January 1933. The opposition was rapidly suppressed, the Nationalists removed from the government, and the Nazis declared the only legal party. In 1934 Hitler succeeded Hindenburg as head of state, and thereafter his position was never seriously challenged. Apart from leading Germany into vicious aggressive war throughout Europe and the middle east, Hitler perpetrated, in the **Holocaust**, the gravest crime against humanity in recorded history. He committed suicide after the fall of Berlin in 1945. **See also**: *Nazism*.

**Hitler**  *Adolf Hitler, infamous German Nazi dictator, the man responsible for the worst crime against humanity in recorded history, the Holocaust.*

❝ I solemnly prophesy that this accursed man will cast our Reich into the abyss and bring our nation to inconceivable misery. Future generations will damn you in your grave for what you have done. ❞

**Erich von Ludendorff**, German general, to Reich president Hindenburg, 1933, on Hitler's appointment to the Reich in the position of Chancellor.

## Hobbes, Thomas (1588–1679)

English political philosopher and the first thinker since Aristotle to attempt to develop a comprehensive theory of nature, including human behaviour. In

*Leviathan* (1651), he advocates absolutist government as the only means of ensuring order and security; he saw this as deriving from the **social contract**. Hobbes analysed everything, including human behaviour, in terms of matter and motion. He is now best remembered for his political philosophy, in which he defended absolute sovereignty as the only way to prevent life from being 'nasty, brutish, and short', as he alleged it was in a state of nature. He based this absolute sovereignty on a social contract among individuals, but the sovereign has duties only to God. Though his views were extreme, his basic idea that there could be no limitation to sovereignty is still a fundamental aspect of the British **constitution**, and he commands enormous respect amongst political theorists to this day.

**Hobbes** *The political philosopher Thomas Hobbes believed that absolute sovereignty was necessary to prevent what he saw as the natural brutishness of human life.*

❝ No arts; no letters; no society; and which is worst of all, continual fear and danger of violent death; and the life of man, solitary, poor, nasty, brutish, and short. ❞

**Thomas Hobbes**, English political philosopher, *Leviathan*.

## Ho Chi Minh (1890–1969)

Adopted name of Nguyen Tat Thanh, North Vietnamese communist politician, prime minister 1954–55, and president 1954–69. Having trained in Moscow shortly after the Russian Revolution, he headed the communist Vietminh from 1941 and fought against the French during the Indochina War 1946–54, becoming president and prime minister of the republic at the armistice. Aided by the communist bloc, he did much to develop industrial potential. He relinquished the premiership in 1955, but continued as president. In the years before his death, Ho successfully led his country's fight against US-aided South Vietnam in the Vietnam War 1954–75.

## Holocaust, the

The annihilation of an estimated 16 million people by the **Hitler** regime between 1933 and 1945, principally in the numerous extermination and concentration camps, most notably Auschwitz (Oswiecim), Sobibor, Treblinka, and Maidanek in Poland, and Belsen, Buchenwald, and Dachau in Germany. Of the victims around 6 million were Jews (over 67% of European Jews); around 10 million Ukrainian, Polish, and Russian civilians and prisoners of war. Romanies, socialists, homosexuals, and others (labelled 'defectives') were also imprisoned and/or exterminated. Victims were variously starved, tortured, experimented on, and worked to death. Millions were executed in gas chambers, shot, or hanged. It was euphemistically termed the final solution (of the Jewish question). The precise death toll will never be known. Holocaust museums and memorial sites have been established in Israel and in other countries.

## homosexuality

Sexual preference for, or attraction to, persons of one's own sex; in women it is referred to as lesbianism. Although some ancient civilizations (notably ancient Greece and Confucian China) accepted homosexuality, other societies have punished homosexual acts. In 12th-century Europe sodomy was punishable by burning and since then homosexuals have suffered varying degrees of prejudice and prosecution. In the latter half of the 20th century **discrimination** against homosexuals has decreased as a result of pressure from campaigners.

**See also**: *gay politics.*

## hostage

A person taken prisoner as a means of exerting pressure on a third party, usually with threats of death or injury. Hostage taking has become a

---

**HELD HOSTAGE**

- In 1979, 63 staff members of the US embassy in Tehran were taken by the Iranians.
- Following the Iraqi invasion of Kuwait August 1990, about 9,000 Westerners were held in Kuwait and Iraq; they were gradually released later that year.
- in 1996–97 80 people were held hostage in the Japanese embassy in Lima, Peru, by Tupamaros (Túpac Amarú Revolutionary Movement) guerrillas.

standard tactic for **guerrilla** groups, though it very seldom achieves their desired results.

## human rights

The civil and political rights of the individual in relation to the state. Under the terms of the United Nations Charter human rights violations by countries have become its proper concern. The Universal Declaration of Human Rights, passed by the General Assembly 10 December 1948, is based on a belief in the inherent rights, equality, and freedom of human beings and sets out in 28 articles the fundamental freedoms – civil, political, economic – to be promoted. The declaration has considerable moral force but is not legally binding on states. Further UN sponsored Human Rights statements include two covenants on human rights from 1966, one on civil and political rights, and one on social and economic rights. The UN 1966 covenant on civil and political rights advocates:

- freedom of thought and opinion
- right to liberty and a fair trial
- right to privacy
- right to self-determination
- freedom from discrimination on grounds of gender, race, religion, nationality, or political orientation
- protection from inhuman punishment.

These covenants are legally binding on states that ratify them, and have now received the 35 ratifications they needed to come into being. In 1946 the Economic and Social Council established the Commission on the Status of

---

### SOME OTHER HUMAN RIGHTS ORGANIZATIONS

- Amnesty International, campaigners for the release of prisoners of conscience and for fair trials and humane treatment of all prisoners
- Human Rights Watch, a US nonpartisan pressure group
- Minority Rights Group, an international organization to increase awareness on minority issues
- **European Court of Human Rights** hears cases referred from the European Commission of Human Rights where individual's rights have been violated by a member state.

Women to study the conditions of women throughout the world and recommend improvements. It has drafted a number of Conventions, legally binding on states that ratify them, which have been adopted by UN bodies.

## Hume, David (1711–1776)

Scottish philosopher whose *Treatise of Human Nature* (1739–40) is a central text of British empiricism, the theory that experience is the only source of knowledge. Examining meticulously our modes of thinking, he concluded that they are more habitual than rational. Consequently, he not only rejected the possibility of knowledge that goes beyond the bounds of experience (speculative metaphysics), but also arrived at generally sceptical positions about reason, causation, necessity, identity, and the self. Hume's law in moral philosophy states that it is never possible to deduce evaluative conclusions from factual premises; this has come to be known as the 'is/ought problem'. As a consequence Hume is a founder of the school that came to be known as **utilitarianism**, and, with its moral relativism, largely dominates British political and social thinking. His *History of Great Britain* (1754–62) was popular within his own lifetime but *A Treatise of Human Nature* was indifferently received. He also wrote the *Enquiry Concerning the Principles of Morals* (1751), and many essays, some of them of considerable importance to political theory and even the study of international relations.

> ❝ Custom, then, is the great guide of human life. ❞
>
> **David Hume**, Scottish philosopher, *Inquiry Concerning Human Understanding*.

## ideology

A set of ideas, beliefs, and opinions about the nature of people and society, providing a framework for a theory about how people should live, as well as how society is or should be organized. A nation's ideology is usually reflected in the political system it creates. The ideologies of 'primitive' communities take the form of myth. An increased philosophical consciousness began with the Greeks, and, for example, **Aristotle's** political philosophy involved an attempt to convince Greeks that 'natural' man was 'man in society' and that only in an organized society could people find fulfilment; 'man' therefore 'is a political animal'. The spread of Christianity devalued the importance of 'political' as opposed to 'religious' life, but at the same time evolved the old **natural law** into the law of God as the final standard by which the acts of temporal rulers might be judged. The danger of **anarchism** on the one hand, and of ecclesiastical domination on the other, was met in practice by the emphasis laid upon the absolute power of the ruler (see **absolutism**). This, in turn, was countered by the theory of the **social contract** as the basis of security, which, however unhistorical, became a powerful weapon against authoritarian rule in the hands of John **Locke** and others. According to **Marxism**, the material conditions of society determine the ruling ideology of various social classes. Although it is tempting to see one's opponents as 'ideological' and oneself as having 'common sense', the truth is that all political actors have an ideology, even when they are not aware of this.

## immigration and emigration

The movement of people from one country to another. Immigration is movement to a country; emigration is movement from a country. Immigration or emigration on a large scale is often for economic reasons or because of religious, political, or social persecution (which may create refugees), and often prompts restrictive legislation by individual countries. The USA has received immigrants on a larger scale than any other country: more than 50 million during its history. In the UK, Commonwealth Immigration Acts were passed in 1962 and 1968, and replaced by a single system of control under the Immigration Act of 1971. The British Nationality Act 1981 further restricted immigration by ruling that only a British citizen has the right to live in the United Kingdom. **See also**: *citizenship.*

## imperialism

The policy of extending the power and rule of a government beyond its own boundaries. A country may attempt to dominate others by direct rule and settlement – the establishment of a colony – or by less obvious means such as control of markets for goods or raw materials. These less obvious means are often called **neocolonialism**.

The word 'imperialism' was first taken up in the 1890s by the British colonial secretary Joseph Chamberlain, who favoured British expansionist policies, and was adopted into other languages during the period of imperial expansion by European powers from the 1880s to 1914. Imperialism was soon exposed to criticism from the left, in the British economist J A Hobson's *Imperialism* (1902), and from a Marxist perspective in **Lenin's** *Imperialism as the Highest Stage of Capitalism* (1917).

Imperialists claimed that they were expanding civilization to underdeveloped countries, and associated their military and technological strength with a belief in the racial and cultural superiority of Europeans. Lenin's view was that imperialism was a symptom of **capitalism**: capitalists used their control over government to encourage imperial expansion, providing them with new markets, raw materials, and opportunities for investment.

The break-up of previous empires, such as the Austro-Hungarian Empire after 1918, and the British Empire in the second

**imperialism** *A Nazi World War II propaganda cartoon of British colonialism proclaims 'England's Schuld' – 'England's Guilt.' The cartoon draws attention to Britain's imperial power over other countries.*

half of the 20th century, or of large multinational states such as the former Soviet Union after 1991, has led to a greater degree of self-determination (freedom for peoples to govern themselves), but this has brought its own problems. Ethnic groups have been mixed under the old regimes (as with the Russian community in the now independent Estonia), sometimes through state policies. In Africa many borders of nation states still follow lines drawn by imperial (often British) authorities, which often do not take account of ethnic differences. Some of these situations have sparked conflict. Imperial powers are also blamed for having exploited local economies and prevented proper economic development among the population.

## industrial democracy

The idea that employees may have a share in the decisions taken by the firm in which they work, and, therefore, a share of responsibility for its success or failure.

In 1975 the UK government appointed a Commission of Inquiry on Industrial Democracy, chaired by Alan Bullock. The *Bullock Report* (1977) produced an explicit model for adoption by company boards but its suggestions were never taken seriously by British management. Although there are a small number of firms in Britain that operate some form of industrial democracy, it is in mainland European countries, particularly Sweden and Germany, that the most successful examples are to be found. More extreme forms, combined with the abolition of private property, have been advocated by modern socialists trying to avoid the problems of USSR style controlled economies, and some experiments were made in the old Yugoslavia.

## industrialization

The process by which an increasing proportion of a country's economic activity is involved in industry. It is essential for economic development and largely responsible for the growth of cities (**urbanization**). It is usually associated with the **modernization** of developing countries, beginning with the manufacture of simple goods that can replace imports.

## initiative

In politics, an initiative device whereby voters may play a direct part in making laws. A proposed law may be drawn up and signed by petitioners, and submitted to the legislature. A **referendum** may be taken on a law that has been passed by the **legislature** but that will not become operative unless the voters assent to it. Switzerland was the first country to make use of the device.

## inquisitorial system

The inquisitorial system of **criminal law** is standard in the **civil law** world, primarily, that is, in continental Europe, not the UK. It is the trial method in criminal cases. The court, either a single judge or a bench of judges and assessors, seeks to find the truth about the charges brought directly, rather than passively allowing the prosecution and defence to bring the evidence they choose in an effort to convince a jury entirely of laypeople. The court will interrogate witnesses, call for evidence, require the counsel for prosecution and defence to answer certain points or make certain arguments, and will not be satisfied until it believes it has itself found out all that can be found out about the case. In contrast, the mode of criminal trial in the **common law** systems is known as the accusatorial system. The judge has only the duty of seeing a fair trial, of ensuring that the rules of evidence are obeyed, and summing up impartially to the jury. Occasionally there have been demands for the English system to be modified in the direction of inquisitorial justice because of such failures in the common law trial system, and indeed the Scottish criminal law system does have elements of this.

## intelligence

In military and political affairs, information, often secretly or illegally obtained, about other countries. Counter-intelligence is information on the activities of hostile agents. Much intelligence is gained by technical means, such as satellites and the electronic interception of data. The British intelligence services consist of M(ilitary) I(ntelligence) 6, the nickname of the Secret Intelligence Service, which operates mainly under Foreign Office control; the counter-intelligence service, the Security Service, MI 5, which is responsible directly to the prime minister for internal security and has Scotland Yard's Special Branch as its executive arm; and Government Communications Headquarters (GCHQ), which carries out electronic surveillance for the other two branches. The overall head of intelligence in the

> ❝ I still do not think of myself as a spy. Other people will have to judge. ❞
>
> **Melita Norwood**, 87-year-old former KGB agent named 'Hola', after passing British atom secrets to Moscow and recruiting agents in Britain. *Independent on Sunday*, 12 September 1999.

UK is the chair of the Joint Intelligence Committee. The British intelligence services budget for 1994 was £975 million, about half of which was spent on GCHQ and £150 million by MI5. Staff numbered almost 11,000, including 6,500 working at GCHQ and 2,000 at MI5. US equivalents of MI6 include the **Central Intelligence Agency** (CIA) and the National Security Agency; the Federal Bureau of Investigation (FBI) is responsible for US counter-intelligence.

## International Court of Justice (ICJ)
The main judicial organ of the United Nations, in The Hague, the Netherlands. It hears international law disputes as well as playing an advisory role to UN organs. It was set up by the UN charter in 1945 and superseded the League of Nation's World Court. There are 15 judges, each from a different member state. Countries can only be brought before the ICJ if they have previously agreed to be bound by its rulings. Many countries, including the USA, do not accept its jurisdiction.

## international law
Body of rules generally accepted as governing the relations between countries, pioneered by Hugo **Grotius**, especially in matters of human rights, territory, and war.

Neither the League of Nations nor the United Nations proved able to enforce international law, successes being achieved only when the law coincided with the aims of a predominant major power – for example, in the Korean War and the **Gulf War**. The scope of the law is now extended to space – for example, the 1967 treaty that (among other things) banned nuclear weapons from space. The sources of international law include treaties, UN resolutions, acknowledged customs, and principles derived from legal philosophy.

## International Monetary Fund (IMF)
A specialized agency of the **United Nations** that seeks to promote international monetary cooperation and the growth of world trade, and to smooth multilateral payment arrangements among member states. IMF standby loans are available to members in balance-of-payments difficulties (the amount being governed by the member's quota), usually on the basis that the country must agree to take certain corrective measures.

The IMF also operates other drawing facilities, including several designed to provide preferential credit to developing countries with liquidity problems. Having previously operated in US dollars linked to gold, since 1972 the IMF has used the special drawing right (SDR) as its standard unit of account, valued in terms of a weighted 'basket' of currencies. Since 1971, IMF rules have been progressively adapted to floating exchange rates. Its headquarters are in Washington, DC, and it was established under the 1944 Bretton Woods agreement and has been operational since 1947.

## international socialism

The idea of the international brotherhood of the working classes has always been important in socialist and communist doctrines. The revolutionary years of the 19th and early 20th century seemed to point to the necessity of world-wide revolution. Consequently there have been numerous attempts to set up international cooperative organizations of the separate national socialist, communist, and revolutionary groups. The two most important were the Second and Third Internationals, the latter also known as the Comintern. (The First was Marx's own creation in the mid 19th century.) The Second International was formed in Paris in 1889, and though weakened by World War I (when socialist parties who had sworn to oppose capitalist wars all rallied to their respective governments), it was reformed in 1923 and still survives as the Socialist International. This International was reformist and social democratic in nature, and had nothing to do with revolutionary doctrines. The Third International was founded at Lenin's instigation by the newly victorious **Bolshevik** government in Moscow to organize and control communist parties throughout Europe. The two most important Western communist parties, in France and Italy, were caused by splits in their respective socialist parties, who were members of the Second International. The revolutionary Marxist elements left to join Lenin's Comintern.

## Internet

The global computer network connecting governments, companies, universities, and many other networks and users. The technical underpinnings of the Internet were developed as a project funded by the US Defense Advanced Research Project Agency (DARPA) to research how to build a network that would withstand bomb damage. The Internet itself began in the mid-1980s with funding from the US National Science Foundation as a means to allow US universities to share the resources of five regional super-computing centres. The political significance of the Internet lies mainly in its use to disseminate ideas and information throughout communities and across borders. Consequently, in nondemocratic countries, such as China, attempts are made to heavily censor (see **censorship**) Internet information and restrict access.

❝ The way the world public with hypocritical lust follows the most private events on the Internet, that – and I use this expression deliberately – makes me puke. ❞

**Helmut Kohl**, Chancellor of Germany, on the Clinton tapes and allied affairs, *Daily Telegraph*, 22 September 1998.

## Irish Republican Army (IRA)

The militant Irish nationalist organization, the paramilitary wing of **Sinn Fein**, formed in 1919. Its aim is to create a united Irish socialist republic including Ulster. To this end, the IRA has frequently carried out bombings and shootings. The IRA was founded with the aim of making British rule ineffective by the use of armed force; the belief being that political activity alone would not achieve this end. Although the IRA and Sinn Fein share a common goal (a united Ireland), and there is overlapping membership, the IRA has always operated independently and in times of crisis has appeared to be free from political control. It was declared illegal in 1936, but came to the fore again in 1939 with a bombing campaign in Britain. Its activities intensified from 1968 onwards, as the civil-rights disorders ('the Troubles') in Northern Ireland increased. In 1969 the IRA split into two wings, one 'official' and the other 'provisional'. The official wing sought reunification by political means, while the Provisional IRA, or Provos as they became known, carried on with terrorist activities, their objective being the expulsion of the British from Northern Ireland. It is this wing, of younger, strongly sectarian Ulster Catholics, who are now generally regarded and spoken of as the IRA.

❝ This is not just another glorious phase in Irish history. We must win. We can't afford to lose. We will keep the campaign going regardless of the cost to ourselves, regardless of the cost to anyone else. ❞

**Seán MacStíofáin**, chief of staff of the Irish Republican Army's militant Provisional wing, quoted in *Time*, 10 January 1972.

## Iron Curtain

In Europe, after World War II, the symbolic boundary between the capitalist West and communist East during the **Cold War**. The term was popularized by the UK prime minister Winston Churchill from 1945. There were earlier references, however: an English traveller to **Bolshevik** Russia, Ethel Snowden (1881–1951), used the term with reference to the Soviet border in 1920. The Nazi minister Goebbels used it a few months before Churchill in 1945 to describe the divide between Soviet-dominated and other nations that would follow German capitulation.

## Islam

Religion founded in the Arabian peninsula in the early AD 600s. It emphasizes the oneness of God, his omnipotence, beneficence, and inscrutability. Its sacred book is the Koran, which Muslims believe was divinely revealed to Muhammad, the prophet or messenger of Allah. There are two main Muslim sects: Sunni and Shiite. Islam embodies a secular law (the Shari'a or 'Main Path'), a mufti is a legal expert who guides the courts in their interpretation. It is because all legitimate law is religious law that Islamic politics is fundamentally different from western liberal democracies, and indeed cannot be fully democratic.

There is no organized Church or priesthood, although Muhammad's descendants (the Hashim family) and popularly recognized holy men, mullahs, and ayatollahs are accorded respect. As the law is regarded as the voice of God, a renowned lawyer is very near to being a priest. By the late 1950s the industrialized West had exerted enormous and disruptive cultural and economic influences on the traditional Islamic value system of the Muslim world. This has lead to movement, the Muslim Brotherhood calling for a return to puritanism in Islam. It has sought to replace what it sees as an 'ethical vacuum' with Islamic values. The organization came into conflict with Egyptian president Gamal Abdel Nasser in 1956 and with Syrian

> ❝ They were a gift from God. It was a fight against the enemies of God. ❞
>
> **Abu Hassan**, Yemeni Islamic militant, on his gang's kidnapping of 16 Western tourists, (four of whom were killed in a shoot-out with troops), at his trial; *Daily Telegraph*, 14 January 1999.

president Hafez al-Assad in 1980. In both cases, the confrontation led to government outlawing of the group, since the Brotherhood's growing popularity was seen as a threat to the political establishment. The call for Islamic revivalism has also been used by groups seeking power in the Islamic world, often leading to an inaccurate interpretation of Islam. **See also**: *fundamentalism.*

## isolationism

Concentration on internal rather than foreign affairs; a foreign policy having no interest in international affairs that do not affect the country's own interests. In the USA, isolationism is usually associated with the **Republican Party**, especially politicians of the Midwest (for example, the Neutrality Acts 1935–39). In fact George Washington himself recommended a very similar policy at the outset of the Republic. Intervention by the USA in both world wars was initially resisted. In the 1960s some Republicans demanded the removal of the United Nations from US soil. From time to time isolationist tendencies still emerge in the USA, as it did whenever there were strains within NATO.

## Jacobin

Originally a member of an extremist republican club of the French Revolution, founded in Versailles 1789. Helped by Danton's speeches, they proclaimed the French **republic**, had the king executed, and

overthrew the moderate Girondins 1792–93. Through the Committee of Public Safety, they began the Reign of Terror, led by Robespierre. After his execution in 1794, the club was abandoned and the name 'Jacobin' passed into general use for any left-wing extremist.

## jihad

A holy war undertaken by Muslims against non-believers (Arabic 'conflict'). In the Mecca Declaration 1981, the Islamic powers pledged a jihad against Israel, though not necessarily military attack. Jihad is, in fact, an extremely complex concept in Islamic thought, and only partially carries the violent sense most outsiders take it to imply.

## judicial review

In English law, action in the High Court to review the decisions of lower courts, tribunals, and administrative bodies. Various court orders can be made:

- certiorari (which quashes the decision)
- mandamus (which commands a duty to be performed)
- prohibition (which commands that an action should not be performed because it is unauthorized)
- a declaration (which sets out the legal rights or obligations)
- an injunction (which is a temporary order).

It is a powerful means for keeping the public administration within the bounds of the law, and will be enhanced considerably when the Human Rights Act comes fully into force in October 2000. In more general terms, judicial review is used to include all systems where courts are entitled to consider the validity of law, including fully-fledged judicial review of the constitutionality of legislation as under the US **Supreme Court**.

## judiciary

The system of courts and body of judges in a country. The independence of the judiciary from other branches of the central authority is generally considered to be an essential feature of a democratic political system. This independence is often written into a nation's **constitution** and protected from abuse by politicians.

## junta

The military rulers of a country, especially after an army takeover, as in Turkey in 1980. Other examples include:

- Argentina, under Juan Perón and his successors
- Chile, under Augusto Pinochet
- Paraguay, under Alfredo Stroessner
- Peru, under Manuel Odría
- Uruguay, under Juan Bordaberry
- Myanmar since 1988.

Juntas (Spanish 'council') rarely remain collective bodies, eventually becoming dominated by one member. The Spanish word designates a legislative or other assembly that meets either for political purposes or for the passing of laws. In 1808 a junta was elected to undertake the defence of Spain against Napoleon. In English the word is used as a term of contempt for a legislative party, for example the Whig Junta in the reigns of William III and Queen Anne. It is also used nowadays to denote a power group, governing a country, having usually achieved power by revolutionary means. Such power groups are usually associated with military regimes.

## justice

A goal of political activity and a subject of political enquiry since **Plato**. The term has been variously defined as fairness, equity, rightness, the equal distribution of resources, and positive discrimination in favour of underprivileged groups. It is most directly applied to the legal systems of states, and to decisions made by the recognized authorities within them. The distinction is sometimes made between procedural justice, which considers the mechanisms of decision-making where individuals may suffer, and substantive justice, which concentrates on whether the actual result is fair, equitable, or whatever.

> ❝ It is not merely of some importance, but is of fundamental importance that justice should not only be done, but should manifestly and undoubtedly be seen to be done. ❞
>
> **Gordon Hewart**, English lawyer and politician, *Rex v. Sussex Justices*, 9 November 1923.

## Just War

One theory of how war should be conducted, developed by the Catholic Church during the 12th century and reaching some agreed definition by the late 13th century. Major contributions came from the Neapolitan philosopher and theologian Thomas **Aquinas** and Pope Innocent IV. It restricted the occasions for war, and where war was permitted it was only to be conducted in approved circumstances. Generally war between Christians was condemned, and penalties were imposed for engagement in unjust war. Christians were expected to be the defenders, not the aggressors, and have just cause for action. Only a legitimate authority could undertake war. Even today, shorn of its religious overtones, Just War theory is the base for much thinking, and even for international law treatment of warfare.

## Kant, Immanuel (1724–1804)

German philosopher who believed that knowledge is not merely an aggregate of sense impressions but is dependent on the conceptual apparatus of the human understanding, which is itself not derived from experience. In ethics, Kant argued that right action cannot be based on feelings or inclinations but conforms to a law given by reason, the categorical imperative. The political relevance of most of Kant's work is a matter of general moral principle, but he wrote directly on international relations with an influential plan for world peace.

**Kant** *Immanuel Kant, German philosopher.*

It was in his *Kritik der reinen Vernunft/Critique of Pure Reason* (1781) that Kant inaugurated a revolution in philosophy by turning attention to the mind's role in constructing our knowledge of the objective world. His other main works are *Kritik der praktischen Vernunft/Critique of Practical Reason* (1788) and *Kritik der Urteilskraft/Critique of Judgement* (1790).

Born in Königsberg (in what was then East Prussia), Kant attended the university there, and was its professor of logic and metaphysics 1770–97.

> ❝ Who wills the end, wills also (so far as reason has a decisive influence on his actions) the means ... ❞
>
> **Immanuel Kant**, German philosopher, *The Moral Law.*

## Keynesian economics

The economic theory of English economist John Maynard Keynes, which argues that a fall in national income, lack of demand for goods, and rising unemployment should be countered by increased government expenditure to stimulate the economy. Though now largely replaced in liberal democracies by **monetarism**, it was the dominant form of economic policy for 20 years after 1945 in most advanced economies, though the USA never openly admitted to being Keynesian.

## KGB

The secret police of the USSR, the Komitet Gosudarstvennoy Bezopasnosti (Committee of State Security), which was in control of frontier and general security and the forced-labour system. KGB officers held key appointments in all fields of daily life, reporting to administration offices in every major town. On the demise of the USSR in 1991, the KGB was superseded by the Federal Counter-intelligence Service, which was renamed the Federal Security Service (FSB) in April 1995, when its powers were expanded to enable it to combat corruption and organized crime, and to undertake foreign-intelligence gathering. Its main successor is the Russian Federal Security Service (FSB), which focuses on 'economic security' and combating foreign espionage. At its heyday the KGB had at least 220,000 border guards, with reinforcements of 80,000 volunteer militia members. Many KGB officers were also said to hold diplomatic posts in embassies abroad. After the attempted anti-**Gorbachev** coup of 1991, reforms intended to curb the political activities of the KGB were introduced: its leadership was removed and KGB troops were placed under the control of the Defence Ministry; the presidential guard was removed from KGB authority; and government communications were transferred to the aegis of a state committee.

## Ku Klux Klan

US secret society dedicated to white supremacy. It was founded in 1866 to oppose Reconstruction in the Southern states after the American Civil War and to deny political rights to the black population. Members wore hooded white robes to hide their identity and burned crosses at their night time meetings. In the late 20th century the Klan evolved into a paramilitary extremist group and forged loose ties with other white supremacist groups.

## Labour Party

UK political party originally based on socialist principles and formed to represent workers. It was founded in 1900 and first held office in 1924. The first majority Labour government 1945–51 introduced nationalization and the National Health Service, and expanded social security and free access to all levels of education. Labour was again in power 1964–70, 1974–79, and from 1997. The party leader (Tony Blair from 1994) is elected by an **electoral college**, with a weighted representation of the Parliamentary Labour Party (30%), constituency parties (30%), and trades unions (40%). The Labour Party, the Trades Union Congress, and the cooperative movement together form the National Council of Labour, whose aims are to coordinate political activities and take joint action on specific issues.

In 1918 a socialist programme was first adopted, with local branches of the party set up, to which individual members were admitted. Labour took office for the first time as a majority government under Clement Attlee, party leader from 1935, after the 1945 elections. The **welfare state** was developed by **nationalization** of essential services and industries, a system of national insurance was established in 1946, and the National Health Service was founded 1948. The party was defeated in 1951, and did not return to office until 1964–70. It was again in office from 1974--79, but thereafter Labour was split by ideological disagreements and seemed unable to make any headway against the enormously popular Thatcher administrations. In spite of the Conservative government's declining popularity, Labour was defeated again in the 1992 general election. Party membership fell to a low of 260,000 in 1990. Tony Blair was elected in July 1994, in the first fully democratic elections to the post, and launched a campaign to revise the party's constitution and throwaway most of the traditional socialism, under the label of New Labour, which finally won the election of 1997. Labour, under Blair, also won the election of 2001 with a majority of 167 seats. The victory was marred, however, by the lowest electoral turnout in 80 years, just 58%, clear proof to many of voter apathy and dissatisfaction with all of the major political parties.

---

❦ The longest suicide note in history. ❧

**Gerald Kaufmann,** British Labour politician, of the Labour Party's 1983
election manifesto, quoted in Dennis Healey *Time of My Life*.

---

## *laissez faire*

The theory that the state should not intervene in economic affairs, except to
break up a monopoly. The phrase originated from 18th-century French economists whose maxim was *laissez faire et laissez passer* (literally, 'let go and
let pass' – that is, leave the individual alone and let commodities circulate
freely). The degree to which intervention should take place is still one of the
chief problems of economics. The Scottish economist Adam Smith justified
the theory in *The Wealth of Nations* (1776). The 20th century has seen an
increasing degree of state intervention to promote social benefits, which after
World War II in Europe was extended into the field of **nationalization** of leading industries and services. However, from the 1970s, *laissez-faire* policies
were again pursued in the UK, even under 'New Labour', and the USA. The
**European Union**, in common with countries such as France and Germany, is
a good deal less committed to *laissez-faire*.

## language groups

Language groups are often extremely important in politics. Which language
one speaks, or is forced to speak for social advancement, is not only practi-
cally significant as the recognition of a language is a major aspect of the
legitimization of a culture and history. Often where language is politically relevant, one language group is an ethnic minority suppressed by what they see
as an alien conqueror or oppressing **élite**. In such places having to speak the
language of the rulers is not just a practical difficulty, but a symbol of 'un-free-
dom'. Often language goes hand in hand with religion and ethnicity. When
this happens, language groups can become important centres for the focusing
of protest politics in the society, keeping alive **cleavages** that might otherwise
have died away. After class and religion (with which they are, in any case,
often interdefined), linguistic cleavages are the most important source of conflict in modern politics. Belgium, parties of the former USSR, Romania, Spain,
the UK, and the former Yugoslav republics are examples of this, among
European nations alone. In the Third World the situation is even more complex because language may be a vital element in the attempt to construct a

national unity out of a political system that is really only the result of imperialist map-makers.

## law

The body of rules and principles under which **justice** is administered or order enforced in a state or nation. In western Europe there are two main systems: Roman or **civil law** and **common law** (mainly English but with important developments from the USA and the old commonwealth).

> ❝ No one using the law against others can complain if the law is, in turn, used against them. ❞
>
> **Alan Rusbridger**, editor of *The Guardian*, on former Conservative minister Jonathan Aitken, sentenced to 18 months' imprisonment for committing perjury in pursuit of his libel case against *The Guardian* and Granada Television; *The Guardian*, 9 June 1999.

## law and order

A state of society in which there is a regular process of **criminal law** and **civil law** and in which certain agencies, such as the police, are responsible for maintaining domestic peace. Law and order is generally seen by most conservatives as the basic requirement of a state, since without these conditions political freedom and **civil liberties** are impossible. Law and order, in common parlance, has also come to mean the provision of a strong police force and a concern with reducing crime and vandalism. As such, law and order may become an election issue in democracies concerned with rising crime rates. George Wallace campaigned for the US presidency as the candidate of the American Independent Party in 1968, emphasizing concern for law and order; Conservative Party campaigns in the UK have also often laid considerable stress on this theme.

## leadership

The role that involves organizing others and taking decisions. A leader in a work organization may be an autocratic leader, someone who perhaps listens to advice but ultimately makes decisions on his or her own, or he or she may be a democratic leader, allowing others to participate in the decision-making process.

## League of Nations

The international organization formed after World War I to solve international disputes by arbitration. Established in Geneva, Switzerland, in 1920, the League included representatives from states throughout the world, but was severely weakened by the US decision not to become a member, and had no power to enforce its decisions. It was dissolved in 1946. Its subsidiaries included the International Labour Organization and the Permanent Court of International Justice in The Hague, the Netherlands, both now under the auspices of the **United Nations** (UN).

The League of Nations was suggested in US president Woodrow Wilson's Fourteen Points (1917) as part of the peace settlement for World War I. The League covenant was drawn up by the Paris peace conference in 1919 and incorporated into the Versailles and other peace treaties. The member states undertook to preserve the territorial integrity of all, and to submit international disputes to the League. The League enjoyed some success in the humanitarian field, but in the political and diplomatic field, the League was permanently hampered by internal rivalries and the necessity for unanimity in the decision-making process. No action was taken against Japan's aggression in Manchuria in 1931; attempts to impose sanctions against Italy for the invasion of Ethiopia 1935–36 collapsed; no actions were taken when Germany annexed Austria and Czechoslovakia, nor when Poland was invaded. Japan in 1932 and Germany in 1933 simply withdrew from the League, and the expulsion of the USSR in 1939 had no effect on the Russo-Finnish war. Long before the outbreak of World War II, diplomacy had been abandoned in international security in favour of a system of direct negotiation and individual alliances.

## left wing

Basically socialist parties and socialist activists (see **socialism**). The term originated in the French national assembly of 1789, where the nobles sat in the place of honour to the right of the president, and the commons sat to the left. This arrangement has become customary in European parliaments, where the progressives sit on the left and the conservatives on the right. It is also usual to speak of the right, left, and centre of politics, especially when referring to the different elements composing a single party. However the term is entirely relative to the national context, and can lead to someone being regarded as dangerously left wing in one country when they would be seen as centrist or even moderately **right wing** elsewhere.

## legislature

The law-making body or bodies in a political system. Some legislatures are unicameral (having one chamber), and some bicameral (with two). In most democratic countries with bicameral legislatures the 'lower', or popular, chamber is the more powerful but there are exceptions, the most notable being in the USA, where the upper chamber, the Senate, is constitutionally more powerful than the lower, the House of Representatives. Most lower or single chambers are popularly elected and upper chambers are filled by appointees or a mixture of appointed and elected members.

## legitimacy

The justification of a ruling group's right to exercise power. Principles of legitimacy have included **divine right**, popular approval, and, in the case of communist parties, an insight into the true meaning of history. Nowadays very few systems try to claim legitimacy on anything but democratic grounds.

## Lenin, Vladimir Ilyich (1870–1924)

The adopted name of Vladimir Ilyich Ulyanov, Russian revolutionary, first leader of the USSR, and communist theoretician. Active in the 1905 Revolution, Lenin had to leave Russia when it failed, settling in Switzerland in 1914. He returned to Russia after the February revolution of 1917. He led the **Bolshevik** revolution of November 1917 and became leader of a Soviet government, concluded peace with Germany, and organized a successful resistance to White Russian (pro-tsarist) uprisings and foreign intervention 1918–20. His modification of traditional Marxist doctrine to fit conditions prevailing in Russia became known as **Marxism–Leninism**, the basis of communist ideology.

Lenin was born on 22 April 1870 and was a Marxist from 1889. He was sent to Siberia for spreading revolutionary propaganda 1895–1900. He then edited the political paper *Iskra* ('The Spark') from abroad, and visited London several times. In *What is to be Done?* (1902), he advocated that a professional core of Social Democratic Party activists should spearhead the revolution in Russia, a suggestion accepted by the majority (*bolsheviki*) at the London party congress in 1903. From Switzerland he attacked socialist support for World War I as aiding an 'imperialist' struggle, and wrote *Imperialism* (1917).

After the renewed outbreak of revolution February–March 1917, he was smuggled back into Russia in April by the Germans so that he could take up his revolutionary activities and remove Russia from the war, allowing Germany to concentrate the war effort on the Western Front. A complicated power struggle ensued, but eventually Lenin triumphed on 8 November 1917; a Bolshevik government was formed, and peace negotiations with Germany were begun, leading to the signing of the Treaty of Brest Litovsk on 3 March 1918.

From the overthrow of the provisional government in November 1917 until his death, Lenin effectively controlled the USSR, although an assassination attempt in 1918 injured his health. With communism proving inadequate to put the country on its feet, he introduced the private enterprise New Economic Policy in 1921.

**Lenin**  *Lenin led the Bolshevik revolution of 1917 and became the first leader of the USSR.*

> 6 It is true that liberty is precious – so precious that it must be rationed. 9
>
> **Vladimir Lenin**, Russian communist revolutionary leader, quoted in Sidney and Beatrice Webb *Soviet Communism*.

## Leninism

Modification of **Marxism** by **Lenin** which argues that in a revolutionary situation the industrial proletariat is unable to develop a truly revolutionary consciousness without strong leadership. The responsibility for this is taken on by the Communist Party, which acts as the 'vanguard of the proletariat' in leading it to revolution, before then assuming political control in a **dictatorship of the proletariat**. Only when the proletariat achieves a full socialist awareness will the power of the party, and ultimately the state itself, wither away.

## liberal democracy

The type of democracy most developed Western nations claim to practice. It is actually a combination of two values, which do not necessarily go together logically. As far as democracy is concerned, liberal democracy is a form of representative democracy. The usual system is the election by the whole electorate of a small number of representatives, probably organized in political parties, who form a legislative assembly. The majority of this assembly makes the law, and may, in parliamentary systems like those of the UK, Canada, Australasia, India, and others derived from the Westminster model, select some among themselves to form the executive. It is an indirect form of majority rule. The liberal aspect refers to a set of core values, based on the idea of civil rights, seen as central to the political culture, and these may be formally written into a constitution and protected by the courts. Political science research has, however, often shown that the majority of the electorate of Western democracies does not attach much importance to some of these rights, for example aspects of the **due process of law**. Thus the empirical will of the majority may conflict with the vital system values. As a result, liberal democracy cannot be a full-blooded majoritarian system.

## liberalism

The general political and social theory that favours representative government, freedom of the press, speech, and worship, the abolition of **class** privileges, the use of state resources to protect the welfare of the individual, and international **free trade**. It is historically associated with the Liberal Party in the UK and the Democratic Party in the USA. Liberalism developed during the 17th–19th centuries as the distinctive theory of the industrial and commercial classes in their struggle against the power of the monarchy, the church, and the feudal landowners. Economically it was associated with *laissez faire*, or non-intervention. In the late 19th and early 20th centuries its ideas were modified by the acceptance of universal suffrage and a certain amount of state intervention in economic affairs, in order to ensure a minimum standard of living and to remove extremes of poverty and wealth. The classical statement of liberal principles is found in *On Liberty* and other works of the English philosopher John Stuart **Mill**.

## liberation theology

Christian theory of Jesus' primary importance as the 'Liberator', personifying the poor and devoted to freeing them from oppression. Enthusiastically (and sometimes violently) adopted in Latin America, it embodies a Marxist interpretation of the class struggle, especially by **Third World** nations. It has been criticized by some Roman Catholic authorities, including Pope John

Paul II. The movement was initiated by the Peruvian priest Gustavo Gutierrez in his book *The Theology of Liberation* (1969).

## libertarianism
A political theory that upholds the rights of the individual above all other considerations and seeks to minimize the power of the state to the safeguarding of those rights. At its most extreme it sees the state as having no legitimate power to interfere with people's lives, since permission for such interference has not been granted by the individual concerned. Individuals should be free to do whatever they like so long as it does not affect the rights of others. Recent advocates have included the philosopher Robert **Nozick**.

## lobby
An individual or **pressure group** that sets out to influence government action. The lobby is prevalent in the USA, where the term originated in the 1830s from the practice of those wishing to influence state policy waiting for elected representatives in the lobby of the Capitol. Under one guise or another lobby activity is common to all liberal democracies, and can sometimes be seen as distorting public policy away from the common good. Lobby has a second meaning in the UK, to denote a practice whereby certain favoured parliamentary journalists are given unofficial access to confidential news. This itself is often criticized as a way for the government to over influence the public reception of its actions.

## local government
That aspect of government dealing mainly with matters concerning the inhabitants of a particular area or town, usually financed at least in part by local taxes. In the USA and UK, local government has comparatively large powers and responsibilities.

Historically, in European countries such as France, Germany, and the USSR, local government tended to be more centrally controlled than in Britain, although German cities have a tradition of independent action, as exemplified in Berlin, and France from 1969 moved towards regional decentralization. In the UK under reorganization proposals, the emphasis since 1997 is on single-tier unitary bodies, each providing a full range of local services. Wales has 22 unitary councils and Scotland 29, alongside the 3 existing island authority areas; Northern Ireland has a single-tier system of 26 district councils. The latest pattern for England came into effect on 1 April 1998 with the creation of 47 unitary authorities, replacing former borough or city councils which were previously part of two-tier structures. There were also, in 1998, 34 county councils in England, 36 metropolitan borough councils, and 33 London borough councils.

The Labour government, after 1997, announced plans to introduce directly elected mayors for the major cities, (a common system in the USA), and London now has the first such elected mayor. Only 15% of the money spent by local government is raised by local taxes (1995), and central government restricts how much may be raised in this way, thus effectively limiting the autonomy of local government. Council tax is a local tax based on property values but taking account of the number of inhabitants of a property.

### Locke, John (1632–1704)

English philosopher and political theorist. His *Essay concerning Human Understanding* (1690) maintained that experience is the only source of knowledge (empiricism), and that 'we can have knowledge no farther than we have ideas' prompted by such experience. His *Two Treatises on Government* (1690) helped to form contemporary ideas of liberal democracy. This book enjoyed great influence in America and France, being highly influential in the drafting of the American Constitution. It supposed that governments derive their authority from popular consent (regarded as a 'contract'), so that a government may be rightly overthrown if it infringes such fundamental rights of the people as religious freedom. It is nowadays seen as rather more conservative than in the past because of its very strong defence of private property. But the idea of limited government, which clashed with the ideas of Locke's near contemporary **Hobbes** is central to much liberal thinking.

**Locke** *An 18th-century copper engraving of English philosopher John Locke.*

In later life he published many works on philosophy, politics, theology, and economics; these include *Letters on Toleration* (1689–92) and *Some Thoughts concerning Education* (1693).

> 6 Government has no other end but the preservation of property. 9
>
> **John Locke,** English philosopher, *Second Treatise on Civil Government.*

## McCarthyism

Political persecution, or witch-hunt, of the type associated with the US senator Joe McCarthy. At the height of US anxiety about the communist 'threat' during the 1950s, McCarthy accused many public officials and private citizens of being Communist Party members or sympathizers. Most of his evidence was fabricated, but the Congressional committees, where his claims were investigated, destroyed many careers and created an atmosphere of suspicion and paranoia, especially in liberal intellectual circles.

## Machiavelli, Niccolò
### (1469–1527)

**Machiavelli** *Machiavelli's name is synonymous with cunning and amoral statescraft.*

Italian politician and author. His name is synonymous with cunning and cynical statecraft. In his chief political writings, *Il principe/The Prince* (1513) and *Discorsi/Discourses* (1531), he discussed ways in which rulers can advance the interests of their states (and themselves) through an often amoral and opportunistic manipulation of other people. Machiavelli was born in Florence and was second chancellor to the republic (1498–1512). On the accession to power of the Medici family in 1512, he was arrested and imprisoned on a charge of conspiracy but in 1513 was released to exile in the country. *The Prince*, based on his observations of Cesare Borgia, is a guide for the future prince of a unified Italian state (which did not occur until the Risorgimento in the 19th century). In *L'Arte della guerra/The Art of War* (1520), Machiavelli outlined the provision of an army for the prince, and in *Historie*

*Fiorentine/History of Florence* he analysed the historical development of Florence until 1492. Among his later works are the comedies *Clizia* (1515) and *La Mandragola/The Mandrake* (1524). His political theories are often seen as the beginning of true political science, concerned with empirical understanding of how politics actually works, rather than merely moralizing about how it ought to work.

> ❻ One of the most powerful safeguards a prince can have against conspiracies is to avoid being hated by the populace. ❾
>
> **Niccolò Machiavelli**, Italian politician and author, *The Prince* (1513).

## MAD
Abbreviation for mutual assured destruction, the basis of the theory of **deterrence** by possession of nuclear weapons. It relies on the idea that actual comparative levels of nuclear weapons do not matter as long as the weaker side has enough weapons that can be guaranteed to survive a first strike by the stronger to destroy a high proportion of the first striker's population and industrial structure.

## Malcolm X (1926–1965)
Adopted name of Malcolm Little, US black nationalist leader. While serving a prison sentence for burglary 1946–53, he joined the Black Muslims sect. On his release he campaigned for black separatism, condoning violence in self-defence, but in 1964 modified his views to found the Islamic, socialist Organization of Afro-American Unity, preaching racial solidarity. In 1952 he officially changed his name to Malcolm X to signify his rootlessness in a racist society. Having become an influential national and international leader, Malcolm X publicly broke with the Black Muslims in 1964. A year later he was assassinated by Nation of Islam opponents while addressing a rally in Harlem, New York City. His *Autobiography of Malcolm X*, written with Alex Haley, was published in 1964.

> ❻ You can't separate peace from freedom because no one can be at peace unless he has his freedom. ❾
>
> **Malcolm X**, US black nationalist leader, speech, New York City, 7 January 1965.

## mandate

Historically, a territory whose administration was entrusted to Allied states by the **League of Nations** under the Treaty of Versailles after World War I. Mandated territories were former German and Turkish possessions (including Iraq, Syria, Lebanon, and Palestine). When the United Nations replaced the League of Nations in 1945, mandates that had not achieved independence became known as trust territories.

More generally a mandate means any official command; in politics also the right (given by the electors) of an elected government to carry out its programme of policies.

## Mandela, Nelson Rolihlahla (1918– )

South African politician and lawyer, president 1994–99. He was president of the African National Congress (ANC) 1991–97. Imprisoned from 1964, as organizer of the then banned ANC, he became a symbol of unity for the worldwide anti-**apartheid** movement. In February 1990 he was released, the ban on the ANC having been lifted, and entered into negotiations with the government about a multiracial future for South Africa. In May 1994 he was sworn in as South Africa's first post-apartheid president after the ANC won 62.65% of the vote in universal-suffrage elections. He shared the Nobel Peace Prize in 1993 with South African president F W de Klerk. In June 1999 he stepped down as president and was succeeded by ANC president, Thabo Mbeki.

Mandela married the South African civil-rights activist Winnie Mandela in 1958. They separated in 1992 and were divorced in 1996. His autobiography, *Long Walk to Freedom* (1994) was widely acclaimed, and his state visit to Britain in July 1996 was a resounding success.

> ⁶ He had the ability to radiate unusual warmth and charm – when he chose to. ⁹
>
> **F W de Klerk,** Former President of South Africa, on his successor, Nelson Mandela, *Independent on Sunday*, 17 January 1999.

## manifesto

The published prospectus of a party, setting out the policies that the party will pursue if elected to govern. When elected to power a party will often claim that the contents of its manifesto constitute a **mandate** to introduce legislation to bring these policies into effect. In an unprecedented move, the Labour Party in 1996 put its manifesto to a pre-election ballot of its membership. The term is now used in politics as a statement of policy or political theory, (for example Peel's Tamworth Manifesto of 1835 and the Communist Manifesto by **Marx** and **Engels** in 1848). Nowadays, before an election political parties usually issue a manifesto in which they outline the policies they advocate. In some countries, such as the USA and Canada, the manifesto is known as the 'party platform'.

## Mannheim, Karl (1893–1947)
Hungarian sociologist who settled in the UK in 1933. In *Ideology and Utopia* (1929) he argued that all knowledge, except in mathematics and physics, is ideological, a reflection of **class** interests and values; that there is therefore no such thing as objective knowledge or absolute truth. Mannheim distinguished between ruling-class ideologies and those of utopian or revolutionary groups, arguing that knowledge is created by a continual power struggle between rival groups and ideas. Later works such as *Man and Society* (1940) analysed contemporary mass society in terms of its fragmentation and susceptibility to extremist ideas and **totalitarian** governments.

## Maoism
A form of communism based on the ideas and teachings of the Chinese communist leader **Mao Zedong**. It involves an adaptation of Marxism to suit conditions in China and apportions a much greater role to agriculture and the peasantry in the building of socialism, thus effectively bypassing the capitalist (industrial) stage envisaged by **Marx**. In addition, Maoism stresses ideological, as well as economic, transformation, based on regular contact between party members and the general population. His ideas became more influential than orthodox Marxism in much of the Third World, though they lack the theoretical rigour and empirical evidence of the best of Marx's writings.

## Mao Zedong (1893–1976)
Chinese communist politician and theoretician, leader of the Chinese Communist Party (CCP) 1935–76, also known as Mao Tse-tung. Mao was a founder of the CCP in 1921 and became its leader in 1935. He organized the Long March 1934–35 and the war of liberation 1937–49, following which he established a People's Republic and communist rule in China. He was state president until 1959, and headed the CCP until his death. His influence diminished with the failure of his early economic policies, but he

emerged dominant again during the 1966–69 Cultural Revolution, which he launched in order to promote his own anti-bureaucratic line and to purge the party of 'revisionism'.

Mao adapted **communism** to Chinese conditions, as set out in the *Little Red Book* (1960), in which he stressed the need for rural rather than urban-based revolutions in Asia. His writings and thoughts dominated the functioning of the People's Republic 1949–76, and some 740 million copies of his *Quotations* have been printed to date, while his works as a whole total over 2,000 publications. In July 1981 the CCP Central Committee published an authoritative official verdict on Mao Zedong and the last 20 years of his life. It assessed Mao as '70 % good and 30 % bad', praising his contribution to the building of the CCP, PLA, and People's Republic, but criticizing him for becoming tyrannical and obsessed with a misguided leftist line from the mid 1950s, culminating in the disastrous Cultural Revolution. Today, **Maoism** is viewed as just one of the many contributions to Chinese communist thinking.

> 6 Communism is not love. Communism is a hammer which we use to crush the enemy. 9
>
> **Mao Zedong**, Chinese premier, *Time*, 18 December 1950.

## Marcuse, Herbert (1898–1979)

German-born US political philosopher. His theories combining **Marxism** and Freudianism influenced radical thought in the 1960s and 1970s. He preached the overthrow of the existing social order by using the system's very tolerance to ensure its defeat; he was not an advocate of violent revolution. Marcuse was born in Berlin and became an influential member of the Frankfurt School. In 1934 he moved to the USA as a refugee from **Hitler's** Germany and taught philosophy at several universities, including Columbia 1934–40, Brandeis 1954–65, and the University of California at San Diego 1965–79. He wrote several books, including *Eros and Civilization* (1955) and *One-Dimensional Man* (1964).

## Marshall Plan

The programme of US economic aid to Europe set up at the end of World War II and totalling $13,000 billion between 1948 and 1952. Officially known as the European Recovery Programme, it was announced by

Secretary of State George C Marshall in a speech at Harvard in June 1947, but it was in fact the work of a State Department group led by Dean Acheson. The perceived danger of a communist takeover in post-war Europe was the main reason for the aid effort.

## martial law

The replacement of civilian authorities by military authorities in the maintenance of order. In Britain, the legal position of martial law is ill defined but, in effect, when war or rebellion is in progress in an area, the military authorities maintain order by summary means. International law nonetheless contains some rules and restrictions on the use of martial law.

## Marx, Karl Heinrich (1818–1883)

German philosopher, economist, and social theorist whose account of change through conflict is known as historical, or dialectical, materialism (**Marxism**). His *Das Kapital/Capital* (1867–95) is the fundamental text of Marxist economics and his systematic theses on class struggle, history, and the importance of economic factors in politics have exercised an enormous influence on later thinkers and political activists.

In 1844 Marx began his lifelong collaboration with Friedrich **Engels**, with whom he developed the Marxist philosophy, first formulated in their joint works *Die heilige Familie/The Holy Family* (1844) and *Die deutsche Ideologie/German Ideology* (1846), which contains the theory demonstrating the material basis of all human activity. Both joined the Communist League, a German refugee organization, and in 1847–48 they prepared its programme, *The Communist Manifesto*. In the wake of the 1848 revolution, Marx was expelled from Prussia. He then settled in London, where he wrote *Die Klassenkämpfe in Frankreich/Class Struggles in France* (1849), *Die Achtzehnte Brumaire des Louis Bonaparte/The 18th Brumaire of Louis Bonaparte* (1852), *Zur Kritik der politischen Ökonomie/ Critique of Political Economy* (1859),

❝ Religion is the sigh of the oppressed creature, the sentiment of the heartless world, and the soul of soulless conditions. It is the opium of the people. ❞

**Karl Marx**, German social theorist and economic historian, quoted in Ernst Fischer *Marx in His Own Words*.

and his monumental work *Das Kapital/Capital*. In 1864 the International Working Men's Association was formed, whose policy Marx, as a member of the general council, largely controlled. Although he showed extraordinary tact in holding together its diverse elements, it collapsed in 1872 owing to Marx's disputes with the anarchists, including the Russian Bakunin. Marx's philosophical work owes much to the writings of the German G W F **Hegel**, though he rejected Hegel's actual conclusions.

## Marxism

The system of sociological and economic theories developed by the 19th-century German social theorists **Marx** and **Engels**, also known as **dialectical materialism**, under which material conditions are dominant over mental ones, and all is subject to change (from dialectic; see **Hegel**). As applied to history, it supposes that the succession of **feudalism**, capitalism, socialism, and finally the classless society is inevitable. The stubborn resistance of any existing system to change necessitates its complete overthrow in the class struggle – in the case of **capitalism**, by the **proletariat** – rather than gradual modification. Social and political institutions progressively change their nature as economic developments transform material conditions.

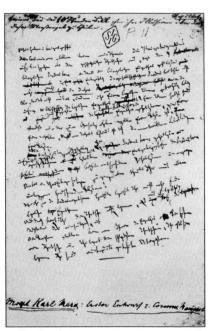

**Marxism** *The manuscript of Marx and Engel's famous* Communist Manifesto.

The orthodox belief is that each successive form is 'higher' than the last; perfect socialism is seen as the ultimate rational system, and it is alleged that the state would then wither away. Marxism has proved one of the most powerful and debated theories in modern history, inspiring both dedicated exponents (**Lenin**, **Trotsky**, **Stalin**, **Mao Zedong**) and bitter opponents. It is the basis of communism.

## Marxism–Leninism

Was the term used by the Soviet dictator **Stalin** and his supporters to define their own views as the orthodox position of **Marxism** as a means of refuting criticism. It has subsequently been employed by other communist parties as a yardstick for ideological purity.

## massive retaliation

The official policy of the administration of US president Dwight D Eisenhower after 1954 and the Korean War. It was the idea that any aggression by the USSR in Europe or elsewhere would be met by a huge nuclear onslaught on the Soviet homeland. This was only plausible because, at that stage, there was no alternative for the West, which had much weaker conventional forces, and because the US nuclear capacity massively outweighed the USSR's. As the USSR's nuclear arsenal grew in the 1960s The USA developed the doctrines of **escalation** and **flexible response**, leading ultimately to mutual assured destruction (**MAD**), in order to preserve the goal of **deterrence**.

## Menshevik

A member of the minority (Russian *menshinstvo* 'minority') of the Russian Social Democratic Party, who split from the **Bolsheviks** in 1903. The Mensheviks believed in a large, loosely organized party and that, before socialist revolution could occur in Russia, capitalist society had to develop further. During the Russian Revolution they had limited power and set up a government in Georgia, but were suppressed in 1922.

## mercantilism

An economic theory, held in the 16th–18th centuries, that a nation's wealth (in the form of bullion or treasure) was the key to its prosperity. To this end, foreign trade should be regulated to create a surplus of exports over imports, and the state should intervene where necessary (for example, subsidizing exports and taxing imports). The bullion theory of wealth was demolished by Adam Smith in Book IV of *The Wealth of Nations* (1776).

## mercenary

A soldier hired by the army of another country or by a private army. Mercenary military service originated in the 14th century, when cash payment on a regular basis was the only means of guaranteeing soldiers' loyalty. In the 20th century mercenaries have been common in wars and **guerrilla** activity in Asia, Africa, and Latin America.

## Militant Tendency

In British politics, a left-wing faction originally within the **Labour Party**, aligned with the publication *Militant*. It became active in the 1970s, with radical socialist policies based on Trotskyism (see **Trotsky**), and gained some success in local government, for example in the inner-city area of Liverpool. In the mid-1980s the Labour Party considered it to be a separate organization within the party and banned it. A number of senior Militants were expelled from the party in 1986, amid much legal conflict. The contested de-selection of the incumbent member of Parliament Frank Field as Labour candidate for Birkenhead, Lancashire, in 1990 led to renewed allegations of Militant infiltration of the Labour Party. In 1991 a Militant Tendency candidate openly contested the Liverpool (Walton) by-election with the official Labour candidate

## military regimes

Autocratic governments where the military controls the country's political system, often after a **coup d'etat**. In military regimes the civil liberties of citizens, and normal political and constitutional arrangements, may be suspended. Although military regimes are autocratic, they may not be **totalitarian**. If they occur because of a national crisis or political emergency (see **emergency powers**) such regimes may have a degree of political legitimacy. Sometimes the leaders of the regime may intend to restore the democratic system of government as soon as it is safe to do so, although the restoration of normal political life is often difficult. Military coups and military regimes are most often associated with Third World countries, though Greece, Poland, Portugal, and Turkey have all experienced periods of military government in the post-war period. In Latin America military regimes have frequently brought experiments with democratic government to an end, although their supporters would claim that military intervention was necessary to end the spiral of hyperinflation, urban terrorism, and disorder which the troubled democracies were experiencing.

## militia

A body of civilian soldiers, usually with some military training, who are on call in emergencies, distinct from professional soldiers. In Switzerland, the militia is the national defence force, and every able-bodied man is liable for service in it. In the UK the Territorial Army and in the USA the National Guard have supplanted earlier voluntary militias.

## Mill, James (1773–1836)

Scottish philosopher and political thinker who developed the theory of **utilitarianism**. He is remembered for his political articles and for the rigorous education he gave his son John Stuart **Mill**. Born near Montrose on the east coast, Mill moved to London in 1802. Associated for most of his working life with the East India Company, he wrote a vast *History of British India* (1817–18). He was one of the founders of University College, London, together with his friend and fellow utilitarian Jeremy **Bentham**.

## Mill, John Stuart (1806–1873)

English philosopher and economist who wrote *On Liberty* (1859), the classic philosophical defence of liberalism, and *Utilitarianism* (1863), a version of the 'greatest happiness for the greatest number' principle in ethics. His progressive views inspired *On the Subjection of Women* (1869). In 1826, as described in his *Autobiography* (1873), he passed through a mental crisis; he found his father's bleakly intellectual **utilitarianism** emotionally unsatisfying and abandoned it for a more human philosophy influenced by the poet Samuel Taylor Coleridge. Mill sat in Parliament as a Radical 1865–68 and introduced a motion for women's suffrage.

In *Utilitarianism*, he states that actions are right if they bring about happiness and wrong if they bring about the reverse of happiness. But unlike classical utilitarianism he tried to incorporate the sense that some ways of being happy were more worthwhile than others. *On Liberty* moved away from the utilitarian notion that individual liberty was necessary for economic and governmental efficiency and advanced the classical defence of individual freedom as a value in itself and the mark of a mature society; this change can be traced in the later editions of *Principles of Political Economy* (1848). His philosophical and political writings include *A System of Logic* (1843) and *Considerations on Representative Government* (1861).

> ❢ If all mankind minus one, were of one opinion, and only one person were of the contrary opinion, mankind would be no more justified in silencing that one person, than he, if he had the power, would be justified in silencing mankind. ❢
>
> **John Stuart Mill**, English liberal philosopher and economist, *On Liberty* (1859).

## Mills, C(harles) Wright (1916–1962)

US sociologist whose concern for humanity, ethical values, and individual freedom led him to criticize the US establishment.

Originally in the liberal tradition, Mills later adopted Weberian and even Marxist ideas. He aroused considerable popular interest in sociology with such works as *White Collar* (1951) and *Listen, Yankee* (1960). His main book in political sociology, *The Power Elite* (1956), depicted the USA as ruled by businessmen, military experts, and politicians. It remains a key text in the study of political **power**.

## minority

Those who are not in a majority in a particular country. Sometimes minorities have a common identity, rather than being united only in their opposition to the majority. Where a minority exists on only one issue, or by virtue of one single characteristic, it is not likely to have political significance. The politically important sense of 'minority' is when a group in society has a set of common interests and beliefs over a wide set of issues, which marks it out as needing, deserving, or at least claiming special treatment that the majority of citizens do not. Minorities are often thought of as having a long term existence, and requiring the establishment of institutional or structural methods to help them. The most common politically important minorities are racial, religious, or ethnic groups in a society who are seen as suffering across a broad spectrum of disadvantages and needing special legal protection and positive discrimination or **affirmative action**. In many societies sexual minorities have become increasingly vocal, particularly since the 1960s (see **gay politics**).

What is important is that the group in question is cut off from, and usually subordinate to, a dominant set of interests against which it needs protection. Occasionally one finds women in general described as a political minority, even though they may be statistically in a majority, because of the way in which they have been historically treated as subordinate to males or lacking full rights.

## modernization

In political science, the capacity of countries from outside the **First World** to develop the economic and political capacity, and the social institutions needed to support a liberal democracy such as is found in parts of the First World. This political science approach risks being biased in terms of Western values, but there is a strong tradition in social and political theory of studying change in this way, much of it derived from Max **Weber**. In fact all the classic sociological theorists of development, **Marx** as much as **Durkheim**, conceive of something like 'modernity' as a stage all societies have to go through. The main thesis is that a form of political division of labour is needed, in which the political system moves from having only a few, all-embracing and authoritative posts, a tribal chieftain perhaps, to highly specific and task specialized roles in a modern bureaucratic and governmental system. At the same time changes in social conditions, especially communications and education, are seen as steadily increasing the capacity of a system to maintain and apply complex modern politics oriented to satisfying as many different political interests as possible.

## monetarism

An economic policy that proposes control of a country's money supply to keep it in step with the country's ability to produce goods, with the aim of curbing inflation. Cutting government spending is advocated, and the long-term aim is to return as much of the economy as possible to the private sector, allegedly in the interests of efficiency. Monetarism was first advocated by the economist Milton Friedman and the Chicago school of economists.

**Central banks** (in the USA, the Federal Reserve Bank) use the discount rate and other tools to restrict or expand the supply of money to the economy. Unemployment may result from some efforts to withdraw government 'safety nets', but monetarists claim it is less than eventually occurs if the methods of **Keynesian** economics are adopted. Additionally, credit is restricted by high interest rates, and industry is not cushioned against internal market forces or overseas competition (with the aim of preventing 'overstaffing', 'restrictive' union practices, and 'excessive' wage demands).

Monetarist policies were widely adopted in the 1980s in response to the inflation problems caused by spiralling oil prices in 1979.

## monetary policy

An economic policy aimed at controlling the amount of money in circulation, usually through controlling the level of lending or credit. Increasing interest rates is an example of a contractionary monetary policy, which aims to reduce inflation by reducing the rate of growth of spending in the economy.

## Monnet, Jean (1888–1979)

French economist. The originator of Winston Churchill's offer of union between the UK and France in 1940, he devised and took charge of the

French modernization programme under Charles **de Gaulle** in 1945. In 1950 he produced the 'Schumann Plan' initiating the coordination of European coal and steel production in the European Coal and Steel Community, which developed into the Common Market, the forerunner of the **European Union**. He is generally regarded as the father of European integration.

## Monroe Doctrine

Declaration by US president James Monroe in 1823 that any further European colonial ambitions in the Western hemisphere would be regarded as threats to US peace and security, made in response to proposed European intervention against newly independent former Spanish colonies in South America. In return for the quietening of such European ambitions, the USA would not interfere in European affairs. The doctrine, subsequently broadened, has been a recurrent theme in US foreign policy, although it has no basis in US or international law.

At the time of the declaration, the USA was militarily incapable of enforcing its sweeping proclamations. The impetus for, and the power behind, the doctrine came from the British, whose commercial interests were at risk in the event of a Franco-Spanish reassertion of colonial influence. President Theodore Roosevelt drew on the doctrine to proclaim a US right to intervene in the internal affairs of Latin American states. Late 20th century US fears of communist influence in Latin America, from the Cuban revolution onwards also relied on this doctrine.

## Montesquieu, Charles Louis de Secondat, Baron de la Brède (1689–1755)

French political theorist and historian, author of *Lettres persanes/Persian Letters* (1721) and *De l'Esprit des lois/The Spirit of the Laws* (1748), a 31-volume philosophical disquisition on politics and sociology as well as legal matters. This advocated the separation of powers within government, a doctrine that became the basis of liberal constitutions. He shares with

> ❝ An empire founded by war has to maintain itself by war. ❞
>
> **Charles Montesquieu**, French philosophical historian, *Considérations sur les causes de la grandeur des Romains et de leur décadence* (1734).

**Locke** the credit for having influenced the framers of the American constitution.

Montesquieu arrived at the concept of the separation of powers, that is, of the legislative, executive, and judicial functions, as a result of experience of living in England, a country whose constitution he much admired but partially misunderstood.

Born near Bordeaux, Montesquieu became adviser to the Bordeaux parliament in 1714. After the success of *Lettres persanes*, which satirizes French legal and political institutions, he adopted a literary career, writing *Considérations sur les causes de la grandeur des Romains et de leur décadence/ Considerations on the Greatness and Decadence of the Romans* (1734).

**Montesquieu** *Charles Montesquieu shares with Locke the credit for having influenced the framers of the American constitution.*

## More, (St) Thomas (1478–1535)

English politician, lawyer, and author. From 1509 he was favoured by Henry VIII and employed on foreign embassies. He was a member of the privy council from 1518 and Lord Chancellor from 1529 but resigned over Henry's break with the pope. For refusing to accept the king as head of the church, he was executed. The title of his political book *Utopia* (1516), sketching an ideal commonwealth, has come to mean any supposedly perfect society (see **utopia**).

Son of a London judge, More studied Greek, Latin, French, theology, and music at Oxford, and law at Lincoln's Inn, London, and was influenced by the humanists John Colet and Erasmus, who became a friend. In Parliament from 1504, he was made Speaker of the House of Commons in 1523. He was knighted in 1521, and on the fall of Cardinal Wolsey became Lord Chancellor, but resigned in 1532 because he could not agree with the king on his ecclesiastical policy and marriage with Anne Boleyn. In 1534 he refused to take the oath of supremacy to Henry VIII as head of the church, and after a year's imprisonment in the Tower of London he was executed.

Also important in the politics of his day were *Dialogue* (1528), a theological argument against the Reformation leader Tyndale; and a *History of Richard III.* He was also a patron of artists, including Holbein. More was canonized in 1935.

## multilateralism

Trade among more than two countries without discrimination over origin or destination and regardless of whether a large trade gap is involved. Unlike bilateralism, multilateralism does not require the trade flow between countries to be of the same value. In strategic and international relations theory multilateralism refers to widespread defensive alliances not dominated by or dependant on one super power.

**More** *The title of More's political book,* Utopia, *about the ideal society, has come to mean any theoretical perfect society.*

## multiparty system

System where several political parties are electorally significant. Party systems are categorized in **comparative government** in complex ways. The original divisions were between one-party states, two-party systems, and 'multi'. This turns out to be too simplistic. The UK, for example, in most early political science work was seen as a two-party system, despite the fact that in the 20th century there was always at least three political parties represented in parliament. So the UK, with a third party, (under various names, getting up to one-quarter of total votes, though usually being unable to alter the balance of power), can no longer be studied as a two-party system leading some commentators to regard Britain as a 'two-and-a-half' party system. West Germany, on the other hand, though it had, between the 1950s and 1983, only three parties in the Bundestag, was seen as a full multiparty system because the small Free Democratic Party (FDP) became a permanent coalition partner after 1969. Basically a multiparty system is one with at least three and usually more, political parties, each of them significant. The best test of when a party must be counted into the system is whether its inclusion or exclusion from government coalitions makes a real difference, and is a real possibility.

### Mussolini, Benito Amilcare Andrea (1883–1945)

Italian dictator 1925–43. As founder of the Fascist Movement in 1919 and prime minister from 1922, he became known as *Il Duce* ('the leader'). He invaded Ethiopia 1935–36, intervened in the Spanish Civil War 1936–39 in support of **Franco**, and conquered Albania in 1939. In June 1940 Italy entered World War II supporting **Hitler**. Forced by military and domestic setbacks to resign in 1943, Mussolini established a breakaway government in northern Italy 1944–45, but was killed trying to flee the country.

Mussolini was originally a journalist, active in the socialist movement, notably as editor of the party newspaper *Avanti* 1912–14. In 1919 he founded the Fascist Movement, whose programme combined violent nationalism with demagogic republican and anti-capitalist slogans, and launched a campaign of terrorism against the socialists. Though anti-capitalist in origin, the movement was backed by agrarian and industrial **élites** in the context of post-war popular unrest. In October 1922 Mussolini came to power by semi-constitutional means as prime minister at the head of a coalition government. In 1925 he assumed dictatorial powers, and in 1926 all opposition parties were banned. During the years that followed, the political, legal, and education systems were remodelled on fascist lines. **Fascism** prefigured other 'totalitarian' regimes, in that it aspired to be an all-embracing ideology, but Mussolini faced constraints on his power – from monarch, church, and industrial élites – which had no real parallel in Hitler's Germany.

> 6 Look at that man's eyes. You will hear more of him later. 9
>
> **Bonar Law**, referring to Mussolini.

## nationalism

Any movement that consciously aims to unify a nation, create a state, or liberate it from foreign or imperialistic rule. Nationalist movements became a potent factor in European politics during the 19th century; since 1900 nationalism has become a strong force in Asia and Africa and in the late 1980s revived strongly in Eastern Europe. Stimulated by the French Revolution, movements arose in the 19th century in favour of national unification in Germany and Italy and national independence in Ireland, Italy, Belgium, Hungary, Bohemia, Poland, Finland, and the Balkan States. Revival of interest in the national language, history, traditions, and culture has accompanied and influenced most political movements.

In political terms, nationalism can be pursued as an **ideology** that stresses the superiority of a nation and its inhabitants compared with other nations and peoples.

Neither religion, language, territory, tradition, nor economic interests can claim monopoly or even predominance in the growth of nationalism. Perhaps the most prevalent influence is community of history, tradition, and culture, difficult to define in general terms but altogether exercising an immensely powerful influence. In recent years the developed nations of Western Europe have seen small nationalist movements within their borders. The Basque movement in Spain being the most violent. France has also experienced minor separatist pressure from movements in Brittany, Corsica, and Alsace. In Canada, French speakers campaign for a *Québec Libre*.

> ❝ Men of England! You wish to kill me because I am a Frenchman. Am I not punished enough in not being born an Englishman? ❞
>
> **Voltaire** (1694–1778) French writer, addressing an angry London mob who desired to hang him because he was French.

## nationalization

The policy of bringing a country's essential services and industries under public ownership. It was pursued, for example, by the UK Labour government 1945–51. Subsequently the trend towards nationalization has slowed and in many countries (the UK, France, and Japan) reversed (see **privatization**). Assets in the hands of foreign governments or companies may also be nationalized; for example, Iran's oil industry, the Suez Canal, and US-owned fruit plantations in Guatemala, all in the 1950s.

Under Tony Blair, the **Labour Party** pledged to restore vital utilities to public ownership or public control but did not commit itself to full nationalization based on the post-1945 model. Once in power, it retreated from its former stance and announced a number of privatization measures, including the Royal Mint, the Commonwealth Development Corporation, and air traffic control.

### Nationalization in the UK
- Bank of England, 1946
- coal, most hospitals transport, and electricity, 1947
- gas, 1948
- iron and steel, 1949
- road haulage denationalized, 1951
- iron and steel denationalized, 1953
- iron and steel re-nationalized in 1977 by Callaghan's Labour government
- aircraft and shipbuilding industries nationalized, 1977
- aircraft and shipbuilding privatized after 1979
- Bank of England denationalized, 1997.

## national socialism
The official name for the Nazi movement in Germany; see **fascism** and **Nazism**.

## nation-state
A nation-state exists when the whole of a geographical area that is the home-land for a people who identify themselves as a community, is governed by one political system. Such contexts are the common experience of today, but are not necessarily any more natural than other forms that have been common in history. There were no nation-states in classical Greece, though there was clearly a Greek nation, which sensed that all Greeks had more in common than a Greek could have with a barbarian. Historically the growth of the nation-state, and its developing legitimacy, came after the collapse of the Roman Empire and only when its successor in the West, the Germanic Holy Roman Empire, could no longer pretend to rule an international collection of

separate sub-states. To some extent the growth of the earliest nation-states, especially France and England, were historical accidents, for the seeds of national identity, especially the linguistic and cultural homogeneity, actually came after rather than preceded the political hegemony of the national governments. Later important nation-states, for example Italy and Germany, although clearly possessing many of the characteristics of nationhood, only united late in the 19th century.

**NATO** See North Atlantic Treaty Organization.

## natural justice
The concept that there is an inherent quality in law that compares favourably with arbitrary action by a government. It is largely associated with the idea of the rule of law. For natural justice to be present, it is generally argued that no one should be a judge in his or her own case, and that each party in a dispute has an unalienable right to be heard and to prepare their case thoroughly (the rule of *audi alterem partem*). It is very similar to US ideas of **due process**.

## natural law
The idea that fundamental laws exist in nature that are common to all humankind. Natural law is distinct from positive law, which is those laws imposed on people by people. Natural law doctrines were once dominant in legal thinking, but they are hard to argue for without a theological basis, and have come to be much less frequently supported.

## Nazism
The ideology based on racism, nationalism, and the supremacy of the state over the individual advocated by the German Nazi party, the *Nationalsozialistische Deut-*

**Nazism** *This Nazi propaganda poster, proclaiming 'Ein neuer Mensch formt eine neue Zeit!' – 'a new man, shaping a new era!' – depicts the blond-haired, blue-eyed Nazi ideal of a 'pure' German race.*

*sche Arbeiterpartei* (National Socialist German Workers' Party) led by Adolf **Hitler** from 1921 to 1945. During the 1930s many similar parties were created throughout Europe and the USA, although only those of Austria and Hungary were of major importance. These parties collaborated with the German occupation of Europe from 1939 to 1945. After the Nazi atrocities of World War II (see **Holocaust**), the party was banned in Germany, but today parties with Nazi or neo-Nazi ideologies exist in many countries.

Nazi-related movements were founded in the UK in 1932 by Oswald Mosley and in 1962 by Colin Jordan (National Socialist Movement); in 1967 the National Front was formed. In the USA the American Nazi Party was founded in 1958 by George Lincoln Rockwell. In a determined attempt to curb right-wing violence, the German government banned six neo-Nazi groups between 1994 and 1995.

## neocolonialism

A disguised form of **imperialism**, by which a country may grant independence to another country but continue to dominate it by control of markets for goods or raw materials. Examples of countries that have used economic pressure to secure and protect their interests internationally are the USA, and to a lesser extent Japan, France, and the UK. Many developing countries, heavily dependent on leading industrial nations, are subject to this new form of imperialism, with significant proportions of their national product being allocated to payment of interest on accumulated foreign debts. This system was analysed in the book *Neo-Colonialism, the Last Stage of Imperialism* (1965) by the Ghanaian leader Kwame Nkrumah.

## neoconservatism

A version of conservatism that emerged in the USA in opposition to the liberal, social, and political attitudes of the 1960s. It advocates a narrow, patriarchal approach to morality and family life, extols the virtues of Western capitalism as a system that encourages individual initiative and freedom, and attacks the notion of the state as the promoter of equality and as a provider of welfare.

## neo-Nazism

The upsurge in racial and political intolerance in Eastern and Western Europe of the early 1990s. In Austria, Belgium, France, Germany, Russia, and Italy, the growth of extreme right-wing political groupings, coupled with racial violence, particularly in Germany, has revived memories of the Nazi period in **Hitler's** Germany. Ironically, the liberalization of politics in the post-Cold War world has

In 1992 five nights of rioting and attacks on a shelter for asylum seekers in Rostock, Germany, was followed by riots in 15 other towns and the bombing of a memorial to commemorate the Holocaust in Berlin.

unleashed anti-liberal forces hitherto checked by **authoritarian** regimes. The most significant parties in Western Europe described by the media as 'neo-Nazi' were the National Front in France, led by Jean-Marie Le Pen, and the National Alliance in Italy (although, by 1998, the National Alliance had become a mainstream Conservative party).

## neutrality

The legal status of a country that decides not to choose sides in a war. Certain states, notably Switzerland and Austria, have opted for permanent neutrality. Neutrality always has a legal connotation. It is unclear whether complete and permanent neutrality is compatible with membership of the UN, which requires a country to be prepared to exercise military force to further UN resolutions. In peacetime, neutrality towards the big power alliances is called **nonalignment**.

## New Deal

The US programme introduced by President Franklin D Roosevelt in 1933 to tackle the Great Depression, including employment on public works, farm loans at low rates, and social reforms such as old-age and unemployment insurance, prevention of child labour, protection of employees against unfair practices by employers, and loans to local authorities for slum clearance. The centrepiece of the New Deal was the Social Security Act of 1935, which introduced a comprehensive federal system of insurance for the elderly and unemployed. Some of the provisions of the New Deal

The New Deal programme was largely designed by a body of professors and other expert advisers (nicknamed the Brain Trust) in 1932. Its aims were helped by a devaluation of the dollar by 40%, by the revitalization of the Reconstruction Finance Corporation set up by Roosevelt's predecessor, Herbert Hoover, that granted the necessary loans, and by the abandonment of the gold standard.

were declared unconstitutional by the Supreme Court (1935–36). The New Deal encouraged the growth of trade-union membership, brought previously unregulated areas of the US economy under federal control, and revitalized cultural life and community spirit. Although full employment did not come until the military-industrial needs of World War II, the New Deal did bring political stability to the industrial-capitalist system. It also transformed the political landscape, making the **Democratic Party** the natural majority party and breaking Republican dominance since 1806.

## New Right

Refers to a resurgence of Conservative and anti-socialist thought in the USA and to a lesser extent in the UK and other advanced industrial democracies that began in the mid-1970s. These included principally a commitment to individualism and the primacy of capitalism and the free market in preference to state policies. Advocates of New Right theories were active in the UK and the USA since the early 1960s, but it was only after the economic crisis of 1973–74 and the electoral success of Margaret Thatcher in 1979 and Ronald Reagan in 1980 that the expression became common.

The fundamental theories of the New Right became the basis for policies such as **privatization** of the public sector, reduction of the **welfare state**, deregulation, monetarism and, to some degree, conservative moralism. The New Right capitalized on disillusionment with national economic planning and an acceptance of the important role of incentives in stimulating economic growth. The **Democrats** in the USA and the **Labour Party** in the UK both needed to defend their policies in view of the spread of these arguments and were forced to revise their own programmes.

The trend in many Western democracies of engaging in extensive privatization programmes became a strategy that has also extended to the new democracies of Eastern and Central Europe. The political influence of the New Right has also grown in France and Italy since the 1970s, and in Australia since the 1980s.

## nonaligned movement

Countries adopting a strategic and political position of **neutrality** ('nonalignment') towards major powers, specifically the USA and former USSR. Although originally used by poorer states, the nonaligned position was later adopted by oil-producing nations. Its 113 members hold more than half the world's population and 85% of oil resources, but only 7% of global GDP (1995).

The origins of the movement can be traced back to the conference of Afro-Asian nations that was held in Bandung, Indonesia 1955, proclaiming anti-colonialism and neutrality between East and West power blocs during the **Cold War** era. Its founders were the Indian prime minister Jawaharlal Nehru, Ghana's prime minister Kwame Nkrumah, Egypt's president Gamal Abdel Nasser, Indonesia's president Achmed Sukarno, and Yugoslavia's president Josif Broz Tito. The first official conference, attended by leaders from 25 countries, was held in Belgrade, Yugoslavia in 1961. Conferences are now held every three years. The movement has no permanent secretariat.

With the end of the Cold War, the chief issues promoted by the movement have been international action against poverty, environmental destruction, nuclear testing, and drug-trafficking. The eleventh conference, held in October 1995 at Cartagena, Columbia, was attended by delegates and heads of state from 113 developing countries, including the South African president Nelson Mandela, the Cuban president Fidel Castro, and the leader of the Palestine Liberation Organization (PLO) Yassir Arafat.

## North Atlantic Treaty Organization (NATO)

Association set up in April 1949 in response to the Soviet blockade of Berlin, to provide for the collective defence of the major Western European and North American states against the perceived threat from the USSR. The collapse of **communism** in Eastern Europe from 1989 prompted the most radical review of its policy and defence strategy since its inception. After the Eastern European Warsaw Pact was disbanded in 1991, an adjunct to NATO, the North Atlantic Cooperation Council (NACC), was established, including all the former Soviet republics, with the aim of building

> In June 1999 NATO mounted the biggest military operation in Europe after World War II, when its forces took over the Serbian province of Kosovo to keep the peace in the region.

greater security in Europe. In 1992 it was agreed that the Organization for Security and Cooperation in Europe would in future authorize all NATO's military responses within Europe. The end of the **Cold War** has lead to complex mechanisms for incorporating other European nations into some form a general alliance with NATO. In May 1997, a NATO–Russia security pact, called the Founding Act on Mutual Relations, Cooperation, and Security, was signed in Paris by all 16 NATO heads of government and Russian president Boris Yeltsin. NATO's secretary general, Javier Solana, announced in July 1997 the historic decision to invite Poland, Hungary, and the Czech Republic to join the alliance, signalling the biggest single expansion in NATO's history. The US Senate voted in early May 1998, by a large majority, to approve the inclusion of the Czech Republic, Hungary, and Poland in NATO. The vote was a foreign policy victory for President Clinton who had carefully steered the policy of NATO expansion through an initially sceptical political establishment. The vote made the USA the fifth country to ratify NATO expansion.

## Nozick, Robert (1938– )
Leading US political philosopher. He argues that the state's existence can be justified only when it is limited to the narrow function of protection against force, theft, and fraud, and to the enforcement of contracts. Any more extensive activities by the state will inevitably violate individual rights. His main work is *Anarchy, State, and Utopia* (1974).

## Nuclear Non-Proliferation Treaty
Treaty signed in 1968 to limit the spread of nuclear weapons. Under the terms of the treaty, those signatories declared to be nuclear powers (China, France, Russia, the UK, and the USA) pledged to work towards nuclear disarmament and not to supply military nuclear technology to non-nuclear countries, while other signatories pledged not to develop or acquire their own nuclear weapons. The treaty was renewed and extended indefinitely in May 1995.

Only 13 countries have not signed the treaty, but three of these (Israel, India, and Pakistan) were widely believed to have developed a nuclear capability although not to have produced any viable devices. In 1998 both India and Pakistan became nuclear powers, after successful testing of weapons. South Africa voluntarily dismantled its six nuclear bombs before signing the treaty in 1991, and Argentina and Brazil abandoned their bomb programmes when democratic governments came to power in the 1980s. The treaty is enforced by the United Nations (UN) and an international crisis was provoked by North Korea's refusal to allow inspection of its civilian nuclear plants by UN inspectors in 1993. Similar difficulties were encountered by UN inspectors in Iraq in the wake of the Gulf War of 1992, although the Iraqis eventually allowed inspections to take place, and again in 1998. Iran is estimated to be 5–15 years away from nuclear capability. In September 1997 Russia agreed to stop producing plutonium for use in nuclear weapons by 2000, and the USA agreed to pay the $150 million cost of converting Russian nuclear weapons to civilian equipment.

## nuclear parity

A way of measuring the relative strengths of the strategic nuclear forces of the USA and the USSR, developed in the 1980s to aid the various process of negotiating nuclear arms reductions. It became clear by the early 1980s that the USSR had redressed the USA's historic advantage, and had achieved, at least, a state of parity. In numerical terms of missiles the USSR was probably ahead, though the USA retained a lead in actual number of warheads, and probably in the technology of targeting. The main fear of the USA was that the combination of accuracy and explosive power achieved by the USSR might have given it the ability to destroy 90% of the land-based US missiles, something the USA could not do to the Soviet forces. The concern that nuclear forces were moving out of parity, making the USA vulnerable, threw doubt on much orthodox strategic thinking and policy making in the USA. In particular the long-established policy of backing **NATO's** weak conventional defense in Germany with the threat of central strategic nuclear warfare came to seem less credible.

## nuclear warfare

Any war involving the use of nuclear weapons. Nuclear-weapons research began in Britain in 1940, but was transferred to the USA after it entered World War II. The research programme, known as the Manhattan Project, was directed by US physicist J Robert Oppenheimer. The worldwide total of nuclear weapons in 1990 was about 50,000, and the number of countries possessing nuclear weapons stood officially at five – USA, USSR, UK, France, and China. After the experience of World War II, the threat of nuclear war, the theory of **deterrence**, and the issue of disarmament, became key features of the **Cold War**.

### Some nuclear warfare terms

- *hydrogen bomb* A much more powerful weapon than the atom bomb, the hydrogen bomb relies on the release of thermonuclear energy
- *neutron bomb or enhanced radiation weapon (ERW)* A very small hydrogen bomb that has relatively high radiation but relatively low blast, designed to leave buildings and weaponry intact
- *nuclear methods of attack* Methods include aircraft bombs, missiles (long- or short-range, surface to surface, air to surface, and surface to air), depth charges, and high-powered landmines

- *intercontinental ballistic missiles (ICBMs)* Missiles that have from 1968 been equipped with clusters of warheads, which can be directed to individual targets known as multiple independently targetable re-entry vehicles (MIRVs)
- *nuclear methods of defence* Methods include antiballistic missile (ABM)
- *Strategic Defense Initiative* Announced by the USA in 1983 to be operative from 2000, but cancelled in 1993; popularly known as the 'Star Wars' programme.

> 6 If only I had known, I should have become a watchmaker. 9
>
> **Albert Einstein** (1879–1955) German-born US physicist reflecting on his role in the development of the atom bomb, *New Statesman.*

## Official Secrets Act

The UK act of Parliament of 1989, prohibiting the disclosure of confidential material from government sources by employees; it remains an absolute offence for a member or former member of the security and **intelligence** services (or those working closely with them) to disclose information about their work. There is no public-interest defence, and disclosure of information already in the public domain is still a crime. Journalists who repeat disclosures may also be prosecuted.

The 1989 act replaced Section 2 of an act of 1911, which had long been accused of being too wide-ranging. Prosecution under criminal law is now reserved for material that the government claims is seriously harmful to national security. Any service member wishing to complain of misconduct within the service is allowed access to an independent counsellor, in turn with access to senior ministers. Investigations under special warrants, issued by the secretary of state in such cases as terrorist acts and organized crime, are also to be regarded as absolutely secret, but the act limits the circumstances of their operation, and there is an independent commissioner and tribunal to prevent abuse of such powers.

## oligarchy

Rule of the few, in their own interests (Greek *oligarchia* 'government of the few'). It was first identified as a form of government by the Greek philosopher **Aristotle**. In his time, although it was acknowledged that an aristocracy often developed into an oligarchy, the two were distinguished. 'Oligarchy' signified the government of the wealthy, who were looked upon as directing their efforts towards their own aggrandisement and the maintenance of their own power and privileges, while 'aristocracy' meant the rule of the best people for the public good.

In modern times there have been a number of oligarchies, sometimes posing as democracies; the paramilitary rule of the Duvalier family in Haiti, 1957–86, is an example.

## ombudsman

An official who acts on behalf of the private citizen in investigating complaints against the government. The post is of Scandinavian origin (the term is Swedish for 'commissioner'); it was introduced in Sweden in 1809, Denmark in 1954, and Norway in 1962, and spread to other countries from the 1960s.

The first Commonwealth country to appoint an ombudsman was New Zealand in 1962; the UK followed in 1966, where the office is know as the Parliamentary Commissioner for Administration. Hawaii was the first US state to appoint an ombudsman in 1967. The UK Local Government

The UK version of the office is relatively weak because a citizen can only have his or her complaint investigated with the support of an MP.

Act 1974 set up a local ombudsman, or commissioner for local administration, to investigate maladministration by local councils, police, health or water authorities. In the 1980s, ombudsmen were appointed to private bodies such as banks 1986, insurance companies 1983, and building societies 1988.

## one-party state

A state in which one political party dominates, constitutionally or unofficially, to the point where there is no effective opposition. There may be no legal alternative parties; for example, in Cuba, or in the former USSR. In other instances, a few token members of an opposition party may be tolerated, as in Mexico; or one party may be permanently in power with no elections. The one-party state differs from the 'dominant-party' state, where one party controls government for an extended period, as the Liberal Democrats did in Japan 1955–93, but where there are openly democratic competitive elections. Since 1989 **pluralism** has spread rapidly throughout the world and one-party states are now rare.

## open-door policy

Economic policy of equal access by all nations to another nation's markets. The term was suggested by US secretary of state John Hay in September 1899 to allow all nations free access to trade with China, and hence a rejection of a sphere-of-influence agreement for Chinese trade that excluded US and British interests. It does not preclude tariffs or other financial restrictions on trade.

## opinion poll

An attempt to measure public opinion by taking a survey of the views of a representative sample of the electorate. Most standard polls take random samples of around a thousand voters, which gives results that should be accurate to within three percentage points, 95% of the time. The first accurately sampled opinion poll was carried out by George Gallup during the US presidential election 1936. Opinion polls have encountered criticism on the grounds that their publication may influence the outcome of an election. Rather than simply predicting how people will vote, poll results may alter voters' intentions, for example, by establishing one party as likely to win and making the voters wish to join the winning side, or by making the lead of one party seem so great that its supporters feel they need not bother to vote. In France, opinion polls cannot be published during the final week of a presidential election campaign.

## Opposition

Commonly means the main party in opposition to the government, usually the second-largest party in the House of **Commons**. The leader of this party has the official title of leader of Her Majesty's Opposition and is assisted by the 'shadow cabinet', which consists of colleagues appointed by the leader to be spokespersons for the party in various policy areas. Since 1989 the leader of the Opposition has received a government salary, starting at £98,000. From 1997 the Opposition is allocated 29 days during each parliamentary session or year to debate any subject it chooses. Called 'supply days' they are technically for discussion of public expenditure. Cooperation and negotiation between the government and the Opposition takes place in discussions between the party business managers, known as whips.

In presenting itself as an alternative government the Opposition does not normally expect to defeat the government in the House of Commons, but to damage the government's credibility so that the electorate will be persuaded to elect the opposition party to power at the next general election. The Opposition also seeks and sometimes succeeds in securing the modification of government policy and may resort to obstructive tactics in Parliament to demonstrate the strength of its feeling.

## Organization for Economic Cooperation and Development (OECD)

The international organization of 30 industrialized countries that provides a forum for discussion and coordination of member states' economic and social policies. Founded in 1961, with its headquarters in Paris, the OECD superseded the Organization for European Economic Cooperation (OEEC), which had been established in 1948 to implement the **Marshall Plan**. The

Commission of the **European Union** also participates in the OECD's work.

The OECD comprises a Council representing all members, an Executive Committee consisting of 14 members who are selected annually, and a Secretariat. The OECD's subsidiary bodies include the International Energy Agency, set up in the face of a world oil crisis (1974). When the USA and Canada became members, its scope was extended to include development aid.

### Members of the OECD
- Australia (from 1971)
- Austria, Belgium, Canada, Czech Republic, Denmark, Finland (from 1969)
- France, Germany, Greece, Iceland, Ireland, Italy, Japan (from 1964)
- Luxembourg, Mexico (from 1994)
- Netherlands, New Zealand (from 1973)
- Norway, Portugal, Spain, Sweden, Switzerland, Turkey, the UK, the USA, Hungary, Poland, and the Slovak Republic (from 1996)
- South Korea (from 1997).

## Organization for Security and Cooperation in Europe (OSCE)

International forum to reach agreement in security, economics, science, technology, and human rights. It was founded in 1972 as the Conference on Security and Cooperation in Europe (CSCE). Its first serious meeting was in Helsinki in Finland in 1975 where it produced the Helsinki Act on East–West Relations. This was regarded as a major thaw in the **Cold War**, and committed members to increasing consultation and cooperation. By mid-1995, having admitted the former republics of the USSR, as well as other new nations from the former communist bloc (with the exception of Yugoslavia whose membership was suspended in July 1992), its membership had risen to 54 states.

Its second major conference in Paris in November 1990 was hailed as marking the formal end of the Cold War. A third conference in Helsinki in July 1992 debated the Yugoslav problem and gave the CSCE the power to authorize military responses of the **North Atlantic Treaty Organization** (NATO). A summit in Istanbul in November 1999 saw OSCE's 54 members sign a European Security Charter (ESC).

## Organization of Petroleum-Exporting Countries (OPEC)

The body established in 1960 to coordinate price and supply policies of oil-producing states. Its concerted action in raising prices in the 1970s triggered worldwide recession but also lessened demand so that its influence was reduced by the mid-1980s. OPEC also aimed to improve the position of

Third World states by forcing Western states to open their markets to the resultant products.

The body's importance in the world market was reflected by its ability to implement oil price increases, from $3 a barrel in 1973, to $30 a barrel in 1980. In the 1980s, OPEC's dominant position was undermined by reduced demand for oil in industrialized countries, increased non-OPEC oil supplies, and production of alternative energy. These factors contributed to the dramatic fall in world oil prices to $10 a barrel in July 1986 (from $28 at the beginning of the year).

### Membership in OPEC

- Algeria
- Gabon
- Indonesia
- Iran
- Iraq
- Kuwait
- Libya
- Nigeria
- Qatar
- Saudi Arabia
- the United Arab Emirates
- Venezuela

## original position

Another term for '**state of nature**' in social contract theory. The term has also become of considerable importance in US constitutional law, particularly associated with the arguments of Judge Robert Bork, the rejection of whose nomination to the Supreme Court by the Senate in 1987 highlighted the controversy over the original position thesis. In this sense the theory states that the words in the US Constitution, agreed upon during 1787, and understood as they would have been at the time, are the binding law of the USA unless specifically altered by a full constitutional amendment. If the words in the 1787 document are not clear enough, they must be interpreted 'restrictively', to import as little judicial initiative as possible. Those who support the original position idea want to reduce judicial activism, to prohibit the creation of citizen rights or governmental duties by the courts as opposed to the legislatures. It is opposed by those who point out that 18th century thinkers cannot have had any idea of the problems faced by the USA 200 years later, and who think the constitution should not be put in such a straightjacket.

## Ostpolitik

The German foreign policy (German 'eastern policy') introduced by Willy Brandt in 1971, which sought reconciliation with Eastern Europe as a means of improving contacts between East and West Germany. It was seen as part of a general **détente** between the East and West.

## pacifism

The belief that violence, even in self-defence, is unjustifiable under any conditions and that arbitration is preferable to war as a means of solving disputes. In the East, pacifism has roots in Buddhism, and nonviolent action was used by Mahatma Gandhi in the struggle for Indian independence. Pacifist sentiment in Europe before and during World War I persuaded many to become conscientious objectors and refuse to fight, even when conscripted. In some countries they were imprisoned and even executed. As a result of the carnage in the war, pacifism became more acceptable in the 1920s and 1930s, and organizations like the Peace Pledge Union in Britain were initiated. During World War II, conscientious objectors who refused to bear arms were often placed in noncombatant units such as the British Pioneer Corps, or in medical units.

> ❝ Sometime they'll give a war and nobody will come. ❞
>
> **Carl Sandburg**, *The People, Yes* (1936).

## paramilitary

A uniformed armed force found in many countries, occupying a position between the police and the military. In France such a force is called the Gendarmerie and in Germany the Federal Border Guard. In recent years the term has been extended to include illegal organizations of a **terrorist** or **guerrilla** nature.

## Pareto, Vilfredo (1848–1923)

An Italian economist and political philosopher. A vigorous opponent of **socialism** and **liberalism**, he justified inequality of income and rule by **élites** on the grounds of his empirical observation (Pareto's law) that income distribution remained constant whatever efforts were made to change it. In some ways a classical liberal, his ideas nevertheless influenced **Mussolini**, who appointed him senator in 1922. As a political scientist he developed an influential theory according to which societies were always governed by élites, even if they appeared democratic in form. This was part of a general theory of society as a self-regulating and interdependent system that operates independently of human attempts at voluntary control. He is more famous as the founder of welfare economics, where he put forward a concept of 'optimality', which contends that optimum conditions exist in an economic system if no one can be made better off without at least one other person becoming worse off.

## parliament

Common term for the legislative body of a country (from the French 'speaking'). The world's oldest parliament is the Icelandic Althing, which dates from about 930. The UK Parliament is usually dated from 1265. The legislature of the USA is called Congress and comprises the House of Representatives and the Senate. The French parliament is actually called the National Assembly, 'parlement' having a quite different historic meaning in French. In the UK, Parliament is the supreme legislature, comprising the House of **Commons** and the House of Lords. The origins of Parliament are in the 13th century, but its powers were not established until the late 17th century. The powers of the Lords were curtailed 1911, and the duration of parliaments was fixed at five years, but any parliament may extend its own life, as happened during both world wars. The UK Parliament meets in the Palace of Westminster, London.

> ❛ The only safe pleasure for a parliamentarian is a bag of boiled sweets. ❜
>
> **Julian Critchley**, English Conservative politician, *Listener*, 10 June 1982.

## parliamentary government

Sometimes also known as **cabinet government**, the form of government in which the executive, for example the British prime minister and cabinet, are members of the **legislature**. Such a government has to have a majority in the legislature, which can dismiss them by a vote of no confidence. This is known as the 'fusion of powers' as distinct from the 'separation of powers', in which the three branches of government the **executive**, legislature, and **judiciary** are separated in terms of personnel and constitutional powers.

The separation of powers is one of the major characteristics of the US system of government. Most countries in Western Europe and the Commonwealth have adopted some form of parliamentary government, although there are significant variations in practice. The French political system is a hybrid of parliamentary government and the US presidential-congressional system. The French president is directly elected by universal suffrage and is not constitutionally responsible to the French parliament, whilst the prime minister and other ministers may not be members of the Senate or the National Assembly. They are, however, constitutionally responsible to the National Assembly and may participate in its proceedings.

> ❝ [Political skill] is the ability to foretell what is going to happen tomorrow, next week, next month, and next year. And to have the ability afterwards to explain why it didn't happen. ❞
>
> **Winston Churchill**, UK prime minister, *The Churchill Wit* (1965).

## parliamentary socialism

The doctrine that radical reform of capitalist societies, along socialist lines, could be achieved only by legitimate power gained through electoral victory. It is linked with ideas such as gradualism, and was seen by many socialist and Marxist thinkers as **revisionism**, a selling out to the capitalist powers. In the UK parliamentary socialism, though always part of the **Labour Party's** assumptions, was most effectively argued by the **Fabians** and opposed by left-wing elements of the trades unions and radical groups. The radical argument against parliamentary socialism is that taking part in the ordinary process of electoral politics perverts the socialist drive of activists, and the party ceases to be a real representative of the working classes. Those opposed to parliamentary socialism often fear a process of 'co-option' will take place, in which the socialist leaders are taken to the heart of the ruling class, given authority and privilege, and cease to understand, or really care for, their working class constituents. In political science this thesis is known as the iron law of **oligarchy**.

## parliamentary sovereignty or parliamentary supremacy

The doctrine that Parliament has 'the right to make or unmake any law whatever and no person or body is recognized by the Law of England as having the right to override or set aside the legislation of Parliament'. This definition comes from A V Dicey (1835–1922), in his book *Law of the Constitution* (1885), still regarded by many as the guiding text to the British constitution. Any act of Parliament, properly passed by both Houses of Parliament (or by the House of **Commons** under the terms of the Parliament Acts 1911 and 1949), and which receives royal assent, is legally binding on all people and property that comes within the jurisdiction of the UK.

No court may question the validity or constitutionality of an act of Parliament, though the courts can interpret an act, and make sure the administration is only doing what an act permits. These powers are to be considerably enhanced by the Human Rights Act of 1998. In practice, however, parliamentary sovereignty is limited by political reality – in no democracy could a parliament totally ignore public opinion. The UK's closer integration within the **European Union** has meant that, during recent decades, there has been some cession of parliamentary sovereignty, as EU regulations, policed by the **European Court of Justice**, take precedence over national laws. Further sovereignty has been ceded since 1997 by the new Labour government, which has devolved certain powers to new assemblies in Scotland, Wales, and Northern Ireland.

### participatory democracy
An alternative label for **direct democracy**.

### party list system
A method of **proportional representation**. Voters are asked simply to choose one party in the ballot. The total votes cast on a national or regional basis then decides how many of the legislators they get. Either the entire country can be treated as one constituency (as in Israel and the Netherlands), or large multi-member constituencies can be used (as in Italy). The number of votes cast for a party, is divided by the total number of votes cast. This proportion of the seats to be filled is allocated to the party from a list of candidates submitted by the party and ranked in the order that the party wishes them to be elected. The system gives great power to the party managers, who can more or less decide themselves which of their candidates will get elected, and ensure obedience to the party line through this mechanism.

### party system
Refers to the way political parties interact in a national political system. The most useful classification is based on the extent to which a party system is

competitive. The old USSR, with only one legal party was a **one-party state**. Alternatively, electoral competition may exist between a number of parties, with only one having any chance of governing over a lengthy period. In India for example, the Congress party governed continuously for 30 years, these are known as one-party dominant systems.

In countries such as the USA, vigorous electoral competition exists between two major parties, each of which wins office from time to time, hence the nomenclature 'two-party system'. Western European countries, however, have **multiparty** systems involving electoral competition between three or more parties. In general, party systems are a reflection of the **cleavages** in the society in which they exist. A widely fragmented society, such as France, exhibiting many deep social cleavages, is likely to have a fragmented party system. More homogeneous societies, such as Britain, are more likely to produce a two-party system.

> ❝ In politics as in religion, it so happens that we have less charity for those who believe the half of our creed, than for those that deny the whole of it. ❞
>
> **Charles Caleb Colton**, *Lacon* (1825).

## patriarchal society
Society in which men control larger social and working groups and also government (Greek 'rule of the father'). The definition has been broadened by feminists to describe the dominance of male values throughout society.

## *perestroika*
The concept in the last years of the Soviet Union that there should be wide-ranging economic and political reforms (from the Russian 'restructuring'). The idea was initiated in 1985 by Mikhail **Gorbachev**. Originally, in the economic sphere, *perestroika* was conceived as involving 'intensive development' concentrating on automation and improved labour efficiency. It evolved to cover market indicators and incentives ('market socialism') and the gradual dismantling of the Stalinist central-planning system, with decision taking being devolved to self-financing enterprises.

## Plato (*c.* 427–347 BC)
Greek philosopher and political theorist, a pupil of Socrates, teacher of **Aristotle**, and founder of the Academy school of philosophy. He was the

author of philosophical dialogues on such topics as metaphysics, ethics, and politics. Plato's philosophy has influenced Christianity and European culture, directly and through both Christian thinkers, leaders of the Renaissance, and countless others.

Of his work, some 30 dialogues survive, intended for performance either to his pupils or to the public. The principal figure in these ethical and philosophical debates is Socrates and the early ones employ the Socratic method, in which he asks questions and traps the students into contradicting themselves. It is impossible to say whether Plato's Socrates is a faithful representative of the real man or an articulation of Plato's own thought.

**Plato**  *Plato, arguably the most famous Greek philosopher. The bust is a Roman copy of a Greek original.*

His political philosophy is expounded in three treatises that describe ideal states: *The Republic, The Laws,* and *The Statesman.* His most famous political idea was that a good society should be ruled autocratically by philosophers, as only they could both know what was right and be trusted to do it.

---

❝ There is only one good, namely knowledge and only one evil, namely ignorance. ❞

**Plato**, Greek philosopher, *Dialogues.*

---

## plebiscite

Another word for a **referendum** or direct vote by all the electors of a country or district on a specific question (from the Latin *plebiscitium* 'ordinance, decree'). In modern politics a plebiscite is an expression of popular opinion obtained by vote from all the electors of the state. It tends to be used of decisions over which state a population should owe allegiance to.

Plebiscites were employed by the **League of Nations** under a section of the Treaty of Versailles to decide the national destiny of areas involved in peculiar difficulties. In 1935 a plebiscite took place in the Saar district to discover the wishes of the inhabitants regarding their nationality, and it resulted overwhelmingly in favour of German as against French nationality. In 1955 a referendum rejected a Franco-German agreement for 'Europeanization' of the Saar (later it was agreed that the Saar should return to Germany, and it did in 1957). Sometimes references are made to 'plebiscitory democracy' meaning a political system in which extensive use is made of referenda so as to involve the electorate more fully in government. Switzerland sometimes comes close to this idea.

## pluralism
The view that decision-making in contemporary liberal democracies is the outcome of competition among several interest groups in a political system characterized by free elections, representative institutions, and open access to the organs of power. This concept is opposed by **corporatism** and other approaches that perceive power to be centralized in the state and its principal **élites.** It also contradicts the pure definition of democracy, which would not allow for such influence by **pressure groups**. The word can also simply mean a society that accepts the equal validity of several different ethnic or other groups rather than stressing one homogenous culture.

## police
The civil law-and-order force. In the UK, it is responsible to the Home Office, with 56 autonomous police forces, generally organized on a county basis. Mutual aid is given in circumstances such as mass picketing in the 1984–85 miners' strike, but there is no national police force such as the French Gendarmerie or the Italian Carabiniere. Unlike most other police forces, the British are armed only on special occasions, but arms issues are being raised more and more frequently.

> ❦ There is a sleeping cop in all of us. He must be killed. ❧
>
> Graffiti written during French student revolt, May 1968.

## police state
A political system where those in power use naked force by police, secret police, and sometimes the military, to control and dominate the population. A

police state is identified by its contempt for ordinary notions of the rule of law, as well as by totally ignoring any idea of civil liberties. It is the immediate power of the executive, or whoever controls the repressive forces, to inflict punishment, even death, on particular individuals or groups, without having to show them guilty of breaking formally constituted law, that characterizes such a state. As an inevitable consequence of such political behavior, the police themselves come to wield unchecked power on their own behalf, as well as on behalf of their political masters, with consequential corruption and an even wider spreading of terror. The two best known and most fully developed police states in modern times have been Nazi Germany and the USSR under Stalin, where the Gestapo and the NKVD (later known as the KGB) respectively exercised direct power over anyone even suspected of opposing or even disapproving of the political system.

## polis

In ancient Greece, a city-state and the political and social centre of most large Greek communities (Greek 'city'). Membership of a polis as a citizen, participation in its cults and festivals, and the protection of its laws formed the basis of classical Greek civilization, which was marked by intense intercity rivalries and conflicts until the Hellenistic period. The word is used in political science as an alternative to 'political system' to indicate the very basic need of humanity to live in some form of body organized by power relations and community.

## Politburo

A contraction of 'political bureau', the executive committee (known as the Presidium 1952–66) of the Supreme Soviet in the USSR, which laid down party policy. It consisted of about 12 voting and 6 candidate (nonvoting) members. It wielded all real power in the USSR, whatever other organs might appear to have constitutional authority.

## political correctness (PC)

Shorthand term for a set of liberal attitudes about education and society, and the terminology associated with them. To be politically correct is to be sensitive to unconscious **racism** and **sexism** and to display environmental awareness. However, the real or alleged enforcement of PC speech codes ('people of colour' instead of 'coloured people', 'differently abled' instead of 'disabled', and so on) at more than 130 US universities by 1991 attracted derision and was criticized as a form of thought-policing. It is almost invariably used dismissively, to suggest an over done, artificial, or unwilling acceptance of the views of a liberal élite.

## political culture

The totality of ideas and attitudes towards authority, discipline, governmental responsibilities and entitlements, and associated patterns of cultural transmission such as the education system and even family life. The importance of all these factors, and the reason for linking them together into one concept, is that they give good measure of how people will react to political issues. The classic study into political culture across several countries, *The Civic Culture*, showed that some societies seemed to transmit a general distrust for authority, and to create very low levels of political hopefulness in their citizens, while others, rightly or wrongly, bred citizens who felt they could trust politicians and that they themselves had a fair say in determining policy and political decisions. All sorts of matters can be relevant in applying this concept, from the discipline systems in schools to child-rearing patterns.

## political development

The idea that just as we can talk about economic development, there is an objective path of political progress through which societies moved towards further political sophistication. It was a major research topic in political science in the 1950s and 1960s, but is now less fashionable. Political development had obvious serious problems in avoiding a purely ideological bias in which nations were seen as more developed the more they came to resemble Western liberal democracies. Particularly in the USA, a great deal of effort was put into comparative government studies with a developmental approach, and much of this was organized around the popular sociological theories of the day, which were all forms of **functionalism**. The idea is very similar to **modernization**.

## political obligation

The theory of why, and when, a person is morally obliged to obey a government. There are a series of alternative theories to account for the requirement to obey governments. Probably the most commonly referred to is the idea of consent, but arguments ranging from divine right to **force majeure** have also been presented. Political obligation is at the heart of social contract political philosophies, in which its exact form depends upon the description of the hypothetical **state of nature**. There is no general argument that can satisfy everyone, but there seems to be a widespread acceptance that obedience of a state's laws is preferable to anarchy. Only where laws restrict very personal liberties, such as racial integration in South Africa (see **apartheid**) might the citizen's obligation to obey the state be regarded as nullified in international circles.

## political party

An association of like-minded people organized with the purpose of seeking and exercising political power. A party can be distinguished from an interest or **pressure group**, which seeks to influence governments rather than aspire to office. Political parties seem to have been largely a product of the 19th century. Certainly the idea of 'party' was disapproved of by earlier political theorists, who saw such bodies as likely to increase social tension, rather than as crucial to political effectiveness. The origin of political parties may be traced to the existence of political factions that appear to have

> Edmund Burke defined a political party as: 'a body of men united for promoting by their joint endeavours the national interest, upon some particular principle upon which they are all agreed'.

existed in all states and political systems as far back as the ancient world. No matter what form of government exists, groups of individuals, with varying interests in common, tend to coalesce to influence or to direct the exercise of power. Inevitably, therefore, the distinction between parties and pressure groups is blurred. Parties tend to be of one or other of two types. Some were created and remain controlled by parliamentarians while others were grass roots bodies created to get representatives elected in the first place. Parties are essential to competitive democracy to raise funds, select candidates, and articulate opposing policy views. They also, however, tend to dominate governments and elections at the cost of independent minded politicians. Though they vary enormously in structure and type of influence, political parties are the main ingredients of all political systems with any pretence whatsoever to be democratic.

## political science

A collective term for a series of subdisciplines, including political theory, **comparative government**, **political sociology**, international relations and, political history. Political science includes the study of the nature, distribution, and dynamics of **power**, usually at the national or international level, but sometimes at a very 'micro' level. The techniques of the discipline range from highly mathematical and statistical analyses of data to logical and conceptual analysis of political morality. As an academic discipline the subject is as least as old as **Aristotle** who called it 'queen' of sciences. The first professorship in the subject was set up in Sweden in the 17th century. Gradually a separate discipline emerged from the previous conglomeration of law, economics, and philosophy, so that by the end of the 19th century most US and many German universities had professors and departments of politics or political science. Britain was relatively late to develop this trend, and despite the creation earlier of the London School of Economics and Political Science, any widespread study and teaching of the subject is a post-1945 phenomenon.

## political sociology
A subdiscipline of political science. Political sociologists tend to concentrate on the behaviour, beliefs, and formation of the masses, while other branches of political science look much more to the behaviour and attitudes of political élites. Thus a major area of political sociology (and perhaps the best developed area in the whole of political science) is the study, by survey research and statistical analysis, of electoral behaviour in Western democracies. Political sociologists are probably the most 'theoretical' of the political scientists conducting empirical research, mainly because of the influence of the great founding fathers of sociological theory, **Marx**, **Weber**, and **Durkheim**, all of whom made serious attempts at theoretical explanation of political phenomena.

## political union (EU)
Even though the **European Union** was founded as a predominantly economic body, its founders always hoped that a political unity of some sort would grow as the member states increasingly integrated their economies. The original impetus for a Western European movement after 1945 was essentially political, because it was seen as a way of preventing future European wars. In recent years enthusiasm for some degree of institutionalized political union has grown in some circles, especially the Commission of the European Union (the EU's civil service). Initially the demand was just for much closer cooperation on foreign policy, to be achieved by agreement between heads of government or in the Council of Ministers. But as economic integration grew the demands for political union increased. There is a general agreement that some degree of further political integration is

desirable, but how great and of what sort is not only controversial between member states, but also inside most of them as well.

## popular front
Any political alliance of liberals, socialists, communists, and other centre and left-wing parties. This policy was propounded by the Communist International in 1935 against **fascism**, and was adopted in France and Spain, where popular-front governments were elected in 1936. (In France it was overthrown in parliament in 1938, and in Spain it fell with the defeat of the Republic in the Spanish Civil War in 1939.) In Britain a popular-front policy was advocated by Labour politician Sir Stafford Cripps and others, but rejected by the **Labour Party**. The resistance movements in the occupied countries during World War II represented a revival of the popular-front idea, and in post-war politics the term tends to recur whenever a strong right-wing party can be counterbalanced only by an alliance of those on the left.

## population control
Measures taken by some governments to limit the growth of their countries' populations by trying to reduce birth rates. Propaganda, freely available contraception, and tax disincentives for large families are some of the measures that have been tried. The population control policies introduced by the Chinese government are the best known. In 1979 the government introduced a 'one-child policy' that encouraged family planning and penalized couples who have more than one child. It has been only partially successful since it

> While population increase remains a worldwide problem, the demographic problem for the developed world has reversed, with births below population replacement levels in several wealthy countries, and in Russia.

has been difficult to administer, especially in rural areas, and has in some cases led to the killing of girls in favour of sons as heirs.

## populism
Generally means a political policy or appeal intended to garner as many mass votes as possible by appealing to often irrational or emotional elements in the popular mind, especially by making racist, authoritarian, and jingoistic appeals. One feature of populist politics is that such

politicians feel no need to make their promises consistent and achievable – thus they might offer both huge tax cuts and massive welfare expenditure. A more restricted sense, in US history, was a late 19th-century political movement that developed out of farmers' protests against economic hardship. The Populist (or People's) Party was founded 1892 and ran several presidential candidates. It failed, however, to reverse increasing industrialization and the relative decline of agriculture in the USA.

## positive law

An opposite to **natural law**, a term found at least as early as Thomas **Hobbes**. The term refers to legislated rules that are observed and enforced in a particular society. Whether or not some rule is a positive law is an empirical question. A positive law is simply anything that is applied as law, regardless of its morality or source. Some legal theorists, called 'legal positivists', restrict the whole of legal study, and the whole legitimacy of law, to positive law. A law, for them, is simply the command of a sovereign (that is, anyone powerful enough to enforce it), and no other sort of law is anything more than metaphysical speculation.

## positivism

A theory that confines genuine knowledge within the bounds of science and observation. The theory is associated with the French philosopher Auguste **Comte** and empiricism. On the basis of positivism, Comte constructed his 'Religion of Humanity', in which the object of adoration was the Great Being; that is, the personification of humanity as a whole. His political theory dismissed all political argument as meaningless unless purely factual and technical. Positivism has had considerable influence on the social sciences by making them relinquish moral issues in favour of description and empirical research into measurable political phenomenon.

## postmodernism

As a political science and sociological concept, rather than artistic or cultural trend, it is the development of theories that stress the role of individual subjective experience, and the ever changing, because historically conditioned, nature of social reality. Post-modern approaches reject both traditional left wing concentration on material factors, like classes, and also more conservative beliefs, like that of absolute morality.

## Poujade, Pierre-Marie (1920– )

French entrepreneur and rightwing politician, often seen as the paradigm of **populism**. His 'Poujadist' movement made a dramatic entry into French politics in the 1956 parliamentary elections (when the youngest deputy elected on Poujade's ticket was Jean-Marie Le Pen, later to become leader of a French extreme **neoconservative** party) before fading in 1958. He came from a monarchist and anti-republican family. Beginning in 1953 with direct action against tax inspections, and organized from 1954 as the Union for the Defence of Tradesmen and Artisans (UDCA), Poujadism came to denote a militant and nationalist protest against France's modernizing state, spreading out from its anti-taxation core to embrace the cause of a French Algeria. He published his political credo in *J'ai choisi le combat/I chose to fight* in 1956.

## power

Social, economic, or political power is at the heart both of actual political conflict and of the discipline of political science. The safest definitions are highly formal. One very common definition of power in modern political science is 'the ability of A to make B do something B would not choose to do'. There are major problems in measuring power. Some argue that only open conflicts between identified interests can be taken as evidence for the use of power. Others think that power can be exercised so as to make people want what it is in the interests of the rulers for them to want. We have an intuitive understanding of power as something that can both come 'out of the mouths of guns', but also out of the mouths of people, (as with 'powerful' orators), which can be wielded evilly but also for good, and which does ultimately depend on the ability to change peoples' preferences.

## pragmatism

A philosophical tradition that interprets truth in terms of the practical effects of what is believed and, in particular, the usefulness of these effects. The US philosopher Charles Pierce is often accounted the founder of pragmatism and it was further advanced by William James. In politics it is often claimed to be a viable and preferable alternative to an ideological position, made attractive by seeming to be a matter of 'common sense' rather than ideals. Pragmatism is itself an **ideology**.

## president

The usual title of the head of state in a **republic**; the power of the office may range from the equivalent of a merely ceremonial constitutional monarch to the actual executive head of the government. In the **constitution** of the USA the head of the federal government is called 'president'. This is the most common meaning of the word, the head by election of a modern republic, such as the USA, France, and Switzerland.

The president of the USA has more power than any similar official elsewhere, though, under the Fifth Republic, the French president's powers are almost as extensive. The US president is commander-in-chief of the US army and navy.

> 〝 Persistence in one opinion has never been considered a merit in political leaders. 〞
>
> **Cicero**, *Ad Familiares*, 1st century BC.

## pressure group

An association that puts pressure on governments, businesses, or parties to ensure laws and treatment favourable to its own interest. The forms of pressure vary; they can involve supplying funds for election campaigns or mobilizing public opinion. Whatever particular technique is used, the idea is to make a politician's re-election dependent on favouring the group. Pressure groups have played an increasingly prominent role in contemporary Western democracies. In general they fall into two

The US National Rifle Association has such extensive membership and finance that they can virtually block any reform of their area of interest, gun control.

types: groups concerned with a single issue, such as nuclear **disarmament**, and groups attempting to promote their own interest, such as oil producers or single parents. Some political scientists maintain that group competition of this form is the very key to understanding modern politics.

## primary

In presidential election campaigns in the USA, a state-wide **ballot** in which voters indicate their preferences for who should be the candidate for each of the two main parties. The most important primaries are the presidential primaries, held in 41 states, beginning with New Hampshire in February and continuing until June; they operate under varying and complex rules. Primaries are also held to choose candidates for other posts, such as Congressional seats.

In the presidential case, usually the number of votes received by a candidate governs the number of delegates who will vote for that person at the national conventions in July/August, when the final choice of candidate for both **Democratic** and **Republican** parties is made. Some delegates remain loyal to the last ballot while others make deals to benefit the state or local situation as the field of candidates narrows. Some primaries are 'closed', being restricted to actual members of the party, others are 'open' to any registered voter.

## privatization

The policy or process of selling or transferring state-owned or public assets and services (notably nationalized industries) to private investors. Privatization of services involves the government contracting private firms to supply services previously supplied by public authorities. Supporters of privatization argue that the public benefits from theoretically greater efficiency from firms already in the competitive market, and the release of resources for more appropriate use by government. Those against privatization believe that it transfers a country's assets from all the people to a controlling minority, that public utilities such as gas and water become private monopolies, and that a profit-making state-owned company raises revenue for the government. In many cases the trend towards privatization has been prompted by dissatisfaction with the high level of subsidies being given to, often inefficient, state enterprise. The term 'privatization' is used even when the state retains a majority share of an enterprise. The policy has been pursued by the post-1979 Conservative administration in the UK, and by recent governments in France, Japan, Italy, New Zealand, and elsewhere. By 1988 the practice had spread worldwide, with communist countries such as China and Cuba selling off housing to private tenants.

In 1997, privatizations worldwide were expected to go beyond the $100 billion mark for the first time, up 14% from the 1996 record and up 28% from 1995. This was announced in Paris in a report by the Organization for Economic Cooperation and Development. The largest privatization in 1996 was Deutsche Telekom ($13.3 billion) and the largest for 1997 was France Telecom.

### Industries in the UK privatized since 1979:

- British Telecom
- British Gas Corporation
- British National Oil Corporation
- British Airways
- British Airports Authority
- British Aerospace
- British Shipbuilders
- British Steel
- British Transport Docks Board

- British Water Board
- Enterprise Oil
- Jaguar
- National Freight Company
- Rover Group
- Water Supply
- Electricity and gas companies
- British Rail

## proletariat

In **Marxist** theory, those classes in society that possess no property (Latin *proletarii* 'the class possessing no property'), and therefore depend on the sale of their labour or expertise (as opposed to the capitalists or **bourgeoisie**, who own the means of production, and the petty bourgeoisie, or working small-property owners). They are usually divided into the industrial, agricultural, and intellectual proletariat. In Marxist social theory because the proletariat, with no capital, are doomed to become ever poorer, they will eventually form the revolutionary class that will overthrow capitalism. The term *proletarius* was traditionally applied in Classical Rome, to the poorest class of citizens, whose only wealth was their offspring (*proles*).

**proletariat** *A contemporary cartoon from the 1917 Russian revolution entitled* 'The Proletarian's Hammer in Action'.

## proportional representation (PR)

An electoral system in which distribution of party seats corresponds to their proportion of the total votes cast and minority votes are not wasted (as opposed to a simple majority or 'first past the post' system). There is a wide variety of methods of proportional representation, varying both in how exactly proportional they are, and in how much power they give to parties to discipline their candidates. PR is sometimes seen as the cause of **multiparty** systems and even a cause of government instability, but both judgements are over simplifications. PR of one form or another is the norm for electoral systems, though both the USA and Britain, and most members of the Old Commonwealth depend mainly on the 'first past the post' election system. The most important methods of PR include:

- *Party list (PLS)* Parties put up several candidates in a multi-member constituency, and seats are won according to the total party vote.

- *Additional member system (AMS)* Half the members are elected from lists by proportional representation, and half fight for single-member 'first past the post' constituencies

- *Single transferable vote (STV)* Candidates are numbered in order of preference by the voter, and any votes surplus to the minimum required for a candidate to win are transferred to second preferences and further preferences, until the required number of elected candidates is achieved.

## protectionism

The imposition of heavy duties or import quotas by a government as a means of discouraging the import of foreign goods likely to compete with domestic products. Price controls, quota systems, and the reduction of surpluses are among the measures taken for agricultural products in the **European Union**. The opposite practice is free trade.

## public good

A service, resource, or facility, such as street lighting, that is equally accessible to everyone for unlimited use and which cannot be denied to anyone if it is to be provided at all. Because of these characteristics, the private sector is reluctant to provide public goods. Consumers are likely to want to be free riders, hoping that they can benefit from the good without having to pay for it. Public goods are therefore normally provided by government and paid for by everyone through the taxation system. Commonly given examples of public goods are defence, the judiciary, and the police. Originally the free rider problem meant that services such as fire protection were provided only by insurance companies to those who had insured with them and the fire brigades would turn away from a fire in an uninsured house. How to overcome the free rider problem is a major topic in political theory.

## race

A term sometimes applied to a supposedly physically distinctive group of people, on the basis of their difference from other groups in skin colour, head shape, hair type, and physique. Formerly, anthropologists divided the human race into three hypothetical racial groups: Caucasoid, Mongoloid, and Negroid. Scientific studies, however, have produced no proof of definite genetic racial divisions. Race is a cultural, political, and economic concept, not a biological one. Genetic differences do exist between populations but they do not define historical lineages, and are minimal compared to the genetic variation between individuals. Most anthropologists today, therefore, completely reject the concept of race, and social scientists tend to prefer the term 'ethnic group' (see **ethnicity**).

It has proved impossible to measure mental differences between groups in an objective way, and there is no acceptable scientific evidence to suggest that one race is superior to others. The attempt to categorize human types, as in South Africa for the purposes of segregation, is inevitably doomed by the absence of any straightforward distinction. Since humans can all interbreed to produce fertile offspring, they must all belong to the same genetic species.

## racism

A belief in, or set of implicit assumptions about, the superiority of one's own race or ethnic group, often accompanied by prejudice against members of an ethnic group different from one's own. Racism may be used to justify discrimination, verbal or physical abuse, or even **genocide**, as in Nazi Germany, or as practised by

Some 11,000 incidents of racial abuse were reported in the UK in 1993–94, although the real level of racially motivated attacks was believed to have been about 140,000. By far the greatest number of racist incidents occurred in London, which accounted for almost half (5,124) of the total.

European settlers against American Indians in both North and South America. Many social scientists believe that even where there is no overt **discrimination**, racism exists as an unconscious attitude in many individuals and societies, based on a stereotype or preconceived idea about different ethnic groups.

> ❝ The collective failure of an organization to provide an appropriate and professional service to people because of their colour, culture, or ethnic origin. ❞
>
> **William MacPherson**, Chairman of the Lawrence Inquiry, providing a definition of 'institutionalized racism', *Daily Telegraph*, 23 February 1999.

## radical

Anyone with opinions more extreme than the main current of a country's major political party or parties, or some general consensus. It is more often applied to those with left-wing opinions, although the radical right also exists. In politics, the term came into use originally as a synonym for 'liberal', but is capable of application to any politician or political supporter whose political creed involves some root-and-branch reform. In recent years the meaning of the term has changed, since radical outlooks have emerged that are no longer identifiable with liberal, socialist, or communist policies; for example, the various 'New Left' trends and 'sexual radicals'.

## *raison d'état*

An overwhelmingly important state motive for an action (French for 'stroke of the state'). Where there is something of vital importance to the entire well-being of a state that all ordinary moral or political restrictions on government actions must be dropped, it is a *raison d'état*. It derives from debates on international law in the 17th century and has become somewhat discredited. The 'state' itself is very much to the forefront when a *raison d'état* argument is invoked, it is the continued existence of the very basic structure of authority and legitimacy that is at stake. The *raison d'état* argument is more often used and found in international politics than in domestic politics.

## *raison de guerre*

The acceptance that armies will ultimately do whatever they have to do to win (French for 'reason of war'). First developed as an argument in the 17th century, at the time that international **law** was beginning to be developed by writers like **Grotius.** *Raison de guerre* is a derogation from the rules of inter-national law, and especially from the theory of just **war**. The concept is linked closely to the more general doctrine of **raison d'état**, that the protection of a state and the furtherance of its interest will always dominate in foreign policy. A weaker version of *raison de guerre* allows acts that would normally be con-sidered immoral and uncivilized. For example, the Allied bombing of Monte Cassino in World War II, and the consequent destruction of one of Europe's finest monasteries and libraries, was justified by the doctrine of *raison de guerre*.

## ratification

Process of formal approval, usually of treaties, by the legislature of a polit-ical system. Thus in the USA, for example, treaties negotiated by the president must be ratified by a two-thirds vote of the Senate and in some cases, such as the Treaty of Versailles after World War I and the SALT II treaty on arms control, Senate support was not forthcoming. Similarly Constitutional amendments in the USA need to be ratified by a vote in each of the state legislatures.

## Rawls, John (1921– )

US political theorist. In *A Theory of Justice* (1971), one of the most influential books in 20th century political thought, he revived the concept of the **social contract** and its use to work out the basic principles of a just society. He argued that if we were to make political choices 'behind a veil of ignorance', so that we did not know which position we were to occupy in society, we would choose to live in a society in which there was equal liberty and the minimum of social and economic inequalities. His ideas have influenced politics throughout the world.

## reactionary

A pejorative term applied to those people who are seen as resistant to change and progress.

## realignment

A concept in political science usually referring to the change of basic vot-ing loyalties by groups in the electorate. These loyalties, often inherited in a fairly automatic way from parents and reinforced by peer-group pressure, last for decades and result in a high predictability in electoral behaviour. From time to time, however, social change, major events like wars, or economic disruption cause sudden breaks in these semi-automatic electoral regularities. When this happens a realignment may occur, shifting the bulk of whole socio-demographic groups to new party loyalties. For example, the economic collapse in the USA after the Wall Street crash, made the 1932 presidential election a realigning election in which new voting loyalties, known as the **New Deal** coalition, were formed and which lasted until at least the 1960s. Realignment should not be confused with dealignment, a similar process but one that sees voters being cut loose from any stable ties to parties, so that their vote loses long-term predictability.

## realpolitik

Belief that the pragmatic pursuit of self-interest and power, backed up by force when convenient, is the only realistic option for a great state (German *Realpolitik* 'politics of realism'). The term was coined in 1859 to describe the German chancellor Bismarck's policies. Modern international relations theory has developed the idea of neo-realism which insists that, whatever their rhetoric, most countries always do in fact operate in this way.

## recall

Process by which voters can demand the removal from office of elected officials, as in some states of the USA.

## referendum

Procedure whereby a decision on proposed legislation is referred to the electorate for settlement by direct vote of all the people. It is most frequently employed in Switzerland, the first country to use it, but has become increasingly widespread. Similar devices are the **recall**, whereby voters are given the opportunity of demanding the dismissal from office of officials, and the **initiative**.

Typically referenda are used to decide major constitutional matters, which are seen as too vital to be left to the ordinary play of party politics. In 1975 Britain used a national referendum to determine whether or not to remain a member of the European Economic Community; similarly in 1992 several European countries (Ireland, Denmark, France, and Spain) held referenda on whether to ratify the Maastricht Treaty on closer European economic and political union. In some cases the referendum precedes executive or legislative action and in others it is a ratification of an executive or legislative act, which may have no legal force until approved by a referendum. Referenda are used in many states of the USA and in a number of cases are combined with the 'initiative', by which measures may be proposed by a specified number of electors for enactment or enforce the submission to a referendum of proposals made by the state **legislature**.

## refugee

According to international law, a person fleeing from oppressive or dangerous conditions (such as political, religious, or military persecution) and seeking refuge in a foreign country. According to the UK Asylum and Immigration Appeals Bill (1992), **asylum** will only be granted to those refugees, as defined by the **Geneva Convention**, whose life and/or liberty are in danger in the country they have come from. The Geneva Convention only applies to victims of persecution, not to those fleeing civil war or violent disturbances at home. The Bill thus excludes the vast majority of refugees in the UK currently granted exceptional leave to remain, and leaves open to the government whether to abolish exceptional leave altogether or to curtail severely its use. A distinction is usually made by Western nations between 'political' refugees and so-called 'economic' refugees, who are said to be escaping from poverty rather than persecution, particularly when the refugees come from low-income countries. The latter group often become illegal immigrants; (see **immigration and emigration**). International law recognizes the right of the persecuted to seek asylum but does not oblige states to provide it.

> In 1995 there were an estimated 27 million refugees worldwide. An estimated average of 10,000 people a day become refugees. Women and children make up 75% of all refugees and displaced persons.

> The term was originally applied to the French Huguenots who came to England after toleration of Protestantism was withdrawn with the revocation of the Edict of Nantes 1685.

### Some major refugee movements in 20th-century Europe

- Jews from the pogroms of Russia 1881–1914 and again after the revolution
- White Russians from the USSR after 1917
- Jews from Germany and other Nazi-dominated countries 1933–45
- Victims of the civil wars in Croatia and Bosnia-Herzegovina, 1991
- Many Chinese fled the mainland after the communist revolution, 1949

- Latin Americans fleeing from Cuba, Colombia, Brazil, Chile, Argentina, and Central America when new governments took power
- Boat people leaving Vietnam after the victory of the North over the South
- Refugees from ethnic violence in Burundi and Rwanda, 1994
- 1.3 million Bosnian refugees distributed across Europe, 1996
- 750,000 million Hutu refugees fled war-torn eastern Zaire (now the Democratic Republic of Congo) for Rwanda, November 1996.

## religion

A code of belief or philosophy that often, but not necessarily, involves the worship of a god or gods. Belief in a supernatural power is not essential; it is absent in, for example, Buddhism and Confucianism, but faithful adherence to the code is usually considered to be rewarded as for example, by escape from human existence (Buddhism), by a future existence (**Christianity**, **Islam**), or by worldly benefit. Religion has been a major component of the politics of all societies until the 20th century, and has occasioned some of the most bitter and vicious wars of all time. Religious **cleavages** still partially explain the party systems of many developed countries, though **secularization** has enormously decreased the influence religious identity has on the vote. The USA, which remains more overtly religious than Europe, may be the only developed **liberal democracy** in which politicians still generally feel obliged to demonstrate that they are good church-going religious believers.

## representation

A form of government that in theory gives the representatives chosen a wider **mandate** than that granted to ordinary delegates or to the holders of proxies. This has always been a contentious issue in political theory, with conservative thinkers such as Edmund **Burke** tending to argue that voters should select the best man in their constituency and then allow him to exercise his own choices on issues. In contrast the left, suspicious of the danger that their candidates might be seduced by an upper class life style once in parliament, have tended to want to give them specific instructions on how to vote. Since the end of the 19th century the representative system has been frequently criticized, and in many countries it has been modified by **proportional representation** in parliamentary and other elections, and also by the use of the **referendum**.

## representative democracy

A form of indirect rule by the majority of the electorate. In this system, the usual form of democracy in the modern world, (the only widespread form of democracy in actual practice), political decisions are made by a small number of people elected by the whole electorate. The usual system is to divide the nation into geographical constituencies, each sending one or more representatives to the legislative assembly. In each constituency several will compete to be elected and, depending on the details of the electoral laws, the person or persons most popular with the voters will be elected. It may also be the case that the political executive is elected by the people, especially as in a presidential system like that of France or the USA. It is contrasted to **direct** (or participatory) **democracy**.

## republic

A country where the head of state is not a monarch, either hereditary or elected, but usually a **president**, whose role may or may not include political functions.

A republic may be an **aristocracy**, **oligarchy**, or **democracy**. The earliest republics, those of Greece and Rome, were mainly aristocratic city-states as were the medieval republics of Venice, Florence, Genoa, and other Italian towns.

---

**SOME REPUBLICS IN HISTORY**

- France from 1793 to 1805, from 1848 to 1853, and from 1870 to the present time
- Mexico 1824 to 1863, and from 1867 to the present time
- Spain from 1873 to 1874, and again from 1931 to 1947 when it became theoretically a monarchy
- Portugal from 1910
- Poland from 1916
- China from 1912
- Germany from 1918
- Italy from 1945.

---

## Republican Party

One of the two main political parties of the USA, formed in 1854. It is more right-wing than the **Democratic Party**, favouring capital and big business and opposing state subvention and federal controls. The party was founded by a coalition of slavery opponents, who elected their first president, Abraham Lincoln, in 1860. Towards the end of the 19th century the Republican Party was identified with US **imperialism** and industrial expansion. With few intermissions, the Republican Party controlled Congress from the 1860s until defeated by the New Deal Democrats in 1932. The Republican Party remained in eclipse until the election of Dwight D Eisenhower in 1952. The party, attracting increasing support from the Christian right and in the formerly Democrat-dominated southern states, enjoyed landslide presidential victories for Ronald Reagan and also carried the Senate 1980–86. George Bush won the 1988 presidential election but faced a Democratic Senate and House of Representatives and in 1992 lost the presidency to the Democrat Bill Clinton. In 2002, George W Bush (son of former president George Bush) was elected president after defeating Democrat Al Gore in a hotly disputed contest and with a smaller share of the popular vote than his rival. The presidency was conceded to Bush 36 days after the election, following a narrow decision by the divided US supreme court.

### revisionism
Usually a political theory derived from **Marxism** that moderates one or more of the basic tenets of Karl **Marx**, and is hence condemned by orthodox Marxists. The first noted Marxist revisionist was Eduard Bernstein, who in Germany in the 1890s questioned the inevitability of a breakdown in capitalism. After World War II the term became widely used by established communist parties, both in Eastern Europe and Asia, to condemn movements (whether more or less radical) that threatened the official party policy. It has come, more generally, to refer to any re-thinking of a once dominant theoretical position in the social sciences. Thus an important school of thought about the origins of the **Cold War** has been labelled revisionist because it challenges some of the earlier US assumptions which put the blame entirely on the Russians.

❝ Half a truth is better than no politics. ❞

**G K Chesterton**, English writer, 'The Boy', *All Things Considered* (1908).

### revolution
Any rapid, far-reaching, or violent change in the political, social, or economic structure of society. It is usually applied to political change: the French

Revolution, where an absolute monarchy was overthrown by opposition from inside the country and a popular uprising; and the Russian Revolution, where a repressive monarchy was overthrown by those seeking to institute widespread social and economic changes based on a socialist model. In 1989–90 the Eastern Bloc nations demonstrated against and voted out the Communist Party, in many cases creating a pro-democracy revolution.

A political revolution is a fundamental change in the internal constitution of a country brought about by the inhabitants. A revolution is thus to be distinguished both from conquest and from a mere **coup**. However the question of what constitutes a fundamental change is central and can only be answered by reference to the kind of analysis to which the user subscribes. Thus for a Marxist a true revolution might only be one in which one class seizes power from another, and following this view it would be possible for there to be major political upheavals involving armed conflict which were not revolutions.

> ❻ The successful revolutionary is a statesman, the unsuccessful one a criminal. ❾
>
> **Erich Fromm**, German psychoanalyst, *Escape From Freedom* (1941).

## rights

An individual's automatic entitlement to certain freedoms and other benefits, usually, in liberal democracies such as the USA and UK, in the context of the individual's relationship with the government of the country. The struggle to assert political and **civil rights** against arbitrary government has been a major theme of Western political history.

## rights, natural

The doctrine, deriving from medieval philosophy but articulated by John **Locke**, that claims human beings as individuals have certain absolute moral claims or entitlements. Locke identified three natural rights: to life, liberty, and property. The first two are also included in the Universal Declaration of Human Rights, and most states pay at least lip service to the concept of rights. The doctrine of natural rights has been criticized on the grounds that no rights are absolute and that natural rights are a myth. Much theoretical work has been done to establish that some rights really are natural, in that they flow from the very basic requirements of any ordered civil life and are essentially nonoptional, at least in the long run. Such a move is necessary now it is no longer possible to ground a political theory on religious premises.

## right wing

The more **conservative** or **reactionary** section of a political party or spectrum. The term originated in the French national assembly in 1789, where the nobles sat in the place of honour on the president's right, whereas the commons were on his left, hence **left wing**. Any such labelling is entirely relative to a country's **political culture**.

## Roman Catholicism

One of the main divisions of the Christian religion, separate from the Eastern Orthodox Church from 1054, and headed by the pope. Membership is concentrated in Western and Southern Europe, Latin America, and the Philippines. In February 2000 Rome reported the number of baptized Roman Catholics to be 1.045 billion, an increase of 40 million since 1998.

The Protestant churches separated from the Catholic Church with the Reformation in the 16th century. In response to the Reformation, in the 16th and 17th centuries, the Catholic Church undertook the campaign of education and coercion known as the Counter-Reformation. An attempt to update Catholic doctrines was condemned by

**Roman Catholicism** *An anti-Catholic picture from the Reformation in the 16th century shows the pope on the throne in the shape of an ass with bagpipes.*

Pope Pius X in 1907, though the Second Vatican Council (1962–66) made the church more liberal and very slightly more democratic. Further moves in this direction have been rejected by John Paul II. Politically, the policy of the Roman Catholic Church has been to establish working relationships with national governments, both Catholic and non-Catholic. It can fairly be said that, with the exception in Latin America of **liberation theology**, the Catholic Church has always favoured the right wing in politics, whether electoral or other. The Holy See maintains official representatives of varying rank in most European

The political prestige of the Holy See was enhanced by the Lateran Treaty of 1929 with the Italian government, when the Vatican City was recognized as a sovereign state.

countries, as well as in many non-European states (papal representatives abroad being known as nuncios or legates), while most of these states have accredited representatives at the Vatican.

## Rousseau, Jean-Jacques (1712–1778)

French social philosopher and writer. His book *Du Contrat social/ Social Contract* (1762), emphasizing the rights of the people over those of the government, was a significant influence on the French Revolution. As the name applies, it adopted the then standard theoretical method of trying to work out what sort of a **social contract** would have led free people to set up a state. As such his work is usually contrasted with that of **Hobbes** and **Locke**. Rousseau was born in Geneva, Switzerland. His *Discourses on the Origins of Inequality* (1754) made his name: he denounced civilized society and postulated the paradox of the superiority of the

**Rousseau** *An 18th-century steel engraving of Jean-Jacques Rousseau.*

'noble savage'. In the *Social Contract* he argued that government is justified only if sovereignty stays with the people. He thereby rejected representative democracy in favour of **direct democracy**, modelled on the Greek **polis** and the Swiss canton, and stated that a government could be legitimately overthrown if it failed to express the general will of the people. The idea of the 'general will', central to the *Social Contract,* and the idea of '**alienation**', from his *Discourse on the Origins of Inequality,* have become central concepts in political theory. He was the first in a line of theorists of positive **freedom** and of the corrupting nature of society, which leads ultimately to **Marxism**.

> ❝ Man is born free, and everywhere he is in chains. ❞
>
> **Jean-Jacques Rousseau**, French philosopher and writer, *Social Contract.*

## rule of law

The doctrine that no individual, however powerful, is above the law. The principle had a significant influence on attempts to restrain the arbitrary use of power by rulers and on the growth of legally enforceable human rights in many Western countries. It is often used as a justification for separating legislative from judicial power. Above all, it restricts the police, and any other state agency to acting only as specifically empowered by general legislation. It is used also in the international relations arena to suggest the need for states to be governed by something approaching international law rather than by sheer self interest.

## sanction

Economic or military measure taken by a state or number of states to enforce international law. The first use of sanctions, as a trade embargo, was the attempted economic boycott of Italy 1935–36 during the Abyssinian War by the **League of Nations**. Although sanctions seem preferable to war as a way of controlling law-breaking states, they are not as painless to the innocent as they sometimes seem. Typically a state suffering from sanctions manages to continue much of its offensive behaviour and to maintain, for example, a strong military. Welfare and similar provisions to the poor, as well as health services however suffer badly. Other examples of sanctions are:

- economic boycott of Rhodesia, after its unilateral declaration of independence in 1965, by the United Nations (UN)

- measures taken against South Africa on human-rights grounds by the UN and other organizations from 1986 (the majority of these were repealed in 1993, the UN's in 1994)

- economic boycott of Iraq in 1990 in protest over its invasion of Kuwait, following resolutions passed by the UN

- UN embargo in force against the military regime in Haiti 1993–94 (the Organization of American States and the USA imposed their own embargos against the regime from 1991)

- international sanctions against Serbia 1992–95 in protest against its backing of the Bosnian Serbs

- sanctions resulting from the situation in the province of Kosovo in 1998

- sanctions in 1998 against India and Pakistan after their respective nuclear tests.

## Schumpeter, Joseph A(lois) (1883–1950)

Austrian-born US economist and sociologist. In *Capitalism, Socialism and Democracy* (1942) he contended that Western **capitalism**, impelled by its very success, was evolving into a form of **socialism** because firms would become increasingly large and their managements increasingly divorced from ownership, while social trends were undermining the traditional motives for entrepreneurial accumulation of wealth. The book also set out a minimal definition of democracy adopted by empirical political scientists, in which the mass of people are only involved periodically in choosing between parties that are alternate governments and have no further say in politics. This was developed extensively by Anthony **Downs**, and began the dominant mode of modern political science, known as 'rational choice' theory. Schumpeter was born in Moravia, now the Czech Republic, and migrated to the USA in 1932. He was deeply interested in mathematics and he took part in the founding of the Econometric Society in 1930. His writings established him as an authority on economic theory as well as the history of economic thought. Among other standard reference works, he wrote the *History of Economic Analysis*, published posthumously in 1954.

## second ballot
A modification of the simple plurality voting method, it requires that candidates secure an overall majority of votes (that is, 50% + 1) before they can be elected. Thus in France, for example, after a first **ballot** for the National Assembly, a second ballot is held in those constituencies where no candidate had achieved an overall majority, and in which candidates with less than 12.5% of the votes withdraw, thereby freeing their supporters to vote for a candidate more likely to be elected. At presidential elections in, for example, Austria, France, and Poland there is, if necessary, a run-off between the top two candidates remaining in contention after the first ballot. The candidate gaining most votes in the second ballot, whether or not they have achieved a majority, is duly elected. The advantage of this system is that it does give voters who have supported unsuccessful candidates in the first ballot the chance to express a second choice. It also encourages alliances and less formal arrangements between parties, as those with broadly similar ideologies will often agree that the less successful of their candidates will withdraw from the contest in each constituency and encourage their supporters to vote for the other. Minor parties, or parties with no obvious alliance partners, tend to do much less well in second ballots.

## secularization
Process through which religious thinking, practice, and institutions lose their religious and/or social significance. The concept is based on the theory, held

❢ Nothing is so fatal to religion as indifference. ❢

**Edmund Burke**, Letter to William Smith (1795).

by some sociologists, that as societies become industrialized their religious morals, values, and institutions give way to secular ones and some religious traits become common secular practices. The theory rests partly on the idea that religion requires small close face-to-face communities typical of rural life to flourish, and industrialization and urbanization destroy this background. The main problem with secularization as an explanatory theory is that the first industrialized and urbanized society, the USA, remains more religious than any Western European society. Nonetheless the plain fact of secularization, with its extensive political consequences, is undeniable.

---

❝ Knowledge and history are the enemies of religion. ❞

**Napolean I**, *Maxims* (1804–15).

---

### secular state
A state that has no official ties to any religious movement. The UK is not secular because there is an officially established church, the Church of England, just as the Scandinavian countries have established Lutheran churches whose ministers are very nearly civil servants. The USA, however, with an article of its constitution expressly forbidding the creation of an established church, is a secular state. In practice the term has more to do with the extent to which governing parties are really independent of religious affiliation. With this alternative definition, the UK, the USA, and Scandinavia are essentially secular. In contrast, Italy could not be so regarded, even though **Roman Catholicism** ceased to be the official state religion in 1985, because the major party of government since World War II, the Christian Democrats, have close ties to the church.

### select committee
Any of several long-standing committees of the UK House of **Commons**, such as the Environment Committee and the Treasury and Civil Service Committee. These were intended to restore parliamentary control of the executive, improve the quality of legislation, and scrutinize public spending and the work of government departments. Select committees represent the major parliamentary reform of the 20th century, and a possible means – through their all-party membership – of avoiding the automatic repeal of one government's measures by its successor. Departmental ministers attend to answer questions, and if information is withheld on a matter of wide concern, a debate of the whole House may be called. It is generally felt that the committees lack adequate power to enforce attendance and gain information, at least

compared to the very strong US congressional committees. They also lack adequate research staff and still suffer from too much party discipline.

## Senate

In ancient Rome, the 'council of elders'. Originally consisting of the heads of patrician families, it was recruited from ex-magistrates and persons who had rendered notable public service, but was periodically purged by the censors. It is now a commonly used title for the higher of two parliamentary chambers in a bicameral legislature, as in the USA, Canada, Italy, and France. The title is used to indicate the sense of an older, wiser body divorced from the pressures of electoral politics.

## separation of powers

Limiting the powers of government by separating governmental functions into the executive, legislative, and judiciary. The concept has its fullest practical expression in the US constitution. Most modern political systems at least claim to abide by some degree of separation of powers. The original theory of separation of powers comes from **Montesquieu**.

## sexism

Belief in (or set of implicit assumptions about) the superiority of one's own sex, often accompanied by a stereotype or preconceived idea about the opposite sex. Sexism may also be accompanied by **discrimination** on the basis of sex, generally as practised by men against women. The term, coined by analogy with **racism**, was first used in the 1960s by feminist writers to describe language or behaviour that implied women's inferiority. Examples include the

**sexism** *A picture postcard of 1948 draws on sexist stereotypes about women's job roles and depicts women as affable but mindless sex objects.*

contentious use of male pronouns to describe both men and women, and the assumption that some jobs are typically or appropriately performed only by one sex.

## shuttle diplomacy
In international relations, the efforts of an independent mediator to achieve a compromise solution between belligerent parties, travelling back and forth from one to the other. The term came into use in the 1970s. In 1990–91 shuttle diplomacy was practised by US secretary of state James Baker in the period leading up to, and following, the **Gulf War**, and has become an extensive feature of relations between the USA and other countries. It has become popular in part because of growing distrust for professional diplomats, but more because the person shuttling can represent the very personal power of the US President.

## social contract
The idea that government authority derives originally from an agreement between people in a pre-social state (often called the **state of nature**) by which they set up political authority. The agreement can be between ruler and ruled in which the former agrees to provide order in return for obedience from the latter, or between those who are to be ruled, collectively laying down their rights in favour of a third party. The method of thinking has been used to support both absolutism (Thomas **Hobbes**) and representative democracy (John **Locke**), and direct democracy (Jean-Jacques **Rousseau**). It is not essential that such a contract or state of nature ever actually existed – the idea is to carry out a thought experiment, and as such the technique has been revitalised by, amongst others, John **Rawls**. The term was revived in the UK in 1974 when a head-on clash between the Conservative government and the trades unions resulted in a general election enabling a Labour government to take power. It now denotes an unofficial agreement (hence also called 'social compact') between a government and organized labour that, in return for control of prices, rents, and so on, the unions would refrain from economically disruptive wage demands.

## social democracy
Political ideology or belief that hopes for the gradual evolution of a democratic form of socialism within existing political structures. The earliest was the German Sozialdemokratische Partei (SPD). Parties along the lines of the German model were founded in the last two decades of the 19th century in a number of countries, including Austria, Belgium, the Netherlands,

Hungary, Poland, and Russia. The British **Labour Party** is in the social democratic tradition. As no revolutionary socialist party could remotely expect to be elected nowadays, the title is somewhat redundant – only democratic socialists have any real political role. Furthermore the extent to which such parties are today even socialist, as opposed to liberal reformist, can be doubted.

## socialism

Political movement aiming to establish a classless society by substituting public for private ownership of the means of production, distribution, and exchange. The term has been used to describe positions as widely apart as **anarchism** and **social democracy**. Socialist ideas appeared in classical times; in early

ДУХ ВЕЛИКОГО ЛЕНИНА И ЕГО ПОБЕДОНОСНОЕ ЗНАМЯ ВДОХНОВЛЯЮТ НАС ТЕПЕРЬ НА ОТЕЧЕСТВЕННУЮ ВОЙНУ... (Я. Сталин)

**socialism** *Joseph **Stalin**, who sought to make socialism a reality in Russia. His name has given rise to the term Stalinism, used to describe any very authoritarian socialist movement or leader.*

Christianity; among later Christian sects such as the Anabaptists and Diggers; and, in the 18th and early 19th centuries, were put forward as systematic political aims by Claude Saint-Simon, François Fourier, and Robert Owen, among others. The late 19th and early 20th centuries saw a division between those who reacted against **Marxism**, leading to social-democratic parties, and those who emphasized the original revolutionary significance of **Marx's** teachings. The Russian Revolution took socialism from the sphere of theory to that of practice. The inability of national socialist movements ever to unite internationally has been their great weakness, facilitating the

> 6 Why is it always the intelligent people who are socialists? 9
>
> **Alan Bennett**, British playwright, *Forty Years On.*

outbreak of World War I, as well as halting the rise of **popular fronts** in France and Spain in 1936–38, thus hastening the rise of **fascism** and **Nazism**. In Western Europe after World War II a communist takeover of the Portuguese revolution failed 1975–76, and elsewhere, as in France under François Mitterrand, attempts at socialist-communist cooperation petered out. However, most countries in Western Europe have a strong socialist, or social democratic, party; for example, the Social Democratic Party in Germany, the **Labour Party** in the UK, the Socialist Worker's Party in Spain, and the Panhellenic Socialist Movement in Greece.

> ❝ As with the Christian religion, the worst advertisement for Socialism is its adherents. ❞
>
> **George Orwell**, English novelist, *The Road To Wigan Pier*.

## social mobility

The movement of groups and individuals up and down the social scale in a classed society. The extent or range of social mobility varies in different societies. Individual social mobility may occur through education, marriage, talent, and so on. Group mobility usually occurs through change in the occupational structure caused by new technological or economic developments. The **caste** system of India and the **feudalism** of medieval Europe are cited as examples of closed societies, where little social mobility was possible. The class system of Western industrial societies is considered relatively open and flexible. Indeed social mobility is theoretically inevitable in a meritocratic system, but in practice social class seems to remain very highly a matter of inheritance. At the beginning of the 21st century, for example, the proportion of children from the poorest homes going to élite universities in Europe – the main avenue to high status jobs – was tiny compared to the proportion of the upper middle class doing so. What social mobility has occurred in modern developed economies has largely been because structural change in the shape of the industrial base has reduced the proportion of less skilled jobs in favour of far more white collar jobs.

## social security

State provision of financial aid to alleviate poverty. The term 'social security' was first applied officially in the USA, in the Social Security Act 1935. In Britain it was first used officially in 1944, and following the Beveridge

Report of 1942, a series of acts was passed from 1945 to widen the scope of social security. Basic entitlements of those paying National Insurance contributions in Britain include an old-age pension, unemployment benefit (known as jobseeker's allowance from October 1996), widow's pension, incapacity benefit, and payment during a period of sickness in one's working life (Statutory Sick Pay). Other benefits, which are non-contributory, include family credit, income support, child benefit, and attendance allowance for those looking after sick or disabled people. Entitlements under National Insurance, such as unemployment benefit, are paid at flat rates regardless of need; other benefits, such as income support, are 'means-tested', that is, claimants' income must be below a certain level. The concept of such payments developed in the later 19th century in Europe. In the 1880s Germany introduced compulsory accident and sickness insurance as well as old age pensions. Britain intro-

Figures for 1999 showed that the number of people claiming sickness benefits in the UK in May exceeded the number of the unemployed. Almost 3 million people were on sickness benefits, becoming the largest single group amongst UK's 6 million claimants.

duced non-contributory old-age pensions from 1909, and compulsory health and unemployment insurance from 1911. The US social-security legislation was passed to enable the federal government to cope with the effects of the Depression of 1929. Similar measures are found in all liberal democracies – the pressure of electoral politics makes this inevitable, as did the state ideology in the former communist societies. **See also:** *welfare state.*

## Solidarity
The national confederation of independent **trades unions** in Poland, formed under the leadership of Lech Wałesa September 1980 (Polish Solidarnosc). Solidarity emerged from a summer of industrial disputes caused by the Polish government's attempts to raise food prices. The strikers created a trade union movement independent of the Communist Party, and protracted negotiations with the government led to recognition of Solidarity in exchange for an acceptance of the leading role of the Communist Party in Poland. Continuing unrest and divisions in Solidarity's leadership led to the declaration of martial law in December 1981; the union was banned

and its leaders were arrested. Wałesa was released in December 1982, and Solidarity continued to function as an underground organization. It was legalized again in April 1989 following a further wave of strikes under its direction and round-table talks with the government. In the elections of June 1989 it won almost every seat open to it, and became the senior partner in a 'grand coalition' government formed in September 1989 with Tadeusz Mazowiecki as prime minister. In December 1990, after a damaging break with Mazowiecki, Wałesa became Poland's president. Wałesa left the confederation in December 1990, and by mid-1991 Solidarity found itself opposing some of its former leader's economic policies and with diminished national influence. It had 2.8 million members in 1991.

Solidarity's achievements inspired the successful 'people power' movements in other Eastern European countries during 1989, as well as the formation of more independent labour unions in the USSR.

## sovereignty

A state having absolute authority within a given territory. The possession of sovereignty is taken to be the distinguishing feature of the state, as against other forms of community. The term means both the ultimate source of authority within a state, such as a parliament or monarch, and the independence of the state from any outside authority. Various theories of sovereignty have been put forward to justify the exercise of such power. Amongst them those deriving from the **social contract** and the utilitarian positions are most important in modern discussions of the issue. In the 19th century when it was felt that the only limitations properly imposed on political power were those that were self-imposed, the assertion of a nation's sovereignty implied freedom from internal influence

> Sovereignty has been contentious in the UK for some time because of the conflict between those who wish further to integrate the country with the European Union, and those who cling to the idea that this involves a dangerous loss of sovereignty.

by other powers. Since World War II increasing international interdependence and the growth of the influence of multinational corporations on domestic economies has led to a drastic reduction in the sphere of autonomous sovereignty.

## soviet

Originally a strike committee elected by Russian workers in the 1905 revolution; in 1917 these were set up by peasants, soldiers, and factory workers. The soviets sent delegates to the All-Russian Congress of Soviets to represent their opinions to a future government. They were later taken over by the **Bolsheviks**. The noun (Russian 'council') became an adjective in Western political language, meaning communist.

## Stalin, Joseph (1879–1953)

Adopted name of Joseph Vissarionovich Djugashvili (Stalin is Russian for 'steel'), Soviet politician. A member of the October Revolution committee of 1917, Stalin became general secretary of the Communist Party in 1922. After **Lenin's** death in 1924, Stalin sought to create 'socialism in one country' and clashed with **Trotsky**, who denied the possibility of socialism inside Russia until revolution had occurred in Western Europe. Stalin won this ideological struggle by 1927, and a series of five-year plans were launched to collectivize industry and agriculture from 1928. All opposition was eliminated in the Great Purge of 1936–38. During World War II, Stalin intervened in the military direction of

**Stalin** *Joseph Stalin, whose name, as in 'Stalinist'; has come to be used to describe any very authoritarian socialist leader.*

the campaigns against Nazi Germany. He managed not only to bring the USSR through the war but to help it emerge as a superpower, although only at an immense cost in human suffering to his own people. After the war, Stalin quickly turned Eastern Europe into a series of Soviet satellites and maintained an autocratic rule domestically. His role was denounced after his death by Nikita Khrushchev and other members of the Soviet regime. As dictator in the 1930s, he disposed of all real and imagined enemies. His **anti-Semitism** caused, for example, the execution of 19 Jewish activists in 1952 for a 'Zionist conspiracy'. His name has come to be used, as in 'Stalinist', to describe any very **authoritarian** socialist movement or leader.

## Stalinism

A totalitarian version of **communism** based on the political methods of Joseph **Stalin**. Power is exclusively in the hands of the Communist Party, which is organized on rigidly hierarchical lines. The leader is presented, by state propaganda, as the selfless and benevolent parent of the nation. Economic policy is based on enforced industrialization and the **collectivization** of agriculture. The general population is controlled by a vast bureaucracy and all opposition and internal debate is ruthlessly repressed by the secret police.

## standing committee

A committee of the UK House of **Commons** that examines parliamentary bills (proposed acts of Parliament) for detailed correction and amendment. The committee comprises members of parliament from the main political parties, with a majority usually held by the government. Several standing committees may be in existence at any time, each usually created for a particular bill. They should not be confused with the **select committees**, which are semi permanent groupings of parliamentary experts on different policy areas.

A system of standing committees operates in the US **Congress**, but the distinction between standing committee and select committee is not made. All parliamentary systems require some sort of committee structure – the UK standing committee system is by no means uniformly used.

## state

Territory that forms its own domestic and foreign policy, acting through laws that are typically decided by a government and carried out, by force if necessary, by agents of that government. It can be argued that growth of regional international bodies such as the **European Union** (formerly the European Community) means that states no longer enjoy absolute **sovereignty**. The classic definition of a state is given by R M MacIver (*The Modern State* (1926): 'An association which, acting through law as promulgated by a government endowed to this end with coercive power, maintains within a community territorially demarcated the universal external conditions of social order.' There are four essential elements in this definition:

- that people have formed an association to create and preserve social order
- that the community comprising the state is clearly defined in territorial terms

- that the government representing the people acts according to promulgated laws
- that it has power to enforce these laws.

The state is, in fact, a theoretically difficult concept; it has to be separated from government, from political system, and from civil society, for it has authority over all of these, though the government is the agent of the state. Civil servants and military, for example, will probably owe their allegiance not to the government of the day but to the state. Some Conservative theorists indeed see the state as having legitimate interests above, and separate from, the interests of the citizens as individuals or collectively. Such an idea originated from **Hegel**, but others have developed it, sometimes in extreme ways.

## state of nature

The state of nature is an imaginative reconstruction of how human society might have been before the creation of organized political society. It is a powerful concept in many brands of political theory, but especially social contract theory. A reconstruction is used to deduce what the major drawbacks of living in a pre-political environment would be, and thereby to decide what rules for organized political life would recommend themselves to those in a position to make such a choice. Naturally, much depends on the original description of how people unconstrained by political authority behave. Taking a very pessimistic view of human nature, as did Thomas **Hobbes**, will produce recommendations for the best form of political organization very different from those given by a political theorist like John **Locke**, who thought that people would be able to cooperate fairly well without government, and would thus only agree to a rather limited form of political control. Arguments about the form of the state of nature are entirely hypothetical, the technique can be of great analytic power, even though it is now accepted that humans have never lived outside of at least a rudimentary state.

## status

An individual's social position, or the esteem in which he or she is held by others in society. Both within and between most occupations or social positions there is a status hierarchy. Status symbols, such as insignia of office or an expensive car, often accompany high status. Formal social status is attached to a certain social position, occupation, role, or office. Informal social status is based on an individual's own personal talents, skills, or personality. These two forms of social prestige may be separate or interlinked. Sociologists distinguish between ascribed status, which is bestowed by birth, and achieved status, the result of one's own efforts. The German sociologist Max **Weber** analysed social stratification in terms of three separate but interlinked dimensions: **class**, status, and **power**. Status is seen as a key influence on human behaviour, on the way people evaluate themselves and others. Nowadays the usual social science class definitions in fact involve status elements as well as purely economic measures, because even in a capitalist country wealth may not fit overall social authority and power that well. Thus, for example, a High Court judge has a salary much less than that of many unqualified but successful traders on the stock market but his or her status is higher, as is his or her power, both on and off the bench.

## strategy

A long term view of goals and courses of action (as opposed to tactics, which deals with the short range). Strategy and tactics are military terms, though they can be applied in any conflict situation. One can contrast politicians who are concerned only with electoral tactics (how best to win the imminent general election), from those who have a political strategy (for example, how to restructure the economy).

## stratification

The way in which a social system is hierarchically ordered. The most common and obvious form of stratification is a class system, but race, and, at times, religion or even language, can be forms of stratification. Social stratification has much to do with the nature of politics and partisanship in a society because political parties often base themselves on the strata.

## strike

Stoppage of work by employees, often as members of a **trades union**, to obtain or resist change in wages, hours, or conditions. A similar but weaker measure is work to rule, when production is virtually brought to a halt by strict observance of union rules. Strikes may be 'official' (union-authorized) or 'wildcat' (undertaken spontaneously), and may be accompanied by a sit-in or work-in, the one being worker occupation of a factory and the other continuation of work in a plant the employer wishes to close. In a 'sympathetic' strike, action is in support of other workers on strike elsewhere, possibly in a different industry. In the UK, under the Thatcher government, various measures to curb trade-union power to strike were introduced, for example, the act of 1984 that provided for loss of immunity from legal action if a secret ballot of members is not held before a strike. However, profit-sharing and co-ownership have been increasingly adopted, and in any case trades union membership has slumped in all advanced capitalist economies. A general strike (where members of several unions act collectively) was last held in the UK in 1926 for the first and last time. The last serious major strike was the miner's strike of 1984–85.

> In the UK, 1.3 million working days were lost in 1996 through industrial disputes, in contrast to the 1970s, when the average loss was 12.9 million days, peaking at 29.5 million during the 'Winter of Discontent' in 1979. The UK's labour relations record during the 1990s has been one of the best among developed OECD countries.

## structural functionalism

Anthropological theory formulated by Alfred Radcliffe-Brown, which argued that social structures arise and are maintained in order to facilitate the smooth and harmonious functioning of society as a whole. It is really a development of **functionalism** and the work of Emile **Durkheim**. Similar theories, sometimes called 'Systems Theory' were extensively used by political scientists in the 1950s and 1960s, but have now become less fashionable.

## subsidiarity

The devolution of decision-making within the **European Union** from the centre to the lowest level possible. Since the signing of the Maastricht Treaty on European union in 1991, which affirms that, wherever possible, decisions should be 'taken as closely as possible to the citizens', subsidiarity has been widely debated as a means of countering trends towards excessive **centralization**. It is akin to the core ideas of **federalism**.

## superpower

A state that through disproportionate military or economic strength can dominate smaller nations. The term was used to describe the USA and the USSR from the end of World War II, when they emerged as significantly stronger than all other countries. With the collapse of the Soviet Union in 1991, the USA is, arguably, now the world's sole superpower. It is however clearly a relative concept, and regional superpowers clearly exist.

## supply-side economics
A school of economic thought advocating government policies that allow market forces to operate freely, such as **privatization**, cuts in public spending and income tax, reductions in trade-union power, and cuts in the ratio of unemployment benefits to wages. Supply-side economics developed as part of the monetarist critique of **Keynesian** economics. Supply-siders argue that increases in government expenditure to stimulate demand and reduce unemployment, advocated by Keynesians, are ineffective in the long term because intervention distorts market forces and creates inefficiencies that prevent the 'supply side' of the economy from responding to increases in demand. Critics, however, argue that failure of supply to respond to increases in demand may result from the failure of market forces to take account of social costs and benefits. This may require increased public spending on infrastructure, training, and research and development. Supply-side policies also create a more uneven distribution of income and wealth, as happened in the USA and the UK in the 1980s.

## Supreme Court
Is the highest US judicial tribunal, composed since 1869 of a chief justice (William Rehnquist from 1986) and eight associate justices. Appointments are made for life by the president, with the advice and consent of the Senate, and justices can be removed only by impeachment. In Britain, the Supreme Court of Judicature is made up of the Court of Appeal and the High Court. Canada also has a Supreme Court. In both the North American Republics the Supreme Court is a major political institution because it interprets the constitution, and has the power to strike down democratically passed legislation.

## syndicalism
A political movement in 19th-century Europe that rejected parliamentary activity in favour of the idea of direct action, culminating in a revolutionary general strike to secure worker ownership and control of industry (from French *syndicat* 'trade union'). After 1918 syndicalism was absorbed in **communism**, although it continued to have an independent existence in Spain until the late 1930s. The idea originated under Robert Owen's influence in the 1830s, acquired its name and its more violent aspects in France from the philosopher Georges Sorel, and also reached the USA.

## systems theory

A version of functionalism, popular in the 1950s and 1960s, and especially associated in political studies with the works of the US academic David Easton (1917–   ). It thinks of a political system as being a mechanism by which popular demands and popular support for the state were combined to produce those policy outputs that best ensured the long-term stability of the political system itself. Along with **functionalist** and **structural functionalist** theories, systems theory was often seen as unduly conservative because of its stress on stability rather than change. The basic idea, that political systems could be seen as analogous to operating mechanical systems, with feedback loops and clear goals, has continued to be useful in some areas of political science.

## tactical voting

While most people cast their vote for the candidate they would prefer to win the election, there are situations when it may be rational not to do so. If someone prefers a party which has no hope at all of being elected in that constituency, he or she may vote for a second preference in order to stop the most disliked party getting in. Weak parties sometimes urge their supporters to vote tactically, but it is uncertain whether tactical voting has more than a minimal effect at British general elections. The results of by-elections, however, often suggest that many voters have changed their traditional support to make a protest, with the candidate of the party in government the usual victim. There are some electoral systems where tactical voting certainly exists, and has a strong impact. Typical is the French case where elections are often held in two stages. In presidential elections only two candidates may proceed from the first to the **second ballot**, and in National Assembly elections only those with more than 12.5% of the votes in the first round may proceed (in practice, candidates with more votes than this often withdraw, acknowledging that they cannot win). The unsuccessful candidates from the first round may then urge their supporters to vote for the candidate among those who remain that they most favour. Although this sometimes rebounds and their voters go elsewhere, it allows for tactical alliances either at the constituency level or nationwide that can have a profound electoral impact.

## taxation

The raising of money from individuals and organizations by the state in order to pay for the goods and services it provides. Taxation can be direct (a deduction from income) or indirect (added to the purchase price of goods or services, that is, a tax on consumption). The standard form of indirect taxation in Europe is value-added tax (VAT). Income tax is the most common form of direct taxation, though taxes on companies are a major source of revenue. The proportions of direct and indirect taxation in the total tax revenue vary widely from country to country. By varying the effect of a tax on the richer and poorer members of society, a government can attempt to redistribute wealth from the richer to the poorer. A progressive tax is one that falls proportionally more on the rich; most income taxes, for example, have higher rates for those with higher incomes. A regressive tax, on the other hand, affects the poor proportionally more than the rich. Many sales taxes are in effect regressive because

**taxation** *An 18th-century caricature of the increase in taxation in Britain to finance the war against France.*

the poor need to spend a larger proportion of their income on necessities. The UK tax system has been criticized in many respects; alternatives include an expenditure tax, which would be imposed only on income spent, and the tax credit system – under which all are guaranteed an income bolstered as necessary by social-security benefits, taxation beginning only above that level. This would eliminate the 'poverty trap', by which the unemployed receiving state benefits may have a net loss in income if they take employment at a low wage.

> ❧ The point to remember is that what the government gives it must first take away. ❧
>
> **John S Coleman**, address to the Detroit Chamber of Commerce.

## terrorism

Systematic violence in the furtherance of political aims, often by small **guerrilla** groups. Terrorist groups include those dedicated to a political programme for their country, usually involving the overthrow of the regime. Systematic violence used to press a single-issue cause, such as anti-abortionism or animal rights, may also be seen as terrorism. Terrorism may also be directed by an ethnic majority against a minority ruling group (as in South Africa or the former Rhodesia) or against an occupying force (as with Afghan resistance to Soviet occupation). Terrorist organizations that

---

**UNLAWFUL DETENTION**

In English law, under the Prevention of Terrorism Act of 1984, people arrested may be detained for 48 hours; the secretary of state can extend the period of detention for a maximum of five further days. This procedure, which results in the holding of those suspected of terrorism for up to seven days with no judicial control, was condemned as unlawful by the **European Court of Human Rights** in 1988. By 1991, 18,000 people had been detained but only 250 charged with offences.

---

represent the interests of an ethnic group in a particular region are often separatist. Left-wing revolutionary groups have included the Baader-Meinhof gang in Germany or the Red Brigades in Italy. Terrorists representing ethnic groups or peoples have included Palestinian, Kurdish, and Kosovan Albanian groups.

State terrorism involves sponsorship of violence against another state. Iran funds and trains members of the Islamic fundamentalist Hezbollah movement, active in suicide bombings throughout Israel in opposition to the 1993 Palestinian–Israeli peace accord. Libya has long supported terrorist activity against Western states, supplying arms to the Provisional **IRA** (**Irish Republican Army**) in Northern Ireland and being implicated in the bombing of a US airliner over Lockerbie, Scotland, in December 1988.

---

❝ Those who cannot face ideas resort to bombs. ❞

**Ghazi Algosaibi**, Saudi Arabia's ambassador to Britain, quoted in *Time*, 27 January 1997, after a letter bomb exploded at the London office of an Arabic newspaper.

---

## Thatcherism

A political outlook comprising a belief in the efficacy of market forces, the need for strong central government, and a conviction that self-help is preferable to reliance on the state, combined with a strong

Elements of Thatcherism, particularly the emphasis on controlling public expenditure and promoting opportunities for personal achievement, have even been incorporated into the policy approach of the 'New Labour' government of Tony Blair, from 1997.

element of **nationalism**. The **ideology** is associated with the former UK prime minister Margaret Thatcher, but partly stems from an individualist view found in Britain's 19th-century Liberal and 20th-century Conservative parties, and is no longer confined to Britain. Thatcher incorporated elements all of her own, as with her stress on traditional 'family values' and her very specific commitment to **monetarist** economic policies. Since leaving public office, Thatcher has established her own 'Foundation'.

> ❝ Mrs Thatcher is doing for monetarism what the Boston Strangler did for door-to-door salesmen. ❞
>
> **Denis Healey**, British politician, House of Commons, 1977.

## theocracy

A political system run by priests, as was once found in Tibet. In practical terms it means a system where religious values determine political decisions. The closest modern examples have been Iran during the period when Ayatollah Khomeini was its religious leader 1979–89, and Afghanistan since the Talibaan came to power in 1996. The term was coined by the historian Josephus in the 1st century AD. Any Islamic society has a tendency towards theocracy because the state versus church distinction found in liberal Christian societies has much less legitimacy in Islamic doctrine.

## Third World

Sometimes called the developing world, covers those countries that are less developed than the industrialized free-market countries of the West and are concentrated in Asia, Africa, and Latin America.

The early 1970s saw the beginnings of attempts by Third World countries to act together in confronting the powerful industrialized countries over such matters as the level of prices of primary products. The nations regarding themselves as a group that had been exploited in the past by the developed nations and having a right to catch up with them. Third World countries have relatively undeveloped modern industrial sectors, mainly producers of primary commodities for the Western industrialized countries, and their populations are poor and chiefly engaged in agriculture. Typically they experience high population growth and mortality rates; poor educational and health facilities; high levels of underemployment and, in some cases, political instability.

Third World countries, led by the Arab oil-exporting countries, account for over 75% of all arms imports. The economic performance of developing countries in recent years has been mixed, with sub-Saharan Africa remaining in serious difficulties and others, as in Asia, making significant progress.

> The Third World has 75% of the world's population but consumes only 20% of its resources. In 1990 the average income per head of population in the northern hemisphere was $12,500, 18 times higher than that in the southern hemisphere.

In Southeast Asia the four so-called 'dragons' of Hong Kong, South Korea, Singapore, and Taiwan developed to such an extent that they are known as newly industrialized countries (NICs), with per-capita incomes comparable to many developed states. Malaysia and Thailand are also developing quickly, along with, more erratically, Argentina, Brazil, Chile, Mexico, and Peru.

## Tocqueville, Alexis Charles Henri Clérel de (1805–1859)

French politician, sociologist, and historian. He was the author of the first analytical study of the strengths and weaknesses of US society, *De la Démocratie en Amérique/Democracy in US* (1835). Although he admired the US political system in many ways, he feared that mass democracy, with no counter-veiling **élite**, would force conformity and what he termed 'the tyranny of the majority'. Many of the features of US politics that he noted are still commented on by modern political scientists as making the USA unusual, as for example the involvement of courts in politics and their high religiosity. Elected

**Toqueville** *Alexis de Toqueville was the author of* Democracy in America, *the first analytical study of US society.*

to the Chamber of Deputies in 1839, de Tocqueville became vice-president of the Constituent Assembly and minister of foreign affairs in 1849. He retired after Napoleon III's coup in 1851. No other 19th-century liberal thinker saw the problems of contemporary democratic society quite as clearly as de Tocqueville.

> ❝ Americans are so enamoured of equality that they would rather be equal in slavery than unequal in freedom. ❞
>
> **Alexis de Tocqueville**, French politician and political scientist, *Democracy in America.*

### torture

The infliction of bodily pain to extort evidence or confession. In the 20th century torture was still widely (though, in most countries, unofficially) used. The **human-rights** organization Amnesty International investigates and publicizes the use of torture on prisoners of conscience. Torture was legally abolished in England about 1640, but allowed in Scotland until 1708 and in France until 1789. Modern methods akin to torture include brainwashing, which was developed in both the communist and Western blocs in the 1950s, often using drugs. From the early 1960s a method used in the West replaced isolation by severe sensory deprivation; for example, IRA **guerrillas** were prevented from seeing by a hood, from feeling by being swathed in a loose-fitting garment, and from hearing by a continuous loud noise at about 85 decibels. For

The UN 1997 report on torture listed 29 countries where torture was fairly extensive. They included Algeria, Bahrain, China, India, Israel, Myanmar, Nigeria, Pakistan, Peru, Russia, South Korea, Saudi Arabia, Sudan, and Turkey. The UN Investigator on torture likened Israel to South Africa under apartheid and accused it of institutionalizing torture in interrogating Palestinian detainees.

this the **European Court of Human Rights** found the UK guilty of 'inhuman and degrading treatment'. In 1996 Amnesty International concluded that most of the countries cited in its first reports on the worldwide practice of torture 1973 and 1984 were still actively torturing their citizens, and a few more countries had been added to the list. Amnesty estimated torture had reached 'epidemic proportions' in 40 countries with outbreaks being reported in 60 others.

## totalitarianism

Government control of all activities within a country, overtly political or otherwise, as in fascist or communist dictatorships. Examples of totalitarian regimes are:

- Italy under Benito **Mussolini** 1922–45
- Germany under Adolf **Hitler** 1933–45
- the USSR under Joseph **Stalin** from the 1930s until his death in 1953
- Romania under Nicolae Ceauşescu 1974–89.

In such systems every aspect of society, including cultural and leisure activities, trades unions, and often religious organizations, are run by the state or by the ruling political party.

## trade union

An organization of workers that exists to promote and defend the interests of its members. Trades unions are particularly concerned with pay, working conditions, job security, and redundancy. Unions negotiate with employers over any differences they may have, but in the past have often taken industrial action: going on **strike** or working to rule, for example.

The early history of trades unions is one of illegality and of legislation to prevent their existence and they had no legal protection for their funds until the enactment of a series of Trade Union Acts 1871–76.

The Union movement was for many years representative mainly of unions of skilled workers, but in the 1890s the organization of unskilled labour spread rapidly. In 1926, following a protracted series of disputes in the coal industry, a general strike was called in support of the miners; this collapsed and under the Trades Disputes and Trade Union Act of 1927 general strikes or strikes called in sympathy with other workers were made illegal. This was repealed under the Labour government in 1946 and the post-war period was marked by increased unionism among white-collar workers. From the 1960s onwards there were confrontations between the government and the trades unions. In 1979 trade union membership in the UK peaked at 13.5 million, representing 54% of the workforce.

The Thatcher government passed a series of laws that effectively curbed union power and by 1997 union membership had dropped by more than 1.7 million since 1989 and stood at 7.3 million in 1995.

> ❝ Industrial relations are like sexual relations. It's better between two consenting parties. ❞
>
> **Vic Feather**, British trade-unionist, *Guardian Weekly*, 8 August 1976.

## treaty

Written agreement between two or more states. Treaties usually take effect on ratification, a process that takes place after the internal governments have approved the terms of the treaty. Treaties are binding in international law, the rules being laid down in the Vienna Convention on the Law of Treaties 1969.

The treaty-making power in the UK rests on the crown. Thus treaties are made by the crown (the queen acting on the advice of her ministers) with the representatives of the supreme authority of the state with whom the treaty is agreed.

Whether a rule created by a treaty will have legal significance within the law of a particular party to the treaty will depend upon that law. In the UK, British courts will only implement a treaty to the extent that parliament has provided for such implementation. In the USA, treaties are negotiated by the president but must be ratified by the Senate. However, so-called executive agreements that in many cases result in an agreement with another state, binding under international law, may be made without such approval. As such they become part of the law of the land, though their implementation may be difficult without congressional approval. Treaties have always played a significant role in the development of international law.

## tribal society

A way of life in which people govern their own affairs as independent local communities of families and clans without central government organizations or states. They are found in parts of Southeast Asia, New Guinea, South America, and Africa.

As the world economy expands, natural resources belonging to tribal peoples are coveted and exploited for farming or industrial use and the people are frequently dispossessed. **Pressure groups** such as Survival

International and Cultural Survival have been established in some Western countries to support the struggle of tribal peoples for property rights as well as civil rights within the borders of the countries of which they are technically a part. Tribal societies consist of families and clans that are related to their neighbours from one district to the next. Fairly small groups tend to develop their own distinctive languages and customs, and local communities often feud with each other. For these reasons tribal societies have often found it difficult to defend themselves from outsiders.

The tribal way of life enables people to make an adequate living without overexploiting their land and they occupy some of the world's last natural environments, such as the tropical rainforest. The self-sufficiency of a tribal way of life means that there are no great inequalities of wealth or power but it also makes it difficult for people to organize themselves into large groups.

## tribunal

Strictly, a court of justice, but used in English law for a body appointed by the government to arbitrate in disputes, or investigate certain matters. Tribunals usually consist of a lawyer as chair, sitting with two lay assessors.

In English law, there are various kinds of tribunal. Administrative tribunals deal with claims and disputes about rights and duties under statutory schemes. A good example is industrial tribunals dealing with employment rights, such as unfair dismissal claims. Mental health review tribunals make decisions about patients detained in mental hospitals. There are also private or 'domestic' tribunals, internal disciplinary bodies of organizations such as professional bodies and trades unions. Completely different are tribunals of inquiry set up by the government to investigate matters of public concern; for example, the King's Cross Fire Disaster Inquiry and the Cleveland Child Abuse Inquiry (1988), and the Prison Overcrowding and Riots Inquiry (1990).

## Trotsky, Leon (1879–1940)

The adopted name of Lev Davidovitch Bronstein, a Russian revolutionary. He joined the **Bolshevik** party and took a leading part in the seizure of power in 1917 and in raising the Red Army that fought the Civil War 1918–20. In the struggle for power that followed **Lenin's** death in 1924, **Stalin** defeated Trotsky, and this and other differences with the Communist Party led to his exile in 1929. He settled in Mexico, where he was assassinated at Stalin's instigation. Trotsky believed in world revolution and in permanent revolution, and was an uncompromising, if liberal, idealist.

Trotsky became a Marxist in the 1890s and was imprisoned and exiled for opposition to the tsarist regime. He lived in Western Europe from 1902 until the 1905 revolution, when he was again imprisoned but escaped to live in exile until 1917, when he returned to Russia and joined the Bolsheviks. Although as a young man Trotsky admired Lenin, when he worked with him organizing the revolution of 1917, he objected to Lenin's dictatorial ways. He was second in command until Lenin's death, and was minister for foreign affairs 1917–18 and minister for war 1918–25. Trotsky's later works are critical of the Soviet regime; for example, *The Revolution Betrayed* (1937). His greatest work is his magisterial *History of the Russian Revolution* (1932–33).

---

❝ Any contemporary of ours who wants peace and comfort before anything has chosen a bad time to be born. ❞

**Leon Trotsky**, Russian revolutionary, quoted in *Observer*, 26 March 1933.

---

## Trotskyism

A form of **Marxism** advocated by Leon **Trotsky**. Its central concept is that of permanent revolution. In his view a proletarian revolution, leading to a socialist society, could not be achieved in isolation, so it would be necessary to spark off further revolutions throughout Europe and ultimately worldwide. This was in direct opposition to the Stalinist view that socialism should be built and consolidated within individual countries. Trotskyism developed in an attempt to reconcile Marxist theory with actual conditions in Russia in the early 20th century, but it was never officially accepted within the USSR. Instead it found much support worldwide, primarily in Third World countries.

## tyrant

Technically, a number of men who seized power in their own ancient Greek cities, the first wave of tyrants occurring in the 7th and 6th centuries BC. They opposed the older hereditary aristocratic rulers. Many of them were highly competent rulers, vigorously promoted trade and commerce, and actively promoted public building and the arts. They often provided a bridge between the older aristocratic **oligarchies** and the less exclusive or more democratic systems that followed the fall of the tyrannies. The word *tyrannos* was used by the Greeks in the sense of 'arbitrary ruler', whose power had been gained unconstitutionally, as opposed to a legitimate monarch. In many ways they were **populist** rulers, who harnessed and in due course unleashed popular forces which their less gifted successors could not control. The concept of a 'tyrant' as a cruel and oppressive despot grew up later from a general dislike of **authoritarianism**, a loyalty to democracy, and the behaviour of the later Sicilian tyrants.

> ❝ Nature has left this tincture in the blood,
> That all men would be tyrants if they could. ❞
>
> **Daniel Defoe**, (1660–1731), British journalist and writer, *The Kentish Petition.*

## unilateralism

Usually support for unilateral nuclear disarmament: scrapping a country's nuclear weapons without waiting for other countries to agree to do so at the same time. Both the Labour party and the Liberals flirted with this policy from time to time between 1958 and the late 1980s, but it was never official policy for long. Its main supporters in the UK are groups like the Campaign for Nuclear Disarmament (CND).

## United Nations (UN)

An association of states for international peace, security, and cooperation, with its headquarters in New York. The UN was established in 1945 by 51 states as a successor to the **League of Nations**, and has played a role in many areas, such as refugees, development assistance, disaster relief, cultural cooperation, and peacekeeping. Its membership in 1996 stood at 185 states, and the total proposed budget for 1995–96 (raised by the member states) was $2,600 million supporting more than 50,000 staff. The name 'United Nations' was coined by the US president Franklin D Roosevelt. The UN Charter, drawn up at the San Francisco Conference in 1945, envisaged a UN world security system, with the Security Council preserving the wartime alliance of the USA, USSR, and Britain (with France and China also permanent members) in order to maintain the peace. Disagreements between the great powers during the **Cold War** period and consequent blocking of Security Council action through the use of the veto prevented this. The Security Council has used full enforcement action against states only twice in its history: in Korea 1950, and in the **Gulf War**.

> The USA regularly (often alone or nearly so) votes against General Assembly resolutions on aggression, international law, human-rights abuses, and disarmament, and has exercised its veto on the Security Council more times than any other member (the UK is second, France a distant third).

In its peacekeeping role, acting in pursuance of Security Council resolutions, the UN has had mixed success. The number of peacekeeping operations increased from 1 between 1975–85 to 25 between 1985–95; in 1995 its 65,000 peacekeepers cost a total of $2 billion. In 1996 UN forces were largely replaced by NATO units.

**Arms control treaties sponsored by the UN**
- Partial Test Ban Treaty (1963)
- Peaceful Uses of Outer Space Treaty (1967)
- Treaty of Tlateloclo making Latin America a nuclear free zone (1967)
- Nuclear Non-Proliferation Treaty (1968)
- Antarctic Treaty (1969)
- Seabed Arms Control Treaty (1971)
- Biological Weapons Convention (1972).

**The principal UN institutions and agencies**
- General Assembly
- Security Council
- Economic and Social Council
- Trusteeship Council
- International Court of Justice in The Hague, Netherlands
- International Telecommunication Union (ITU)
- World Health Organization (WHO)
- UN Educational, Scientific, and Cultural Organization (UNESCO)
- International Bank for Reconstruction and Development (World Bank)
- United Nations High Commissioner for Refugees (UNHCR) Geneva
- United Nations International Children's Emergency Fund (UNICEF)
- International Labour Organization (ILO).

## urbanization
The process by which the proportion of a population living in or around towns and cities increases through migration and natural increase as the agricultural population decreases. The growth of urban concentrations in the USA and Europe is a relatively recent phenomenon, dating back only

about 150 years to the beginning of the Industrial Revolution (although the world's first cities were built more than 5,000 years ago). Urbanization has had a major effect on the social structures of industrial societies,

In England, about 705 sq km/705,000 hectares of former agricultural land was lost to housing, industrial development, and road building 1945–92.

affecting not only where people live, but also how they live, and urban sociology has emerged as a distinct area of study.

## utilitarianism
Philosophical theory of ethics outlined by the philosopher Jeremy **Bentham** and developed by John Stuart **Mill**. According to utilitarianism, an action is morally right if it has consequences that lead to happiness, and wrong if it brings about the reverse. Thus society should aim for the greatest happiness of the greatest number.

## utopianism
The wish or attempt to create an ideal social and political system. Cooperative communities were suggested by, for example, the French socialist François Fourier and attempted by Robert Owen in Scotland and the USA. Thomas **More** wrote the first known design for a utopia (Greek 'nowhere') in his *Utopia* (1516).

## vote

An expression of preference by a **ballot**, show of hands, or other means. In parliamentary elections the results can be calculated in a number of ways. The main electoral systems are:

- simple plurality or first past the post, with single-member constituencies
- second ballot
- proportional representation.

The qualifications for voting were liberalized during the 20th century. New Zealand was the first country to give women the vote, in 1893, and, among economically advanced states, Switzerland was one of the last in 1971, with Liechtenstein in 1984. The minimum age for voting has also been reduced over the years. The age of 18 has now been adopted by most countries, but a few have adopted an even lower figure. The age qualification in Iran for presidential elections is 15.

## war

An act of force, usually on behalf of the state, intended to compel a declared enemy to obey the will of the other. The aim is to render the opponent incapable of further resistance by destroying its capability and will to bear arms in pursuit of its own aims. War is therefore a continuation of politics carried on with violent and destructive means, as an instrument of policy.

> In the wars of the late 20th century, 90% of casualties have been civilian (in World War II, the figure was 50%; in World War I only 5%).

According to the Stockholm International Peace Research Institute (SIPRI), there were fewer wars in 1995 than at any time since the end of the Cold War in 1989. All 30 of the wars in 1995 were civil wars fought within nations, apparently signalling a further shift from the pattern of inter-state wars, which had characterized the modern era. **See also:** *Just War.*

> ❝ Qui desiderat pacem, praeparet bellum./Let him who desires peace, prepare for war. ❞
>
> **Vegetius**, Roman military writer, *De Re Militare.*

## Weber, Max (1864–1920)

German sociologist, one of the founders of modern sociology. He emphasized cultural and political factors as key influences on economic development and individual behaviour.

Weber argued for a scientific and value-free approach to research, yet highlighted the importance of meaning and consciousness in understanding social action. His ideas continue to stimulate thought on social **stratification**, **power**, organizations, **law**, and **religion**.

Key works include *The Protestant Ethic and the Spirit of Capitalism* (1902), *The Sociology of Religion* (1920), *Economy and Society* (1922), and *The Methodology of the Social Sciences* (1949).

## welfare state
A political system under which the state (rather than the individual or the private sector) has responsibility for the welfare of its citizens. Services such as unemployment and sickness benefits, family allowances and income supplements, pensions, medical care, and education may be provided and financed through state insurance schemes and **taxation**.

## women's movement
The campaign for the rights of women, including social, political, and economic equality with men. Early European campaigners of the 17th–19th centuries fought for women's right to own property, to have access to higher education, and to vote. Once women's suffrage was achieved in the 20th century, the emphasis of the movement shifted to the goals of equal social and economic opportunities for women, including employment. A continuing area of concern in industrialized countries is the contradiction between the now generally accepted principle of equality and the inequalities that remain between the sexes in state policies and in everyday life. **See also:** *feminism.*

> ❛ Whatever women do they must do twice as well as men to be thought half as good. Luckily, this is not difficult. ❜
>
> **Charlotte Whitton**, Canadian writer and politician, *Canada Month,* June 1963.

## World Bank
The popular name for the International Bank for Reconstruction and Development a specialized agency of the **United Nations** that borrows in the commercial market and lends on commercial terms. In 1992 the World Bank made a net transfer of $49.7 million to developing countries. In 1999 it made an appeal for $2 billion to rebuild Kosovo after the Balkan conflict. The bank is located in Washington, DC, and is the second-largest employer there after the Federal government. It is housed in a complex of 19 buildings.

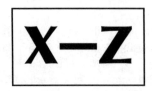

# X–Z

## xenophobia

Fear (phobia) or strong dislike of strangers or anybody foreign or different. Popularly it is used to mean anti-foreign and even facist.

## Zionism

The national liberation movement advocating the re-establishment of a Jewish homeland (the *Eretz Israel*) in Palestine. The movement was founded by the Hungarian writer Theodor Herzl, who in 1897 convened the First Zionist Congress in the Swiss city of Basel. Zionism was the driving force behind the creation of the state of Israel in 1948.

In 1917 the Zionist leaders Chaim Weizmann and Nahum Sokolow gained from Great Britain (which controlled Palestine after the collapse of the Ottoman Empire in World War I) a promise of support for a Jewish homeland. This was enshrined in the Balfour Declaration. Before and during World War II, escalating persecution in Europe led many Jews to embrace Zionism and emigrate. After the war, the United Nations sanctioned the establishment of a Jewish state alongside a homeland for the Arab Palestinian people.

# Appendix

## Noteworthy Political Thinkers

**Althusser, Louis** (1918–1990) Algerian-born French Marxist philosopher who argued that ruling class ideology is a crucial form of class control.

**Arendt, Hannah** (1906–1975) German-born US political theorist and philosopher who considered the moral implications of 20th-century political history.

**Aron, Raymond** (1905–1983) French political and social theorist who was critical of Marxism and emphasized pluralism as essential in any society.

**Bakunin, Mikhail Aleksandrovich** (1814–1876) Russian anarchist and revolutionary who supported communism as part of his "withering away of the state" doctrine.

**Bodin**, Jean (1530–1596) French political philosopher whose six-volume *'De la République/Of the Commonwealth'* is considered the first work on political economy.

**Burke, Edmund** (1729–1797) Irish political theorist who supported the American colonists and denounced the French Revolution.

**Debray, Régis** (1941–  ) French Marxist theorist who was involved with Che Guevara in the 1960s revolutionary movement in Latin America.

**Engels, Friedrich** (1820–1895) German political philosopher who, with Karl Marx, founded the communist movement.

**Gentile, Giovanni** (1875–1944) Italian political philosopher whose writings formed the basis for Mussolini's fascist state in Italy.

**Godwin, William** (1756–1836) English political philosopher whose *'Enquiry Concerning Political Justice'* advocated an anarchic society.

**Gramsci, Antonio** (1891–1937) Italian Marxist who attempted to unify social theory and political practice.

**Hobbes, Thomas** (1588–1679) English political philosopher whose *'Leviathan'* advocated absolutist government as the only means of ensuring order.

**John of Salisbury** (c. 1115–1180) English political thinker whose *'Policraticus'* portrayed the church as the guarantee of liberty against a secular authority.

**Korsch, Karl** (1886–1961) German Marxist philosopher who argued against the theory of dialectical materialism and attempted a reinterpretation of Marxism.

**Kropotkin, Petr Alekseevich** (1842–1921) Russian anarchist who wrote extensively on anarchism, history, and political and social justice.

**Lukács, Geyorgy Szegedy** (1885–1971) Hungarian political philosopher who was one of the founders of Western or Hegelian Marxism.

**Lyotard, Jean François** (1924–   ) French political philosopher who was one of the leading theorists of postmodernism.

**Machiavelli, Niccolò** (1469–1527) Italian political theorist whose works *'Il principe/The Prince'* and *'Discorsi/Discourses'* advocated amoral political manipulation of people.

**Marcuse, Herbert** (1898–1979) German-born US political philosopher who combined Marxism and Freudianism, and whose teaching influenced radical thought in the 1960s.

**Marx, Karl Heinrich** (1818–1883) German political philosopher whose *'Das Kapital/Capital'* is the fundamental text of Marxist economics and politics.

**Michels, Robert** (1876–1936) German social and political theorist whose *'Political Parties'* argued that an "iron law of oligarchy" governs any organization or society.

**Mill, John Stuart** (1806–1873) English social and political theorist who wrote *'On Liberty'*, the classic philosophical defence of liberalism.

**Montesquieu, Charles Louis de Secondat Baron de la Bréde et de** (1689–1755) French political theorist whose *'De L'Esprit des lois/The Spirit of Laws'* advocated the separation of powers within government.

**Nozick, Robert** (1938–   ) US political philosopher who believes the state exists only to protect the rights of individuals.

**Ortega y Gasset, José** (1883–1955) Spanish political philosopher who argued that communism and fascism caused the downfall of Western civilization.

**Pareto, Vilfredo** (1848–1923) Italian political philosopher who opposed socialism and liberalism.

**Scruton, Roger Vernon** (1944–   ) British social and political theorist whose *'The Meaning of Conservatism'* influenced the free-market movements in Eastern Europe.

**Spengler, Oswald** (1880–1936) German political thinker who argued in *'Der Untergang des Abendlandes/Decline of the West'* that civilizations go through cycles of growth and decay.

**Stirner, Max** (pseudonym of Johannes Kaspar Schmidt) (1806–1856) German anarchist thinker who argued that the state, class, and humanity are meaningless abstractions.

**Smith, Adam** (1723–1790) Scottish economist and creator of the discipline of political economy that greatly influenced political theory in later years.

**Tocqueville, Alexis Charles Henri Maurice Clérel de** (1805–1859) French political and social theorist who authored the first analytical study of US society: *'De la Démocratie en Amérique/ Democracy in America'*.

**Trotsky, Leon** (adopted name of Lev Davidovitch Bronstein) (1879–1940) Russian political theorist who believed in permanent world revolution, and who was assassinated by Ramon del Rio, an agent of Stalin.

# Longest Serving Political Leaders

As of 2000.

| Rank | Name | Position | Country | Term(s) | Years |
|---|---|---|---|---|---|
| 1 | Jiang Jie Shi (Chiang Kai-shek) | general and president | China and Taiwan | 1928–75 | 47[1] |
| 2 | Kim Il Sung | communist leader | North Korea | 1948–94 | 46 |
| 3 | Ibrahim Didi | prime minister | Maldives | 1883–1925 | 42 |
| 4 | Fidel Castro Ruz | communist leader | Cuba | 1959– | 41 |
| 5 | Enver Hoxha | communist leader | Albania | 1954–85 | 40 |
| 6= | Omar Bongo | president | Gabon | 1964– | 36 |
| 6= | Francisco Franco Bahamonde | dictator | Spain | 1939–75 | 36 |
| 6= | Antonio de Oliveira Salazar | dictator | Portugal | 1932–68 | 36 |
| 6= | Marshal Tito | communist leader | Yugoslavia | 1943–80 | 36 |
| 10= | Todor Zhivkov | communist leader | Bulgaria | 1954–89 | 35 |
| 10= | Alfredo Stroessner | dictator | Paraguay | 1954–89 | 35 |
| 12 | Felix Houphouet-Boigny | president | Côte d'Ivoire | 1960–93 | 33 |
| 13 | Mobuto Sese Seko | president | Zaire | 1965–97 | 32 |
| 14= | Suharto | president | Indonesia | 1967–98 | 31 |
| 14= | Habib Bourguiba | president | Tunisia | 1956–87 | 31 |
| 14= | Lee Kuan Yew | prime minister | Singapore | 1959–90 | 31 |
| 14= | Josef Stalin | communist leader | Soviet Union (Russia) | 1922–53 | 31 |
| 14= | Moamer al Khaddhafi | revolutionary leader | Libya | 1969– | 31 |
| 19= | John Compton | prime minister | St Lucia | 1964–79 and 1982–96 | 30 |
| 20= | Sheikh Khalifa bin-Sulman al-Khalifa | prime minister | Bahrain | 1970– | 30 |
| 20= | Vere Bird | prime minister | Antigua and Barbuda | 1960–71 and 1976–94 | 29 |
| 22= | Hastings Kauzu Banda | president | Malawi | 1966–94 | 28 |
| 23= | William Tubman | president | Liberia | 1944–71 | 27 |
| 23= | Kenneth Kaunda | president | Zambia | 1964–91 | 27 |
| 23= | Mao Zedong | communist leader | China | 1949–76 | 27 |
| 23= | Klemens von Metternich | chancellor | Austria | 1821–48 | 27 |

[1]During the late 1930s and 1940s, Jiang was leader in only a small nationalist stronghold portion of China.